French Soldiers' Morale in the Phoney War, 1939–1940

The collapse of the French army in 1940 is a well-researched topic in Second World War Studies but a surprising gap in the historiography emerges when it comes to the study of the French military prior to the German offensive of May 1940.

Using various public and private sources in different languages, this book aims to address this gap by studying morale on the frontline and its management by the French Government, the Grand Quartier Général, at the scale of the regiment and on a personal level. This research also investigates German and British propaganda in French and aimed at the French sector of the frontline in order to offer the first comprehensive comparative study of French army morale in any language.

Maude Williams is a French historian working at the University of Saarland in Germany. Her research looks at wartime propaganda and rumours, war evacuations in 1939–1940 and more recently at Franco-German music transfers in the 1960s. She has written several articles on these topics.

Bernard Wilkin is a Belgian historian working at the State Archives of Belgium. His research investigates wartime propaganda and the French army from 1799 to 1945. He is the author of *Aerial Propaganda and the Wartime Occupation of France, 1914–1918* and seven other books.

Routledge Studies in the Modern History of France

Series Editor
Rachel Utley
University of Leeds, UK

Titles in the series:

French Soldiers' Morale in the Phoney War, 1939–1940
Maude Williams and Bernard Wilkin

https://www.routledge.com/Routledge-Studies-in-the-Modern-History-of-France/book-series/FRENCHHISTORY

French Soldiers' Morale in the Phoney War, 1939–1940

Maude Williams and Bernard Wilkin

Hanna Diamond
Jan. 2023

Routledge
Taylor & Francis Group

LONDON AND NEW YORK

First published 2019
by Routledge
2 Park Square, Milton Park, Abingdon, Oxon OX14 4RN

and by Routledge
52 Vanderbilt Avenue, New York, NY 10017

First issued in paperback 2020

Routledge is an imprint of the Taylor & Francis Group, an informa business

British Library Cataloguing-in-Publication Data
A catalogue record for this book is available from the British Library

Library of Congress Cataloging-in-Publication Data
A catalog record has been requested for this book

ISBN 13: 978-0-367-58324-8 (pbk)
ISBN 13: 978-1-138-23274-7 (hbk)

Typeset in Galliard
by Integra Software Services Pvt. Ltd.

Contents

List of figures and tables

Acknowledgements

The authors would like to acknowledge the following people for providing support without which the realisation of this project would have been impossible: Alistaire Nicholas, who has been incredibly helpful and patient while correcting our chapters, Timothy Baycroft, our mentor and friend, James Connolly, a fellow propaganda enthusiast, and Niky Lambert, who agreed to read chapters of this book. We are in debt to Prof. Peter Jackson, who was kind enough to write the foreword. Let us not forget the staff of the *Service Historique de la Défense* and the *Archives de l'État en Belgique*. The support of our families proved essential as usual. We are also grateful to Phileas, the tiny terror.

Foreword

Peter Jackson
University of Glasgow

The legacies of defeat, occupation and collaboration have cast a long shadow over historical understanding of the period before the fall of France. The state of the French army is no exception. This excellent book by two exceptionally talented young scholars does much to clear away the stubborn undergrowth left by decades of historiographical neglect. What emerges is a nuanced and detailed picture of an army struggling to meet the unique and unprecedented challenges thrown up by the Phoney War. Memories of 1914–1918 weighed heavily on the army of the Republic. On the eve of the German invasion, the vast majority of French soldiers were nonetheless 'motivated to fight the Germans to secure peace for the next generations'.

This deeply researched study therefore calls into question long-standing assumptions about French resolve in 1940. For many years historians explained France's military defeat within the context of wider moral judgements concerning the state of French society between the wars. The Third Republic was characterised as a bankrupt regime in which parliamentary politics and narrow self-interest took priority over the national interest and a spirit of collective sacrifice. In contrast to the generation of the Great War, the leaders of inter-war France failed to marshal the energies of the nation in preparation for the inevitable war with Hitler's Germany. The French nation entered a war for which it was neither materially nor psychologically prepared.

For a long time accounts of the fall of France were thus predetermined by a teleology of defeat. France fell because its society was decadent, its political leaders were incompetent and short-sighted, its foreign and defence policies were flawed, its military leadership was deficient and its army was ill-equipped and lacked the will to fight. The defeat, along with the occupation and collaboration that followed, were interpreted as the inevitable consequences of a long process of national decay. These themes were central to the way the defeat was represented by the Vichy regime. After 1944, they continued to provide a general framework for interpretations of French politics and policy that have reverberated down the decades through to the early twenty-first century. Jean-Baptise Duroselle, the long-time *doyen* of international history in France, entitled his magisterial study of French foreign and military policy during this period *La décadence*.

Anthony Adamthwaite, Nicole Jordan, Eugen Weber and Talbot Imlay have all, to a greater or lesser degree, endorsed this line of interpretation.[1]

Since the 1970s this interpretation has come under increasing challenge by scholars who warn against interpreting the history of inter-war France through the lens of 1940–1944. Robert Young underlined the difficult choices facing French civilian and military elites and argued that their policies were rational given the challenges that they faced. Robert Frank's careful analysis of French rearmament policy under the Popular Front showed that on the eve of war France was out-producing Germany in both tanks and aircraft. Several historians identified a process of 'psychological recovery' within French public attitudes during the spring of 1939 that allowed the government of Edouard Daladier to declare war on Germany with the support of the vast majority of the French population. Fabrice Grenard argues that this recovery underpinned French commitment to resist German aggression during the Phoney War. The work of military historians Henry Dutailly and Robert Doughty underlined the inflexibility of French operational doctrine and errors of judgement by the high command in arguing that defeat could be explained without recourse to theories of societal decay. Scholars such as John Cairns, Philip Bell, Martin Alexander, Jeffery Gunsburg and Julian Jackson, meanwhile, present the defeat of 1940 as an Allied defeat rather than a specifically French collapse.[2]

The morale of the French army provides a fascinating window through which to revisit this wider debate while at the same time shedding new light on the experience of French soldiers on the eve of the Battle of France. Maude Williams and Bernard Wilkin have provided us with an original and important study based on extensive research in a wide range of archival and other primary sources. The detailed surveys of the army general staff's *Contrôle postal* are complemented by extensive use of diaries, letters, memoirs and a survey of various media sources. In addition to the national press, official and unofficial soldiers' newspapers have been consulted as well as newsreels from this period. The result is a highly nuanced account that makes fascinating comparisons with the way the French went to war in 1914.

French soldiers accepted war in September 1939 with the same combination of resignation and determination that had prevailed in August 1914. Desertions were a negligible 0.099 per cent of all those mobilised. Reports on the attitudes of French conscripts highlighted a widespread conviction that war was necessary to end to repeated German bids to disrupt the peace of Europe. But the peculiar character of the war made the struggle to maintain this resolve especially difficult. The great galvanising force of the Great War was that it was a struggle to liberate French soil from the German invader. This was not the case during the opening phase of the Second World War. As general Victor Bourret observed in January 1940: 'Officers and men accept the war without enthusiasm but with gravity. They feel its complexity, which is more difficult to understand than in 1914–1918 because the national territory is not occupied.' This, combined with months of inaction and winter weather, took a toll on the morale of French troops.

All of this adds colour and texture to the previous studies – in particular those by Jean-Louis Crémieux-Brilhac and François Cochet – that have underlined the decline in army morale during the winter of 1939–1940. More revealing still is the evidence Williams and Wilkin have uncovered of a recovery in the fighting spirit of the army with the arrival of spring. Neither German nor communist propaganda were effective in sapping this new spirit. In fact, it is clear that the prospect of action against the Germans actually *revived* the fighting spirit of frontline troops. This evidence challenges the prevailing view that the French army was not fit to take the field in spring 1940. It instead adds a new dimension to growing evidence that French troops fought ferociously during the second phase of the Battle of France. As Martin Alexander has shown, the military catastrophe of May-June 1940 is best explained not as the inevitable product of a decadent society, but as 'a failure of command, conception and intellect'.[3]

One of the many strengths of this excellent book is that it highlights the need for more research into the causes of the Fall of France. Thanks to the work of these two rising stars of the next generation of historians, we have a much better understanding, not only of where we are, but also where we need to go in order to better understand this pivotal moment in European history.

Notes

1 J-B Duroselle, *Politique étrangère de la France, 1932–1939. La décadence* (Paris, Seuil, 1979). On this literature see P. Jackson 'Post-War Politics and the Historiography of French Strategy and Diplomacy before the Second World War', *History Compass*, 4/5 (2006), 870–905.
2 Useful historiographical discussions are P.M.H. Bell, 'John Cairns and the Historiography of Great Britain and the fall of France: Il n'y a que le premier pas qui coûte', in M. Alexander and K. Mouré (eds.), *Crisis and Renewal in France, 1918–1962* (Oxford, Berghahn, 2002), pp. 15–27; R.J. Young, *France and the Origins of the Second World War*, (London, Macmillan, 1996), pp. 37–59; Jackson, 'Returning to the Fall of France: Recent Work on the Causes and Consequences of the "Strange Defeat"', *Modern and Contemporary France*, 12, 4 (2004), pp. 513–536 and P. Finney, *Remembering the Road to World War Two: International History, National Identity, Collective Memory* (London, Routledge, 2011), pp. 149–187.
3 M.S. Alexander, 'After Dunkirk: the French army's performance against "Case Red", 25 May to 25 June 1940', *War in History*, 14, 2 (2007), pp. 219–264, quote from p. 258.

Introduction

France and Britain declared war on 3 September 1939, but preparations for conflict on the Franco-German border had been made since 1 September 1939. On both sides of the border, civilians living in the 'red zone' where evacuated while mobilised soldiers moved to the front.[1] The area around the Maginot Line was occupied by the army and civilian workers and, on the German side, *Westwallarbeiter* who carried on fortification work.[2] Despite the declaration of war and the mobilisation, no great offensive was launched until May 1940. Except for a small incursion into German territory between 20 September and 12 October 1939, both armies remained static on the 300 km frontline.[3] This period is known in French as the *Drôle de Guerre* (Phoney War in English, *Sitzkrieg* in German).[4]

It would be incorrect to assume that nothing happened on the Franco-German border during these months. At various places on the frontline both sides lost soldiers. During the Phoney War, 10,410 French military men died (excluding the Navy), equivalent to around 20% of the casualties during May and June 1940.[5] Most died of disease (43%), but 12.7% were killed in action (10.4% in accidents and 3.8% by suicide).[6] Moreover, many soldiers were captured by both sides. However, the war on the Rhine and on the Maginot Line was largely fought with words, pictures and propaganda.

Questions

Who were the men facing each other across the border? How was the French army in the North-East theatre of operations organised? What was the daily life of a French soldier? What factors influenced the French army's morale during this unique period of the war? This book is an attempt to answer these questions and many more. Several short testimonies exist in various publications but no thorough study of French military morale has been attempted. The term 'morale', used in both military and civilian reports to define the psychological state of the soldiers, is difficult to grasp as it encompasses a range of different experiences and emotions.[7]

Studies have argued that the lack of fighting spirit in the French army explained the defeat of May-June 1940. This book refutes such a simplistic explanation.[8] It has been proven by others that the defeat was triggered by four factors: the surprise German assault through the Ardennes, the dynamism of German troops, the misuse of French forces (tanks and planes dispersed, the lack of motorised reserves, too many troops dedicated to the Maginot Line), and outdated strategies based on First World War doctrines.[9] This research is not another strategic assessment but aims to put French soldiers at the centre to understand their world as well as their material and mental well-being.

To get a clear picture of what happened in the mind of an individual, historians rely on sources. Testimonies, written or spoken, are subjective by nature which made an evaluation of morale difficult and required thorough critical analysis. Another problem was the variety of soldiers' situations: serving in the Sarre region was not the same as fighting in the Moselle sector. Thus, a complex picture emerged which required great nuance to offer both a broad and representative study.

Sources

This book is based on several primary sources. The most important was undoubtedly the collection of reports written by the *contrôle postal* (or CP – 2nd Bureau of the *État-Major Général* (EMG)). Its organisation was rooted in the 10 February 1939 decree regarding the *organisation des services de contre-espionnage en temps de paix et en temps de guerre* inspired by the First World War.[10] The CP, originally designed to fight espionage, became a barometer of soldiers' morale. Starting in November 1939, the office released frequent reports about the morale of various units and armies. Precise topics were explored, including morale, operations, enemy propaganda, Alsatian soldiers or material conditions, and quotations extracted from private letters were reproduced.[11] Officers writing these reports were given freedom to introduce or remove categories.

Extracts of letters were particularly useful when trying to penetrate soldiers' thoughts. However, this collection of sources was far from perfect as it offered only a selective picture of life on the frontline.[12] CP reports did not reproduce full letters and said little about the social background of quoted writers. It is clear that the censor who selected quotations for the CP had his own feelings and background, of which we know nothing. Moreover, soldiers knew that their letters were read and, as a result, adapted their description of life on the frontline. They also wanted to protect their relatives, avoiding gruesome details; it is clear that a soldier rarely talked as openly about army problems to his wife than to a fellow military man.[13] To solve these concerns, we also used private diaries. More intimate, they let us follow various soldiers throughout the Phoney War. In recent years, several diaries and letters have been published, giving a voice not only to intellectuals but equally to men of different and more modest social backgrounds.[14] Although, on average, farmers and factory workers wrote less, fortunately, official reports made sure to study their morale.[15]

Frontline newspapers were also used in this book. These informative primary sources are not without their problems. In 1939–1940, they were written by educated men such as priests, officers, or non-commissioned officers.[16] Moreover, they were scrutinised by the army and the government, just like the conventional press. In various issues, spaces were left blank after having been censored.[17] Frontline newspapers were nonetheless an excellent mirror of the daily life at the front and often reflect problems and worries.[18] Speaking to fellow soldiers, these newspapers were forced to stick to the reality of life in the army to be successful. As such, a certain level of authenticity was guaranteed.

To understand broad policies and decision-makers, we consulted administrative documents produced by civilian and military authorities. This type of primary source gave us fundamental indications on how commanders saw their men and what steps were taken to improve morale in the army. The French military did not work in a vacuum. External influences, such as the media, were also analysed. Radio broadcasts, newspapers and newsreels were all included in this study to understand how French soldiers interacted with the outside world. Was propaganda as intense in 1939–1940 as it was during the First World War? German psychological warfare was an important factor on the frontline. It has often been stated that it played a vital part in the defeat. This study will argue that German propaganda was not as effective as previously stated and was certainly not the main explanation for the French defeat of 1940.[19]

The historiography so far

Study of the Phoney War, especially on the Franco-German front, is still limited. As historians like Bruno Cabanes and Édouard Husson stated, 'we know too little about the soldiers, the war culture and the war memory, especially compared to the First World War'.[20] French historians working on the Second World War have often preferred the study of Free France or the Vichy Regime. Only a handful of books have been written on the Phoney War. Recently, Fabrice Grenard looked at politics and society in France, explaining that the population was fully committed to the war effort as soon as September 1939.[21] A few years before, Jean-Louis Crémieux-Brilhac had released a fundamental study of French society during the Phoney War. This book is still the reference in French. Written in the 1990s, his two volumes explored in detail the political and social life of France (volume 1) as well as soldiers and workers in 1939–1940 (volume 2).[22] In addition, Crémieux-Brilhac as well as other French and British researchers, wrote articles in the 1970s about the Franco-British armies and the public opinion.[23] Another more recent book on French soldiers must be mentioned. François Cochet published in 2006 a study of the French army during the Phoney War.[24] This publication is useful to understand the context, but this study of propaganda was superficial. Reproducing several clichés, Cochet argued that French propaganda was weaker than that used by the Germans.

There have also been local studies. Henri Hiegel has looked at life in the Moselle region while others researched local aspects of the Maginot Line or specific French units.[25] Other books are useful for an understanding of propaganda, the British army, or the complex organisation of the French military.[26]

Many aspects of life on the Maginot Line remain nonetheless unknown.[27] We sincerely hope that this book will encourage others to look at this fascinating part of the Second World War.

Content

This book is made up of five chapters, each looking at a specific aspect of life on the frontline. The first studies the organisation of the French Army on the Franco-German front and its living conditions. It will be argued that soldiers faced difficult conditions and a shortage of military supplies. The authorities tried to improve the situation but the cold and the lack of food damaged morale.

The second chapter gives an overview of morale in the army during the Phoney War. Three phases have been identified, each reflecting a major change. Ultimately, it will be shown that French soldiers, despite difficult conditions, were motivated to fight the Germans to secure peace for the next generations.

The next chapter examines strategies used by military authorities to combat idleness and low morale in the French military. Caring deeply about the army's psychological state, commanders launched training campaigns, improved living accommodations and introduced various distractions.

The fourth chapter looks at a crucial aspect of the Phoney War: German propaganda and communist activities targeting the army. Looking at these forms of psychological warfare, this study will highlight their successes, but also their serious limitations.

Finally, the last chapter studies relations between French and British soldiers. The Phoney war was a time of interaction between men of different cultures. The French Government as well as French and British propaganda institutions tried to promote cooperation between allied troops on the frontline. However, French soldiers formed their own views based on personal experience. Using personal documents and military reports, this chapter will argue that French soldiers did not have a homogenous opinion of the British: suspicion, doubt, but also friendship, appeared between the two armies.

The names of the various institutions and units mentioned in this book have been kept in the original language (French or German). A glossary explaining their various roles can be found at the end of the book. Citations have been translated into English by the authors.

Notes

1 'Red zones' were areas along the border and the frontline. Civilians living there were evacuated to protect the population and facilitate the army's work. See: Nicholas Williams, *An 'Evil Year in Exile'. The Evacuation of the Franco-German Border Areas in 1939 under Democratic and Totalitarian Conditions* (Berlin, 2018).

2 On the topic: Nicholas Williams, 'Les évacuations de 1939 en Moselle et en Sarre : cadres et plans stratégiques pour la prise en charge des populations civiles', in: *Vingtième Siècle. Revue d'histoire*, 128 (2015), pp. 91–104.

3 Henri Hiegel, *Ils disent drôle de guerre ceux qui n'y étaient pas … 3 septembre 1939–10 mai 1940* (Sarreguemines, 1983), pp. 219–254.

4 This name appeared for the first time in the newspaper *Gringoire* in October 1939. Roland Dorgelès, *La Drôle de Guerre : 1939–1940* (Paris, 1957), p. 9.

5 Jean Quellien, Françoise Passera, Jean-Luc Leleu, and Michel Daeffler (eds), *La France pendant la Seconde Guerre mondiale: Atlas Historique* (Paris, 2010), p. 37.

6 Ibid.

7 Service Historique de la Défense – Armée de Terre (SHD AT): 27N69. This term was used by the CP (*contrôle postal*) and was already found during the First World War. Jean-Noël Jeanneney, 'Les Archives des Commissions de Contrôle postal aux Armées (1916–1918). Une source précieuse pour l'histoire contemporaine de l'opinion et des mentalités', in: *Revue d'Histoire Moderne & Contemporaine*, 15.1 (1968), pp. 209–233, p. 217.

8 François Fonvieille-Alquier, *Les Français dans la Drôle de guerre* (Paris, 1971).

9 Quellien, Passera, Leleu and Daeffler (eds), *La France pendant la Seconde Guerre mondiale*, p. 41.

10 SHD AT: 7N2486. Décret d'organisation des services du contre-espionnage; Jeanneney, 'Les Archives des Commissions de Contrôle postal aux Armées (1916–1918)', pp. 209–233.

11 SHD AT: 27N69. CP reports from October 1939 to May 1940.

12 Jeanneney, 'Les Archives des Commissions de Contrôle postal aux Armées', p. 217.

13 Ibid.

14 Among others: Jean Paul Sartre, *Carnets de la Drôle de Guerre: Septembre 1939–Mars 1940*, ed. by Arlette Elkaïm-Sartre (Paris, 1995); Georges Sadoul, *Journal de guerre: 2 septembre 1939–20 juillet 1940* (Paris, 1977); Eric Deroo and Pierre de Taillac, *Carnets de déroute 1939–1940 : Lettres et récits inédits* (Paris, 2010); Jean-Bernard Wahl, *Jours Tranquilles et Bruits de Guerre Au Mont Des Welches: Août 1939–Juillet 1940; (Petite) Histoire, La 'Drôle de Guerre' Sur La Ligne Maginot* (Huningue, 2007); Paul Tuffrau, *De la 'drôle de guerre' à la libération de Paris (1939–1944) : Lettres et Carnets* (Paris, 2002).

15 A notable exception is: Gustave Folcher, *Les carnets de guerre de Gustave Folcher, paysan languedocien, 1939–1945*, ed. by Rémy Cazals (Paris, 2000).

16 See for example: *Cambronne, Coup de Bambi, CQ, Hausse 400, Je passe partout, L'Isard de Metz, La rose Maginot, La voix de la voie de 60, Le cheval à vapeur, Le chic à Nied, Le cri du béton, Le pied Lourd, Rouge vert*: Archives Départementales de la Moselle (AD Moselle): 5 R 628.

17 Among others, see: *Isard de Metz*, 15 December 1939.

18 Stéphane Audoin-Rouzeau, 'Les soldats français et la Nation de 1914 à 1918 d'après les journaux de tranchées', *Revue d'Histoire Moderne & Contemporaine*, 34.1 (1987), pp. 66–86, p. 69.

19 Jean-Louis Crémieux-Brilhac, *Les Français de l'an 40. Tome 1. La guerre, oui ou non ?* (Paris, 1990); Max Gallo, *Et ce fut la défaite de 1940: la cinquième colonne* (Paris, 1980).

20 Bruno Cabanes, Édouard Husson, *Les sociétés en guerre: 1911–1946* (Paris, 2003), p. 12.

21 Grenard Fabrice, *La drôle de guerre – L'entrée en guerre des Français* (Paris, 2015).

22 Jean-Louis Crémieux-Brilhac, *Les Français de l'an 40. Tome 1. La guerre, oui ou non ?*; *Tome 2, Ouvriers et soldats* (Paris,1990).

23 Colloque franco-britannique (ed.), *Les relations franco-britanniques de 1935 à 1939 : communications présentées aux colloques franco-britanniques tenus à Londres (Imperial War Museum) du 18 au 21 octobre 1971, Paris (Comité international d'Histoire de la 2ème Guerre mondiale) du 25 au 29 septembre 1972* (Paris, 1975); Comité international d'histoire de la Deuxième Guerre mondiale (ed.), *Français et Britanniques dans la drôle de guerre: actes du colloque franco-britannique tenu à Paris du 8 au 12 décembre 1975* (Paris, 1979).

24 François Cochet, *Les soldats de la drôle de guerre* (Paris, 2004).

25 Henri Hiegel, *La Drôle de Guerre en Moselle, 1939–1940* (Sarreguemines, 1983); Jean-Bernard Wahl, *La Ligne Maginot En Alsace: 200 Km de Béton et d'acier* (Ellange, 2013); Roger Bruge, *Faites sauter la ligne Maginot!*, (Paris, 1975); Jean-Pascal Soudagne and Michel Mansuy, *Comprendre la ligne Maginot: Nord, Ardennes, Lorraine, Alsace, Savoie, Dauphiné, Alpes-Maritimes* (Rennes, 2009).

26 See: Maude Fagot, *La drôle de guerre: Une guerre d'influence. La propagande antibritannique allemande et la guerre psychologique française pendant la drôle de guerre du 3 septembre 1939 au 10 mai 1940* (Master's Thesis, Albert-Ludwig Universität/Université Lumière Lyon II, 2013); Maude Fagot, 'La guerre des ondes entre la France et l'Allemagne pendant la 'drôle de guerre'', in: *Revue Historique 671* (2014), pp. 630–654; Edward Smalley, *British Expeditionary Force, 1939–40*, 2015 (New York, 2015); Jean-Yves Mary and Alain Hohnadel, *Hommes et Ouvrages de La Ligne Maginot* (Paris, 2000).

27 Many topics deserve thorough studies, such as prostitution on the frontline and German prisoners of war.

1 The French Army on the German-French border

For the last twenty years, historians have investigated the military and strategic reasons behind the French defeat of 1940. The lack of co-ordination in the use of artillery and tanks,[1] failure of aerial bombing,[2] the surprise German attack through the Ardennes[3] and the flood of refugees that reduced mobility have been highlighted as potential causes for the disaster.[4] Despite a growing body of literature on May-June 1940, we know little of the men who served on the French side during the Phoney War. Who were they? Where were they? How did they live? How were their units structured? We must understand the hardship and the appalling conditions in which French soldiers lived from September 1939 to appreciate their state of mind at the beginning of May 1940. This chapter will look at the historical background leading to the construction of the fortified line before investigating the state of the French army on the Franco-German frontier in 1939–1940.

Forces involved on the North-East front

The structure and organisation of the French army along the German border faced major changes after the First World War. Indeed, the recovered 'lost territories' (Alsace, Moselle and parts of the Meurthe-et-Moselle) made the 1871–1918 defence line known as 'Séré de Rivières' obsolete.

As map 1.1 shows, the post-1918 border with Germany was considerably longer than before the conflict. This was not the only strategic difficulty of the interwar period. France faced a severe demographic crisis in 1918. By the end of the First World War, the country had a population of 38,670,000, 3,000,000 fewer men than in 1914. As shown in Figure 1.2, the population rose during the interwar period but by 1940 only matched that of 1914.[6]

In summary, the country had fewer men to defend a longer border. This major problem invalidated the French Army's favoured and traditional aggressive doctrine. Many understood that France would have to switch to a defensive strategy to save human resources. General Philippe Pétain was first to advocate a fortified line in 1919. This proposal was brought forward by the War Minister André Lefèvre in March 1920. On 17 May 1920, the *Conseil Supérieur de la Guerre* ordered Generals Humbert and Berthelot to submit specific proposals. Two years

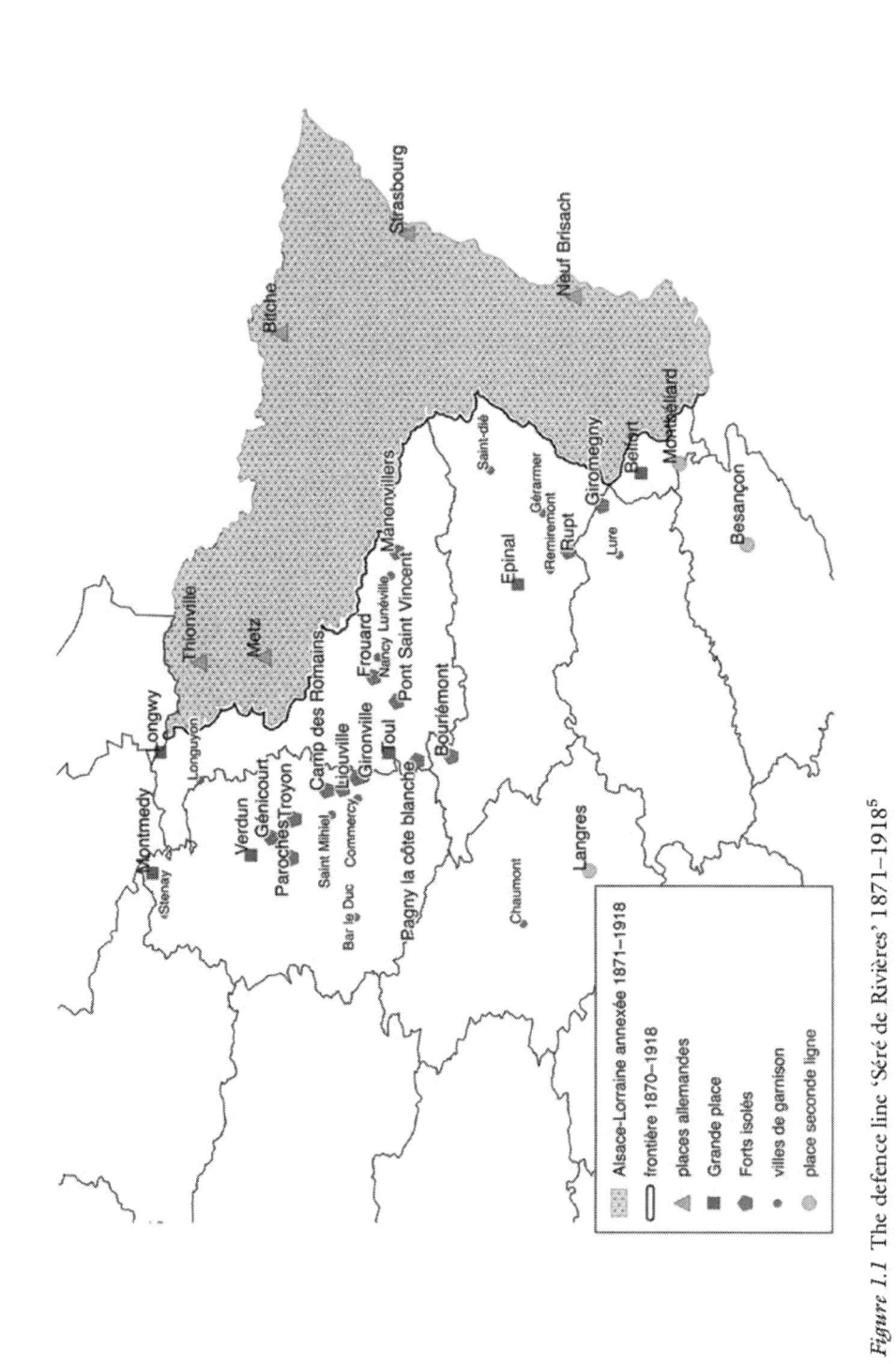

Figure 1.1 The defence line 'Séré de Rivières' 1871–1918[5]

Credit: Maude Williams

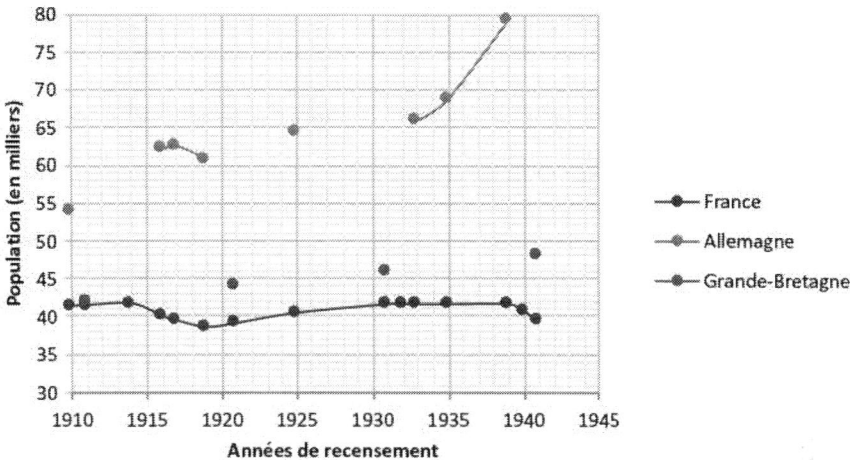

Figure 1.2 The demography of France, Great Britain and Germany, 1910–1945[7]
Credit: Maude Williams

later, the officers presented their research, but disagreements arose between those who favoured aggressive doctrines and mobile warfare and those who supported the fortification of the border. Unable to decide, the CSG formed a commission named the *Commission chargée des études d'organisation de la défense du territoire*, presided over by Marshal Joseph Joffre.[8] This commission was unable to agree on a strategy and therefore failed to deliver results. It was replaced by the *Commission de défense du territoire* on 3 August 1922. A report was delivered to the War Minister in 1923 but failed once again to resolve the dispute. After two years of stagnation caused by the victory of the left and the absence of Marshal Pétain, a new *Commission de défense des frontières* began to study the matter in 1925. By the beginning of 1927, a proposal was delivered to the President of the Council Gaston Doumergue and War Minister Paul Painlevé.[9] It suggested lines of fortifications in the area of Metz-Thionville and Lauter-Haut Alsace.[10] Another commission, the *Commission d'organisation des régions fortifiées*, created on 30 September 1927, examined the project's practicality. In 1930, the new War Minister André Maginot released 2.9 billion francs to build the line bearing his name. The initial plan was executed in two stages and completed by 1934. Additional funds were found to extend the line between 1934 and 1940 so, when the war began, French soldiers were still working on the unfinished Maginot Line.[11]

By 1 September 1939, the North-East front was defended by 60 fortresses, including 27 structures for 500 to 800 men and 6 to 12 artillery pieces. In addition, on the Maginot Line, there was also 33 intermediary strongholds, manned by 100 to 250 soldiers equipped with machine-guns and anti-tank cannons, and 310 bunkers, intended for 30 to 50 men, as well as many pillboxes, each for a handful of men.[12] The northern part of the front was defended by fortresses equipped with artillery, except for the Sarre sector in which the fortifications were less significant. Near the Rhine, artillery was not required as the French relied on the natural defence of the river.[13] It should be noted that the men deployed on the Maginot Line were part of a new branch of the French military: fortress troops. This new designation was introduced on 15 April 1933[14] and included about 415,000 men by 1939–1940.[15] On 1 September 1939, these troops were organised in *Régiments d'infanterie de Forteresse* (RIF). The Maginot Line was divided into three *Régions Fortifiées* (RF): Metz, Lauter and Belfort, each with its own headquarters and commanded by a general.[16] The RIF were subdivided into *Secteurs Fortifiés* (SF)[17] alongside the Franco-German border along with two *Secteurs Défensifs* (SD) (Sarre and Altkirch).[18]

On 16 March 1940 this structure was modified to rationalise the chain of command and simplify the transmission of orders.[20] A number of SF were renamed *Corps d'Armée de Forteresse* (CAF) while others became *Divisions d'Infanterie de Forteresse* (DIF). In the Metz RF, the Crusnes SF became the 42nd CAF; in Lauter RF, the Vosges SF the 43rd CAF and in the Belfort RF, the Bas-Rhin SF the 103rd DIF, the Colmar SF the 104th DIF and the Mulhouse SF the 105th DIF. Each SF or DIF came under an Army Corps, which in turn formed part of an Army and then an Army Group. While most of the soldiers serving on the Maginot Line were part of the RIF there were also artillerymen as well as military engineers, who were required to maintain the equipment.[21]

The organisation of the Maginot Line was new but followed a well-defined hierarchy based on traditional structures. In 1939, the North-Eastern front consisted of four Military Regions: VI (Metz), XX (Nancy), X (Strasbourg) and VII (Besançon). The VIIth Military Region was covered by Army Group 3, General Antoine Marie Benoit Besson,[22] with 8th Army (General Marcel Garchery)[23] in the Haut-Rhin. General Alphonse Georges[24] was responsible for the whole Northern front, which not only included Army Group 2 and 3 but also Army Group 1, deployed from Luxemburg to the North Sea. The French Army was commanded by General Maurice Gamelin[25] but he was replaced by General Maxime Weygand[26] on 17 May 1940.

In September 1939, France mobilised 4,564,000 men,[27] including 725,000 stationed outside mainland France and 700,000 serving at their workplace on 'special duty'.[28] The oldest mobilised soldiers were more than 45 years old. As stated before, demography was not in France's favour. Twenty-nine age groups, or *classes*, were mobilised to compensate for the lack of younger soldiers. This significant crisis becomes obvious when the number of conscripts is compared with that in 1939: 1,250,000 soldiers were between 20 to 25 years old at the beginning of the First World War, as opposed to 600,000 in 1939. Signs of an ageing population were also clearly visible when compared with Germany which only mobilised seven *classes*.[29] It should also be recalled that Great Britain had 897,000 men in 1939 and 1,650,000 in June 1940; only 500,000 of them were deployed in France.[30]

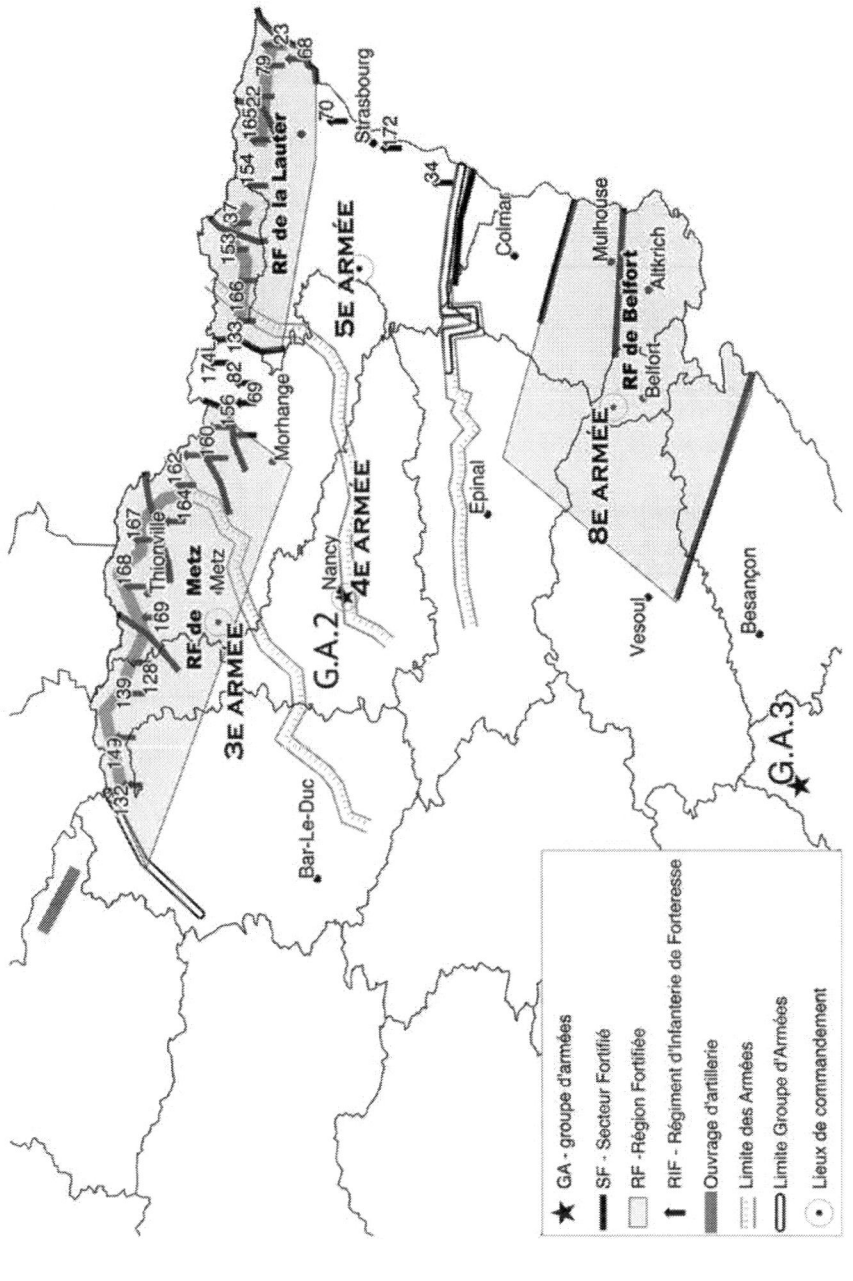

Figure 1.3 Fortified regions and sectors[19]

Credit: Maude Williams

The French army had 20 well-trained and well-equipped active service divisions and another 74 reserve divisions, far less experienced, filled the gaps.[31] New divisions were created and others were transferred to become accustomed to frontline duty. In April 1940, young men serving in fortified regions were sent to mobile divisions and replaced by older soldiers.[32] Several officers were also removed for further training in an attempt to improve their leadership.[33] These changes make it difficult to precisely locate army corps and divisions during the Phoney War. On the North-Eastern front, divisions and their regiments were not only deployed on the Maginot Line but also in forward posts or behind the fortification line.[34] Two periods are particularly useful to understand French troops during the Phoney War: the end of September 1939, just after the Sarre offensive, and the beginning of May 1940, just before the German invasion of the Low Countries. They offer slices of life on the frontline and provide an overview of how the French army changed between September and May. At the end of September 1939, the French and the Germans had respectively 84 and 45 divisions.[35] Along the Sarre and the Palatinate, the French could count on 1,600 cannons against 300. All German tanks were deployed in Poland until November 1939.[36] Moreover, German fortifications, such as the Siegfried line or *Westwall* in German, were unfinished.[37] General Prételat, commanding Army Group 2, launched the Sarre offensive on 7 September 1939 and the front was stabilised between 14 September and 4 October. On 24 September, the Eastern front (stretching from Luxemburg to Switzerland) was occupied by nine *Corps d'Armée* (CA), one *Corps d'Armée Coloniale* (CAC), four *Divisions d'Infanterie Nord-Africaine* (DINA), five divisions of *Divisions d'Infanterie Motorisée* (DIM), 21 Infantry Divisions (DI), four Divisions of Colonial Infantry (DIC) and seven *Eléments Organiques de Corps d'Armées* (EOCA).[38] Most of the men in the Sarre area fell back between 4 and 15 October 1939 and the rearguard withdrew on 16 and 17 October.[40] Between the end of the Sarre offensive and the German offensive of May 1940, the armies faced each other with little fighting.

By 10 May 1940, the French army had undergone several changes. There were 2,240,000 French and colonial troops in 104 divisions on the North-Eastern front where 151 Allied, including British, divisions faced 135 German divisions.[41] Army Group 2 was formed of 10 Army Corps, with 19 French and a Scottish Division, and one DIF within 3rd, 4th and 5th Armies. 8th Army had four divisions and two DIF in two Army Corps as part of Army Group 3.

Noticeable changes had taken place, as seen in map 1.5, for example the 3rd, 4th, 5th DINA, which had fought during the Sarre offensive in September 1939, had been transferred from the Franco-German front to Army Group 1 along the Belgian border.[43]

The Maginot line had drastically changed French attitudes to war. Although little had changed from a geographical perspective, as bunkers and blockhouses discreetly fitted into the landscape, the line of fortification had important human consequences. The Maginot Line was located 8 kilometres from the border with

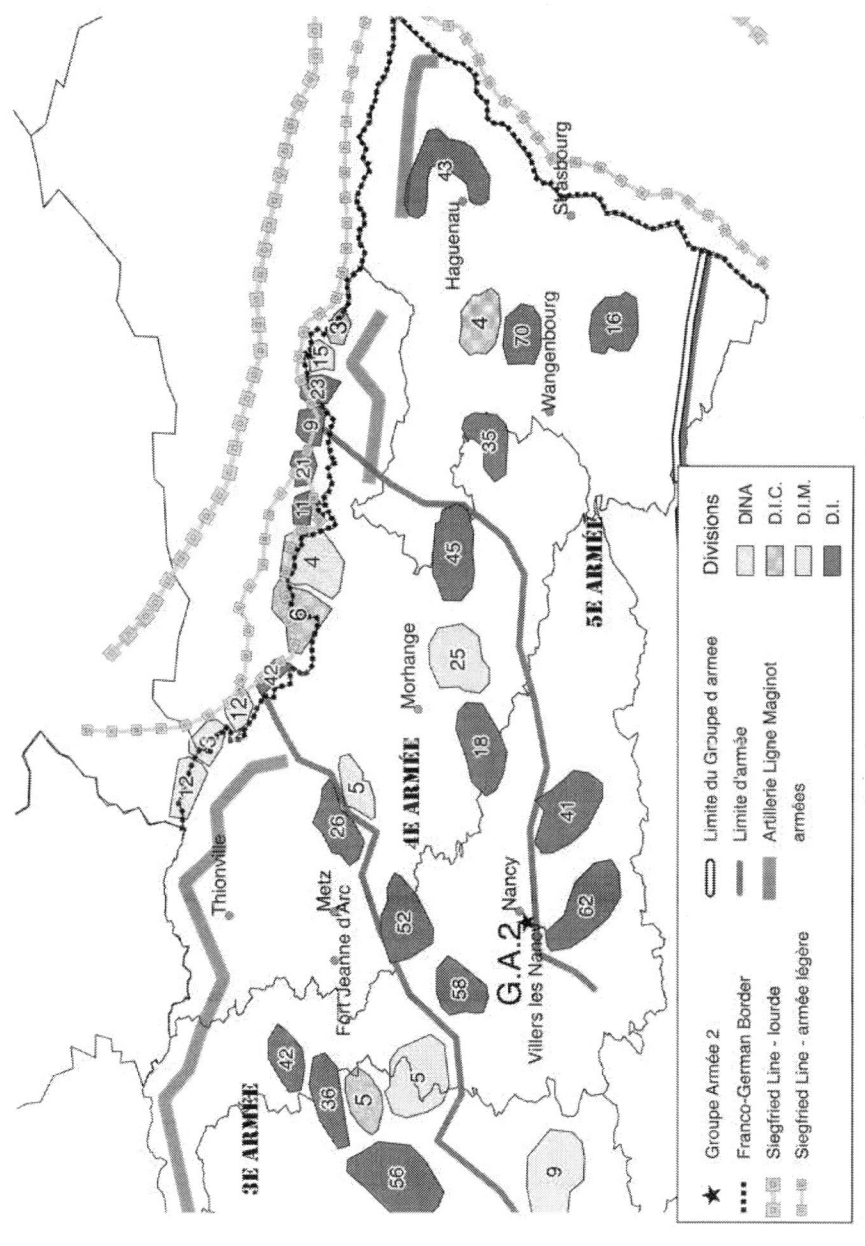

Figure 1.4 The French army on the French-German border on 24 September 1939.[39]
Credit: Maude Williams

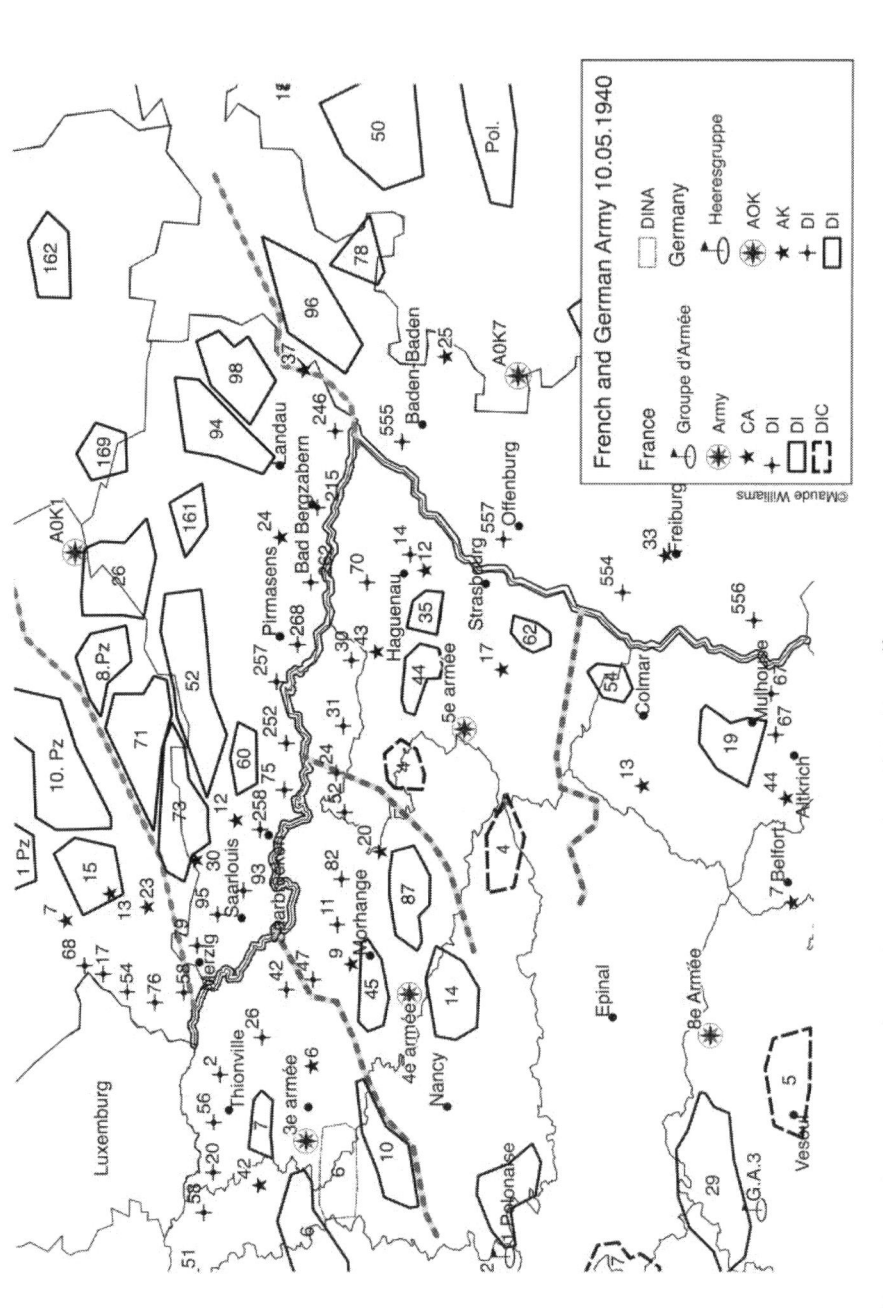

Figure 1.5 The French army on the French-German border in May 1940.[42]

Credit: Maude Williams

Germany, leaving densely populated territory undefended. The area between the line and the border, which included the city of Strasbourg, was known as the 'red zone'. Between 1924 and 1936, the army and the government drew up evacuation plans to prevent civilians from being stuck between opposing armies in case of war.[44] The main objective was to create a no man's land between the Maginot Line and the border. According to this plan, people living in the 'red zone' were to be evacuated to a more secure region of France. In September 1939, more than 600,000 inhabitants of Alsace and Lorraine left their houses for the South-East of France, where they remained until June 1940.[45]

During the first days of the conflict, the army moved up to the front while Alsatian and Lorraine civilians left for their 'inner exile'.[46] Soldiers, gendarmerie and various safeguarding commissions looked after abandoned villages and towns. Those who worked in vital sectors, mainly miners and factory workers, stayed behind.[47] Evacuated civilians sometimes tried to return to their village to check on their property but were quickly caught and escorted from the army zone. In the rear of the Maginot Line, civilians lived, in fear of evacuation, alongside the soldiers. Having understood the history and the structure of the Maginot Line, we can now look at life on the frontline.

Living conditions: hygiene, food and equipment

This chapter must now investigate life on the frontline. Before addressing issues of morale or propaganda, it is vital to understand a basic question: what was life for the troops like between September 1939 and May 1940? 10,410 soldiers lost their lives in France and in the colonies during the Phoney War: 30.1% died of unknown causes, 43% of illness, 3.8% by suicide, 10.4% in accidents and only 12.7% in action.[48] Poor sanitary conditions were responsible for the high number of illness-related deaths. It is important to highlight that living standards were not the same everywhere on the frontline. From September 1939 to May 1940, most men served either on the Maginot Line, in forward posts or in rear bases, living conditions, including hygiene, food and equipment, in these different parts of the front starkly different.

This section will look first at accommodations on the Maginot Line itself. Crews deployed in large and small forts slept in concrete rooms while men serving in smaller defensive positions had wooden barracks or tents for shelter. As a result, those housed in concrete fortifications had better protection from the rain and the cold and enjoyed modern amenities. Life in the long tunnels 'underground' was 'quite particular yet clean, well lit, well organised and comfortable'.[49] Soldiers slept in proper bedrooms equipped with iron bunks[50] or hammocks.[51] Rooms were intended for 18 men but were used by 24 to 32 soldiers. Rest was therefore organised in shifts: two beds being allocated to three soldiers.[52] Non-commissioned officers and officers enjoyed more space: 4 adjutants or 9 sergeants shared a room, only officers were allowed permitted privacy. Living conditions were acceptable but far from perfect, as this soldier's testimony from February 1940 demonstrated:

Our bedroom? Four concrete walls, painted with lime and perhaps white a long time ago, transpiring big drops of shiny sweat condensation. Big globules of water hang from the ceiling, the light turns them into transparent pearls. It is pretty but not very healthy. The bed is parallel to a big pipe located below. I have a tissue to dry these terrible drops. They are particularly annoying at night. At first, they wake me up when they fall on my face, and they force me to cover my body with a blanket. The number one enemy is water but the other is the cold. I wrapped my feet with a newspaper, I have two pairs of socks, but I am cold. The cold makes me suffer, especially at night. I have not been used to sleep standing.... .[53]

Large structures were equipped with other facilities: disciplinary rooms, a decontamination area, a first-aid station, sometimes a surgical room, and more rarely a dental clinic. Showers and toilets, a sign of modernity, were also found in fortresses. It should be recalled that most French families had no bathroom at home at the time.[54] Such comforts were essential for an acceptable life below ground:

I serve on the Maginot Line. It was a bit hard at first but you get used to everything, especially since comfort is not lacking. Electric heating, warm showers, electric cooking.... We are even working on a hair salon.[55]

As the war dragged on, this lifestyle became harder to tolerate:

I can assure you that I have had enough of this underground life. I have been here since 23 August and it is more than enough because, as you know, there is no distraction, and we are only allowed one hour to breathe outside.[56]

Underground, soldiers rarely saw the light of day, complained about being 'continually exposed to artificial lights'[57] and suffered headaches caused by loud sounds and the lack of fresh air.[58] Humidity was a real problem underground. It spoiled the food, damaged the telephones and fostered disease.[59] Heating devices were progressively installed to sanitise the environment.[60]

Serving on the Maginot Line did not always mean being in a concrete structure or having modern facilities. Men deployed in regions without large fortifications, such as the defensive sector of the Sarre on the Alsatian border, experienced a different type of duty and had to endure rougher conditions. Soldiers serving in pillboxes or bunkers had no proper sleeping accommodation.[61] Maurice Charles, adjutant-major in the 154th RIF, wrote the following account after being assigned to a bunker near Phillipsburg (Alsace):

We were told that we would serve on the Maginot Line. [...] Imagine our disappointment when the battalion was ordered to erect its tents in a rain-soaked field. The first night outside was less than brilliant because our men learnt that they would need to build the blockhouses before living inside them.[62]

Indeed, soldiers were often required to build their own accommodations and fortified positions. Tents offered little protection against the cold and the rain. Damp straw and corrugated iron became sought-after luxuries. In Lorraine, the colonel commanding the 63rd RI denounced this situation:

> The lack of corrugated iron and cardboard was badly perceived. Earth and wood were unable to stop water, making it impossible to light a fire in our flooded shelters. Men were constantly struggling with damp.[63]

Wet straw was difficult to endure at night as mattresses were soaked and rotten. To make matters worse, these appalling conditions favoured vermin, including mice and rats.[64] Winter made life on the frontline even more problematic. Prolonged exposure to cold conditions caused illness and frozen feet.[65]

Such Spartan conditions were also to be found at the forward posts.[66] Damp straw, the cold and the lack of proper beds were all responsible for a tough life. Barns were often used to accommodate soldiers:[67]

> Here, it has been very cold for a few days. Many men are unwell. Since Monday, the first-aid post has always been full and men are sent to the hospital on a daily basis. All of this is caused by our living conditions. Most of us sleep in draughty barns.[68]

In a few rare cases, soldiers lived in evacuated villages in Alsace and Lorraine.[69] There, they found comfortable rooms and enough supplies to make life more bearable where civilians had abandoned canned food, fruit and even chicken or pigs in September 1939.[70] There was a great temptation to take more than food. Several cases of pillaging were reported:

> We are in an evacuated village and I am saddened to see how our predecessors have behaved. It is disgusting and sad to see that French soldiers wearing the uniform destroyed, broke, smashed and soiled goods, furniture, china, laundry, etc. Everything in fact they could find here.[71]

It was strictly forbidden to take anything without a requisition order but in reality many soldiers did not care. Commanding officers were in a difficult position regarding civilians' belongings. They knew that their men lacked basic goods but they were supposed to uphold the law. On the other hand, enforcing it might trigger hostility or even disciplinary problems. A superior officer of 4th Army explained the dilemma in a letter:

> We were instructed to take whatever civilians had abandoned in evacuated villages: clothes, mattresses, stoves, etc. It is said that the rear lacks supplies

to host and warm refugees.[72] This decision is not extraordinary but a few comments must be made. First, the evacuation of the population living near the border will forever shame the government. [...] That said, our soldiers occupied the region and slept in villages. I do not have to underline how soldiers behaved, it is not pretty. Three months later, we were finally allowed to use whatever the civilians had left behind. It has been said and repeated: use local resources. Do not pillage, but use everything, this will help our supply units (they needed it badly). Our men enjoyed what they could find everywhere, blankets and mattresses. They did not have to sleep on straw anymore. Today, winter is coming and mud and rain is making life difficult to endure. We must tell our men: these mattresses, you have to give them back. Straw must be enough, we have to return this small comfort. What will make things worse is this official note that states that only mattresses belonging to officers can be retained.[73]

The occupation of abandoned villages by the military was particularly hard for Alsatian and Lorrainer soldiers wearing the French uniform.[74] Leave was used to check on evacuated houses or to recover belongings. They were usually appalled when they discovered how badly fellow French soldiers had behaved:

Last Sunday, I received the authorisation to travel to Huningue. I took a bike and rode 70 km in the afternoon. But I was more demoralised than tired. If you knew in what state my house was. Soldiers had broken the doors to get in. In our flat, the mess and the dirt almost brought me down. On the table, pots were filled with mould, the desk was broken, drawers were opened. Bedsheets were black, soldiers must have slept on them without removing their boots. My two violins below the bed... Prussians would not have done worse. But this was one case among a thousand. Alsatian comrades of my regiment told me worse things and I am ashamed to write them in this letter. This is how they take care of those who sacrifice their lives.[75]

A mixture of sadness and anger was palpable in the correspondence of those who witnessed senseless destruction. Alsatian and Lorrainer soldiers denounced this form of violence in their letters to their family, therefore demoralising entire communities.[76]

Most divisions were deployed behind the Maginot Line. Barns and farms were once again used to accommodate them. Others, the lucky ones, stayed with civilian families or lived in barracks. Jean Zay, a former Minister of National Education and Fine Arts, was given a requisitioned bedroom in a Lorraine village:

I live in a very acceptable bedroom on the ground floor of a middle-class house, a hardware store: a big provincial bedroom, a bit rustic, with a faience boiler. [...] Cupboard with a marble top and a bucket and a pot of water (running water is unknown), a little blue light. [...] I have vast cupboards, a big table, the bed is deep and has many sheets and a quilt.[77]

Life with civilians was both peaceful and emotionally rewarding. Mealtimes were spent together while families enjoyed socialising with soldiers in front of the boiler.[78] In return, members of the military worked in their hosts' farms.[79] Communication was not always easy since the older generation of Alsatians and Lorrainers did not necessarily understand French: 'We do not understand these people because they only speak German, but it is very clear that they hate Hitler.'[80] People from Alsace and Lorraine were more than often perceived as upstanding French citizens. Their hostility toward the German chancellor and their hospitality were sure signs:

> We are now in a small town and were moved by the inhabitants' warm welcome. I stay in the bedroom of a house belonging to a nice family who lived under German rule. Their generosity is so touching that we are embarrassed. They give us the nicest and most comfortable things. Refusing these things would sadden them. They treat us as their own children and it is hard to imagine how patriotic this population can be. This reception is a comfort and we hope that refugees from Alsace and Lorraine are treated as well in the western and central provinces. Really, my stay in this mining area of Lorraine is something I will remember.[81]

Local authorities were equally pleased to see how well soldiers from the 'inside' (a term used by Alsatian and Lorrainer populations for the rest of the country) and civilians lived together:

> Looking at relations between the men and civilians, we were could see very fortunate signs of friendly collaboration, even touching gestures of brotherhood... It has been said that the 'French soldier', the term used to designate a non-Alsatian soldier, was particularly kind, happy, and always ready to help. Burgundians of the 8th Corps were especially liked in the wine region at the foot of the Vosges. A farmer told us: 'the army brought 5 horses to my barn a month ago. At first, they were looked after by Alsatian reservists who believed that they owned everything. They emptied the basement (and even broke the door) and were noisy, badly behaved and unhelpful. They were replaced by Burgundians: they were kind, discreet and far more helpful. When they arrived in the morning to feed the animals, they were careful not to wake the children. These things are noticeable and please us.' In Molsheim, men commanded by General Noël were from Toulouse. They brought their lovely accent, which is being adopted by little Alsatians. It seems that they also brought sunshine and happiness in their luggage. We found them pleasant and they were happy in Alsace.[82]

As these letters suggested, tensions between civilians and soldiers were minimal. This does not mean that life behind the border was without incident. Military men occasionally complained about the lack of hospitality displayed by Alsatian and Lorrainers, especially in the area of Bitche.[83] French soldiers from the 'inside' occasionally suspected pro-German feelings or separatist attitudes in the border region:

> Civilians do not like soldiers very much. I think they prefer those who believe in a 'vital space'. If we have to stay here for long, I am afraid there will be clashes between civilians and the military. In the evening, everybody must be home by 8.30. Posters warn us that women approach soldiers at night and try to obtain information.[84]

While it must be remembered that coexistence was usually harmonious, nevertheless civilians were not entirely comfortable with the presence of soldiers. Stories of pillaging by the French military were shared amongst the population, especially at the beginning of the war. Fortunately, soldiers loudly condemned it, clearly showing that this kind of behaviour was not the norm.

Whilst sleeping conditions varied across the different areas on the front shortages of equipment and clothing were suffered everywhere. Heavy rain and flooding in October and November 1939 gave rise to concerns about the lack of heating devices and coats. Soldiers were continually wet and cold:

> If we had boilers to get warm during the day, considering that we must stay in the dark at night, we could at least dry our coats and other belongings. We do not have any spare, not even a dry sock. We have to make do, 25 to 30 men, with an old kitchen stove in which we burn wood, because coal is lacking.[85]

The lack of good quality boots was another major problem. In October 1939, heavy rain flooded the front, making entire regions muddy and cold: 'everywhere we complain about the lack of waterproof shoes. We are unable to dry them and have cold feet, bronchitis, etc. We ask for a second pair.'[86] On 1 November 1939, 2,000,000 pairs of shoes and 1,500,000 blankets were needed.[87] It was estimated that 700,000 pairs of shoes, 200,000 pants, 65,000 blankets and 15,000 tents were still lacking at the beginning of 1940.[88] The army was clearly unable to respond to the demand. A military cobbler serving in the 173rd Régiment d'Artillerie Lourde Divisionnaire (RALD) of 5th Army seemed rather at a loss: 'I am alone for 200 men and I do not have the material needed. What I can do?'.[89] Budget cuts and delays in mass-production caused the shortages. In November 1939, rubber boots were dispatched to the front, bringing 'great satisfaction' everywhere.[90] Unfortunately, not enough of them were made.[91] Conflicts and protests followed: 'We received pairs of boots, but I only have 20 to give to 40 men. What a mess.'[92] Slowly, new types of raincoats and warm clothes were produced but, once again, not enough were made.[93] The army tried to appease its soldiers by providing clogs. This old-fashioned type of footwear was deemed an insult by those who had to face mud and freezing conditions. Men, unwilling to endure the harsh weather in such poor circumstances, asked their families for help[94]:

Most wrote to their families to request rubber boots. At least, they do not have wet feet. It is nonetheless unfortunate. If we need something, we have to buy it. It seems to me that the army should provide something so we can have dry feet.[95]

In October 1939, cold became a real issue.[96] Soldiers improvised, knitting woollen socks[97] or asking their wives for clothes and blankets. The army tried to provide warm clothes but failed once again to deliver enough items. The situation did improve in March 1940:

> We received extra equipment. We were given an extra pair of shoes, under-wear, a pair of pants, two blankets (a small and a large one, we will use it for protection from the sun in summer). So far, 50% of the men have received nothing.[98]

In March 1940, the temperature rose. Soldiers became less vocal about the equipment but continued to complain about the 'lack of underwear' and about the fact that entire units were so badly equipped that 'their bottoms were stuck in the wind'.[99]

Sleeping conditions and uniforms were major sources of complains but food was also an issue. Soldiers needed energy to build fortifications, pillboxes and bunkers, or just to conduct military patrols. In larger fortifications, food was prepared using pots on electric cookers.[100] Officers and soldiers had different kitchens. In modern facilities, there was a percolator to make coffee and a machine to peel potatoes. Smaller fortifications used gas or coal in the kitchen.[101] The daily allocation of food was calculated precisely: 600g of bread, 400g to 450g of meat (more rarely 500g), 32g of sugar, 32g of coffee (24g if deployed behind the line), 60g of rice or dried vegetables. French soldiers also received daily 50cl of wine and 15g of tobacco.[102]

Rations developed during the Phoney War but they were generally badly received. Between September 1939 and February 1940, meals were heavily criticised. In March 1940, letters from soldiers of the 3rd, 4th and 5th Armies underlined a change.[103] Meat was always the main issue. Beef was considered very bad, almost inedible. It was even blamed for food poisoning: 'Everybody has diarrhoea, some have to go to the loo up to 20 times. The meat is probably responsible for this.'[104] Pork and veal were introduced and slowly replaced beef.[105] Quality improved but quantities and freshness remained significant problems.[106] In various sectors, officers tried to 'grow their own vegetables in order to improve the food'.[107] In winter, food had a tendency to freeze very quickly: 'Since our arrival, we have been badly supplied. Wine, bread, meat, vegetables, everything is frozen.'[108] There was criticism over its monotony: 'Our menus are not varied: rice and beef with a tomato sauce from Monday to Sunday.'[109] Potatoes, both loved and filling, became a rarity: 'rice, noodles, lentils, peas and fatty meat. It is always the same... We have not seen a potato for the last three months.'[110] Soldiers were disappointed by the food and expected better. The Christmas meal of December

1939, the so-called 'Daladier meal', was a pleasant surprise. A soldier serving in the 214th RI of 8th Army described it:

> Yesterday night, we celebrated Christmas and today we enjoyed a generous meal offered by Daladier. Here is the menu: renaissance soup, York ham, 12 oysters, beans, roast beef, salad, jam, biscuits, orange, champagne, coffee, liquors, cigars.[111]

This meal was filmed by the media to show that soldiers were well fed during the Christmas celebrations.[112] But once the celebration was over, bad food returned.

The size of the rations was also denounced by soldiers. In October 1939, they criticised 'the amount of food, especially bread, wine, sometimes meat and tobacco'.[113] The author of the following letter complained about having to march on an empty stomach:

> You know, the last stop they made us do, they did not feed us. We left at 2 in the morning and we arrived at noon and they had not given us anything but a sardine and a little bit of cheese for dinner.[114]

From mid-January 1940, bread was rationed: 'They found it clever to ration bread. I hope that this is a temporary situation. When talking about food, we can say that we have been punished as severely as possible'.[115] The situation became more critical as the war went on:

> If this war continues, unfortunately I fear the worst. A loaf only weights 200 grams. Five soldiers receive only 300 grams each and for the last two days, we have had only 200 grams.[116]

Anger was generalised, as this testimony from the 9th CA of the 4th Army showed:

> It is not surprising to be unwell with what they feed us for the moment... They do not want to give anything. We should have 700g of bread per day. Yesterday evening, we did not have any bread to eat. We had half a loaf for 8. We asked three times for bread, but they refused to give more.[117]

Wealthy soldiers bought their bread[118] in local bakeries or inns:

> I eat in a pub in the evening, because I have never seen such bad food. The meat is hard and it is impossible to swallow it. It has to change because everybody is fed up and it is the responsibility of one person, this is the worst.[119]

Only well-healed soldiers could afford this solution but others found alternative ways to improve their meals. Hunting was forbidden but soldiers did not hesitate to poach if stationed in the suitable area:

Game can be found here and there. Rabbits are afraid because I hunt them day after day and I am not kind. Hares are also hunted. I have been eating game ever since I arrived.[120]

Tobacco was not a problem. A few soldiers complained about it: 'The price of tobacco will rise to 20 *sous*, we protest, especially because we only have three packs for 15 days. It is not enough and we will need to buy more.'[121] But this was not such a major issue and was rarely mentioned in soldiers' letters. Wine, on the other hand, was a much bigger problem. A source of pride, wine was celebrated for its medicinal values and its ability to give courage. It was regarded as an essential and was consumed by most French on a daily basis.[122] Just before the war, a majority of civilians drank about three-quarters of a litre of wine per day. 11.5% consumed more than two litres and 4% three litres.[123] Two million litres were dispatched every day to the front. Soldiers received half a litre a day and an additional quarter from January 1940. Those at the forward posts were entitled to a litre per day.[124] However, wine was often delivered late and in a frozen state as a result of the winter cold. Issues regarding quality and quantity were highlighted: 'Wine, we had some today. A litre for 12 non-commissioned officers and it was full of straw and dust: it was undrinkable.'[125] Rumours soon surfaced. It was widely believed that bromide was mixed with wine to lower the sex drive and 'make loneliness more bearable'.[126] This rumour even featured in frontline newspapers, as can be seen in the following caricature:[127]

Vas donc... hé... Bromuré !

Figure 1.6 A frontline newspaper looking at the bromide rumour[128]

An undetermined number of soldiers, believing in these rumours, only drank water.[129] Overall, wine attracted far less criticism than food. The government took care to satisfy its soldiers in this regard. The deputy-mayor of Béziers, Edouard Barthe, a member of the Socialist and Republican Union, launched a charity to provide 'warm wine for the soldiers' in October 1939.[130] The matter of warm wine even gave rise to a day of national awareness on 3 March 1940.[131] Barthe also headed the parliamentary commission for alcoholic beverages, the propaganda committee in favour of wine and the superior council for alcoholic beverages. In March 1940, he led the fight to grant soldiers a litre of wine per day, 'just as it was during the last war'.[132] Alcohol was readily available near the frontline. Men bought wine in the numerous cafés and outlets.[133] Historian Jean-Louis Crémieux-Brilhac noted that one particular wine dealer sold 2,100 litres of *eau de vie* and 7,430 litres of aperitif in January 1940.[134] Soldiers living with civilians were also offered alcohol and bottles could also be bought on the black market:

> We are in a very small Alsatian locality. Civilians are not very wealthy but are talkative and very French. We are appreciated and they give us glasses and we pay 2 francs a litre![135]

Indeed, wine was not lacking in Alsace. Grape harvest had been good and soldiers had helped.[136] Wine consumption, however, had very negative consequences. As in the First World War,[137] alcoholism was endemic:

> A man was drunk; we receive a lot of alcohol, you need that to make the men march. When a man is depressed, he drinks. He is dead inside because this affects the nerves. It is a strange sight.[138]

This became a real problem by April 1940. Censors working for the CP raised the alarm:

> Letters from several units (in particular the 6th DIC of the 3rd Army, the 4th DIC of the 5th Army, the 85th and 113rd RI of the 45th DI of the 4th Army) give the feeling that many officers drink too much and men have way too much wine (in particular colonial troops and soldiers from Brittany). Most of their money is spent on drink; there are many incidents, including fights and challenges to authority.[139]

In May 1940, alcohol was the trigger in a third of the cases examined by military tribunals.[140] Excess, however, was rarely punished during the Phoney War. In fact, officers and soldiers widely accepted alcoholism as an ordinary fact of life. On 1 March 1940, Paul Reynaud successfully managed, despite pressure from the powerful wine lobby, to ban the consumption and sale of alcohol on Tuesday, Thursday and Saturday.[141] When the defeat of 1940 was investigated at the Riom trial of 1942, renowned medical doctors such as Professor Heuyer declared that 'alcoholism was one of the reasons behind our defeat'.[142] This accusation was exaggerated but highlighted the challenges that military authorities faced during spring 1940.

Wine consumption was not only at the root of disciplinary issues but also health problems. Professor Jacques Parisot, working for the 8th Army at the hospital of Alsace, noticed the following:

> Out of 903 new patients in five months, 163 had alcohol-related problems and alcoholism alone caused 138 cases. Delirium tremens, acute accidents, mental confusion, delirious state, nervous or behavioural problems.[143]

The same could be said of army psychiatric centres, where 20% of the patients suffered from alcoholism.[144] It caused the effects of other complaints such as tuberculosis, gastric and liver malfunction and ulcers to be more severe.[145]

From a medical perspective, the winter of 1939-1940 was a bad one. The cold and food triggered several health issues. Low temperatures caused illnesses such as bronchitis,[146] the flu,[147] meningitis,[148] pulmonary infections[149] or pneumonia.[150] The lack of medicines forced doctors to treat these afflictions with warm drinks and cupping glasses. In several units, the lack of proper footwear led to frozen toes, which were amputated.[151] In January 1940, only 80 of the 180 men serving in the 78th RI of the 34th DI of the 4th Army were still fit. Out of 100 soldiers out of action, 19 had been casualties of war (2 dead and 17 wounded) while the rest were ill or suffering from frozen feet.[152] Bad food and infected water,[153] from a well, caused diarrhoea, stomach pain[154] and typhoid.[155] Scabies was also very common not only in the army but also in military hospitals in January 1940.[156] There were outbreaks of measles and mumps in spring 1940.[157] These illnesses considerably reduced the number of men on the frontline. In January 1940, several letters showed how concerned soldiers serving in frontline units were:

> The flu is progressing. 38 soldiers are ill and 60 are showing up at the doctor every day. We had to evacuate a lot of them... I do not know what kind of flu this is but it is really bad and we quickly go downhill in two days.[158]

Life in the army facilitated cross-contamination. The number of unfit soldiers climbed rapidly with the appearance of contagious illnesses or when men endured poor living conditions. Epidemics were not uncommon and even forced military authorities to cancel leave to protect the rear.[159] Lice, familiarly called 'toto' by French soldiers, also spread on the frontline,[160] recalling what was experienced in the Great War:

> We have lice and had to disinfect everything with cresyl, burned with straw. We were rid of almost all of them but it is disgusting, I had more than a dozen in my handkerchief. [...] I spend my time washing my clothes.[161]

Physical problems were followed by psychological issues. There is no sign of shellshock as in the First World War,[162] but mental-health issues which manifested themselves in nervous tension,[163] overwork,[164] suicide, and depression, were all common. Stories of 'madness', to reproduce the term used by French soldiers, were fairly rare but existed:

> One of my comrades was assigned to the kitchen and was really liked because he was hard-working. He had a crisis of nerves or delirium and knocked out four guys. They had to use morphine to put him to sleep. He came back to us remembering nothing and now he is awaiting his sentence. Another consequence of this war of nerves which drives some crazy.[165]

As stated before, the lack of sun and fresh air was a recurring problem. In the 169th RIF of the SF (Thionville), a soldier wrote: 'You might believe that my lot is better than yours. You are mistaken. You are outside while we have been living inside since 26 August.'[166] One of his comrades described a solution employed as a remedy: 'Yesterday, we marched ten kilometres, the doctor ordered it, because many need fresh air and have a hard time seeing. Our life is the same as in a submarine.'[167] Indeed, a doctor who visited fortified positions of the Maginot Line made a comparison with submarine crews.[168] Those living below ground potentially faced specific risk to their mental health, called *bétonite* (a wordplay based on *béton* – concrete in French).[169] This condition was described by Captain Kasper:

> We noticed a certain amount of apathy which, in a few weeks, became an established state. Men used about 75% of their normal abilities. Intelligence was not affected but anger was heightened and sudden, leading to many conflicts among soldiers.[170]

In the 156th RIF (Faulquemont, 4th Army), 'we noticed 2 cases of madness in 15 days in a fortified position. This was blamed on the lifestyle underground.'[171] Psychological illnesses were difficult to treat. Doctors, nurses and soldiers complained about the lack of medication,[172] bandages[173] and hospital supplies. The lack of medicines was particularly upsetting; soldiers felt neglected, abandoned[174] and were forced to buy their own supplies.[175] Those living with civilians asked for pills.[176] In November 1939, a nurse complained about the 5th Army's hospital:

> The hospital acquired equipment and medication slowly. We had very caring doctors who did the impossible to treat and often save our patients. But what is the situation? One sink, a gas cooker, urinal, no toilet for four rooms including 80 beds and two other rooms with 50 beds, each lacking elementary comfort.[177]

Many other letters confirmed doctors' and nurses' professionalism,[178] but also the lack of equipment,[179] and the organisational chaos.[180] The health situation improved during spring, probably simply because the weather became warmer.[181]

Conclusion

There is no doubt that life in the French Army was difficult during the Phoney War. Soldiers were badly fed, poorly clothed and unsuitably housed. These conditions caused not only the deaths of thousands of men but also mass-demoralisation. It is, however, dangerous to see this as specific to the period or the French Army. We must remember that many problems highlighted in this chapter have been encountered by other armed forces throughout history. For example, Napoleonic soldiers often wore rags instead of uniforms and had to live off the land or starve. In fact, conscripts of the *Grande Armée* were far more likely to die of disease than men conscripted in 1939–1940.[182] The First World War was also marked by its share of logistical complexities and disciplinary problems.[183] The Maginot Line brought nonetheless unique challenges. Psychological and physical problems caused by life underground were far more widespread than in other conflicts. We must continue our exploration of the French Army in 1939–1940 in order to understand internal factors but also outside influences and other variables affecting French morale. Chapter 2 will look at fluctuations in morale and their causes, such as boredom and inaction on the Maginot Line.

Notes

1 Maurice Vaïsse (ed.), *Défaite française, victoire allemande sous l'œil des historiens étrangers* (Paris, 2000).
2 Philippe Garraud, 'L'action de l'armée de l'air en 1939–1940: Facteurs structurels et conjoncturels d'une défaites', *Guerres mondiales et conflits contemporains*, 203 (2001), pp. 7–31.
3 Jean-Louis Crémieux-Brilhac, *Les Français de l'an 40*, Vol. 2, *Ouvriers et soldats* (Paris, 1990), pp. 541–598.
4 Eric Alary, Eric, *L'Exode* (Paris, 2010).
5 Jean-Yves Mary and Alain Hohnadel, *Hommes et Ouvrages de La Ligne Maginot*, Vol. 1 (Paris, 2000), p. 9; Les fortifications du système Séré de Rivières, http://www.fortiffsere.fr/index_fichiers/Page322.htm [accessed 12 April 2017].
6 The population of France collapsed once again from 1940 to 1945.
7 Conférence Universitaire de Démographie et d'Étude des Populations, La population de la France (2005), http://cudep.u-bordeaux4.fr/sites/cudep/IMG/pdf/La_popu lation_de_la_France-2.pdf [accessed 12 April 2017]; https://www.destatis.de/DE/ ZahlenFakten/GesellschaftStaat/Bevoelkerung/Bevoelkerung.html [accessed 12 April 2017]; https://www.ons.gov.uk/peoplepopulationandcommunity/populationandmi gration/populationestimates/adhocs/004356ukpopulationestimates1851to2014 [accessed 12 April 2017].
8 Ibid.
9 Mary and Hohnadel, *Hommes et Ouvrages*, Vol. 1, p. 12.
10 Philippe Garraud, 'La politique de fortification des frontières de 1925 à 1940: logiques, contraintes et usages de la ligne Maginot', *Guerres mondiales et conflits contemporains*, 226 (2007), pp. 5–6.
11 Mary and Hohnadel, *Hommes et Ouvrages*, Vol. 1, p. 18.
12 Garraud, 'La politique de fortification des frontières de 1925 à 1940', p. 10.
13 Jean-Pascal Soudagne and Michel Mansuy, *Comprendre la ligne Maginot: Nord, Ardennes, Lorraine, Alsace, Savoie, Dauphiné, Alpes-Maritimes* (Rennes, 2009), p. 134.

14 Mary and Hohnadel, *Hommes et Ouvrages*, Vol. 1, p. 71.
15 Garraud, 'La politique de fortification des frontières de 1925 à 1940', p. 10.
16 For example, the RF of Metz had 86,000 men at the beginning of September 1939, including 12,969 serving in fortified positions. Mary and Hohnadel, *Hommes et Ouvrages*, Vol. 1, p. 86.
17 SF of Crusnes, Thionville, Boulay, Faulquemont, Rohrbach, Vosges, Haguenau, Bas-Rhin, Colmar and Mulhouse.
18 The Maginot Line had a total of 25 fortified sectors. Jean Quellien, Françoise Passera, Jean-Luc Leleu and Michel Daeffler (eds), *La France pendant la Seconde Guerre mondiale: Atlas historique* (Paris, 2010), p. 32.
19 Mary and Hohnadel, *Hommes et Ouvrages*, Vol. 1, p. 15; 84–85; Jean-Pascal Soudagne and Michel Mansuy, *Comprendre la ligne Maginot: Nord, Ardennes, Lorraine, Alsace, Savoie, Dauphiné, Alpes-Maritimes* (Rennes, 2009), p. 134; Quellien et al. (eds), *La France pendant la Seconde Guerre mondiale*, p. 32.
20 Mary and Hohnadel, *Hommes et Ouvrages*, Vol. 1, pp. 26–27.
21 Stéphane Gaber, *Quatre siècles de fortifications en Lorraine: Des premiers bastions à la ligne Maginot* (Metz, 2012), p. 145.
22 General Marie Benoit Besson (1876–1969) became the 3rd Army Group commander in October 1939.
23 General Marcel Garchery (1876–1961) was Chief of Staff at the Army of the Orient (Levant), commanding troops in Lebanon 1924–1925 and became General Officer commanding the 8th Army in September 1939.
24 General Alphonse Georges (1875–1951) served under General Ferdinand Foch as operations chief in 1918, took part in the Rif War (1920–1926) and became part of the Supreme War Council in 1932.
25 General Maurice Gamelin (1872–1958) was part of Joffre's general staff during the First World War and led from 1924–1929 the French Army in the Levant (today Syria and Lebanon).
26 General Maxime Weygand (1867–1965) served as staff officer under Ferdinand Foch during the First World War.
27 This number is debated. Friser talks of 6.1 million men in Ulrich Liss, *Westfront 1939–1940* (Neckargemünd, 1959). Other figures can be found in Henri Amouroux, *Le peuple du désastre, 1939–1940* (Paris, 1976) and Karl-Heinz Frieser, *The Blitzkrieg Legend: The 1940 Campaign in the West* (Annapolis, 2013), p. 43.
28 The Dalbiez law of 1915 stated that a man could be mobilised at his workplace if contributing to the war economy. François Cochet, *Les Soldats de La Drôle de Guerre, La Vie Quotidienne* (Paris, 2004), p. 31.
29 Ibid., pp. 32–33.
30 Frieser, *Le Mythe de La Guerre-Éclair*, p. 43.
31 Cochet, *Les Soldats de La Drôle de Guerre*, p. 38.
32 Roger Bruge, *Faites sauter la ligne Maginot!* (Paris, 1975), p. 66.
33 Cochet, *Les Soldats de La Drôle de Guerre*, p. 39.
34 Thibault Richard, *Des forêts d'Alsace aux chemins de Normandie* (Condé-sur-Noireaut, 1985), pp. 22–23; Bruge, *Faites sauter la ligne Maginot!*, p. 73.
35 Crémieux-Brilhac, *Les Français de l'an 40*, Vol. 2, p. 400.
36 Ibid., p. 400.
37 Flack, Werner, *Wir bauen am Westwall: ein Fronterlebnis deutscher Jugend im Frieden* (Berlin, 1939).
38 See Fig. 1.4.
39 Hans-Adolf Jacobsen, *Fall Gelb: Der Kampf um den deutschen Operationsplan zur Westoffensive 1940* (Wiesbaden, 1957); Quellien et al. (eds), *La France pendant la Seconde Guerre mondiale*), p. 36; Henri Hiegel, *Ils disent drôle de guerre ceux qui n'y étaient pas ... 3 septembre 1939–10 mai 1940* (Sarreguemines, 1983), p. 430; Klaus

Jürgen Thies, *Der Westfeldzug, 10. Mai Bis 25. Juni 1940: Ein Lageatlas der Operationsabteilung des Generalstabs des Heeres: Neu gezeichnet nach den Unterlagen im Bundesarchiv/Militärarchiv* (Osnabrück, 1994).

40 See Chapter 2.

41 Frieser, *The Blitzkrieg Legend*, p. 43.

42 Jacobsen, *Fall Gelb*; Quellien et al. (eds), *La France pendant la Seconde Guerre mondiale*, p. 39; Klaus Jürgen Thies, *Der Westfeldzug, 10. Mai Bis 25. Juni 1940*.

43 See Fig. 1.5. The Franco-German border on 10 May 1940.

44 Nicholas Williams, 'Les évacuations de 1939 en Moselle et en Sarre : cadres et plans stratégiques pour la prise en charge des populations civiles', *Vingtième Siècle. Revue d'histoire, Sciences Po Les Presses*, 128 (2015), pp. 91–104.

45 For an overview of the Moselle and the Sarre, see the Franco-German research project EDEFFA: Olivier Forcade and others (eds), Exils intérieurs : Les évacuations à la frontière franco-allemande (Paris, 2017).

46 Département de la Moselle (ed.), *Un exil intérieur : l'évacuation des Mosellans de septembre 1939 à octobre 1940* (Lyon, 2009).

47 *Le Populaire*, 17 November 1939.

48 Service Historique de la Défense: Armée de Terre (SHD AT): BAVCC, individual files of deceased French soldiers, quoted in: Quellien et al., *La France pendant la Seconde Guerre mondiale*, p. 37.

49 SHD AT: 27 N 69. CP. SF Vosges (Region of Bitche, Bärenthal), report, 26 October 1939.

50 Gaber, *Quatre siècles de fortifications en Lorraine*, p. 141.

51 Cochet, *Les Soldats de La Drôle de Guerre*, p. 85.

52 Ibid.

53 SHD AT: 27N79. CP, a soldier of the 133rd RIF, 4th Army, report, 2 February 1940.

54 Gaber, *Quatre siècles de fortifications en Lorraine*, p. 141.

55 SHD AT: 27N79. CP, a soldier of the 5th Army, report, 28 November 1939.

56 SHD AT: 27N69. CP, a soldier of the SF Thionville, 3rd Army, report, 3 December 1939.

57 SHD AT: 27N69. CP, a soldier of the 168th RIF, SF Thionville, 3rd Army, report, 3 December 1939.

58 Mary and Hohnadel, *Hommes et Ouvrages de la Ligne Maginot*, vol. 3 (Paris, 2003), p. 32.

59 Bruge, *Faites sauter la ligne Maginot !*, p. 20.

60 Ibid., p. 86.

61 Gaber, *Quatre siècles de fortifications en Lorraine*, p. 144.

62 Maurice Charles, adjudant-major in the 154th RIF, quoted in: Bruge, *Faites sauter la ligne Maginot !*, p. 46.

63 SHD AT: 34N83/9. Quoted in: Crémieux-Brilhac, *Les Français de l'an 40*, Vol. 2, p. 431.

64 SHD AT: 27N69. CP, report, 12 April 1940.

65 SHD AT: 27N69. CP, report, 20 November 1939.

66 Gaber, *Quatre siècles de fortifications en Lorraine*, p. 143

67 SHD AT: 27N69. CP, captain of the 428th Pioneers of the 8th Army, report, 28 November 1939.

68 SHD AT: 27N69. CP, soldier of the region of Ingwiller Niedersulzbach, 43rd RI, 35th DI 8th Army, report, 2 January 1940.

69 'We sleep in the houses of those who evacuated the country'. SHD AT: 27N69. CP. SF Bas-Rhin, report, 26 October 1939.

70 SHD AT: 27N69. CP, 4th Army, report, 14 October 1939.

71 SHD AT: 27N69. CP, report, 28 November 1939.

72   Indeed, the government organised a mission to collect supplies in the evacuated zones to distribute to the refugees in the South-West.
73   SHD AT: 27N69. CP, report, 20 November 1939.
74   SHD AT: 27N69. CP, Alsatian soldiers of the 5th and 8th Armies, report, 10 January 1940.
75   SHD AT: 27N69. CP, an Alsatian soldier to his family, 35th RI, 14th DI, 8th Army, report, 21 December 1939.
76   Maude Williams, *Kommunikation in Kriegsgesellschaften am Beispiel der Evakuierung der deutsch-französischen Grenzregion 1939/1940* (PhD Thesis: Tübingen/Sorbonne Université, 2016).
77   Jean Zay, *Lettres de la Drôle de Guerre* (Paris, 2015), p. 20.
78   SHD AT: 27N69. CP, report, 2 January 1940.
79   *L'Illustration*, 27 April 1940.
80   SHD AT: 27N69. CP, report, 13 November 1939.
81   SHD AT: 27N69. CP, soldier of the 306th RI, 3rd Army, Lorraine, report, 26 October 1939.
82   Archives Départementales du Bas-Rhin (ADBR): 98 AL 450. Institut d'Études Européennes, Psychological situation in Alsace and military influence, 23 October 1939.
83   SHD AT: 27N69. CP, report, 26 October 1939.
84   SHD AT: 27N69. CP, soldier based in Obermodern (Region of Bouxviller), 5th Army, report, 24 November 1939.
85   SHD AT: 27N69. CP, Captain of the 428th Pionner, 8th Army, 28 November 1939.
86   SHD AT: 27N69. *Grand Quartier Général* (GQG), 2nd Bureau, report, 7 November 1939.
87   Crémieux-Brilhac, *Les Français de l'an 40*, Vol. 2, p. 429.
88   Ibid., p. 429.
89   SHD AT: 27N69. GQG, 2nd Bureau, report, 20 November 1939.
90   Ibid.
91   Ibid.
92   SHD AT: 27N69. GQG, 2nd Bureau, Sergeant of the 5th Army, report, 24 November 1939.
93   SHD AT: 27N69. GQG, 2nd Bureau, report, 28 November 1939.
94   SHD AT: 27N69. GQG, 2nd Bureau, a soldier of the 220th RI, 67th DI, 8th Army, report, 2 January 1940.
95   SHD AT: 27N69. CP, 5th Army, SF Rohrbach, report, 29 October 1939.
96   SHD AT: 27N69. GQG, 2nd Bureau, report, 7 October 1939.
97   SHD AT: 27N69. GQG, 2nd Bureau, 31st DI, 8th Army, report, 16 November 1939.
98   SHD AT: 27N69. GQG, 2nd Bureau, 241st RAI, 23rd DI, 5th Army, report, 25 March 1940.
99   SHD AT: 27N69. GQG, 2nd Bureau, a sergeant of the 71st RI, 19th DI, 8th Army, report, 25 March 1940.
100 Gaber, *Quatre siècles de fortifications en Lorraine*, p. 140.
101 Ibid.
102 Crémieux-Brilhac, *Les Français de l'an*, Vol. 2, p. 431.
103 SHD AT: 27N69. GQG, 2nd Bureau. report, 25 March 1940.
104 SHD AT: 27N69. GQG, 2nd Bureau, a sergeant of the 66th RI, 18th DI of the 4th Army, report, 9 December 1939.
105 SHD AT: 27N69. GQG, 2nd Bureau, 45th CA, 8th Army, report, 15 April 1940.
106 SHD AT: 27N69. GQG 2nd Bureau, report, 12 April 1940.
107 SHD AT: 27N69. GQG 2nd Bureau. 45th CA, 8th Army, report, 15 April 1940.

108 SHD AT: 27N69. GQG 2nd Bureau, a non-Commissioned officer of the 32nd RAC, 7th DI, 4th Army, report, 15 January 1940.
109 SHD AT: 27N69. GQG 2nd Bureau, a soldier serving in the SF Haguenau, 5th Army, report, 15 January 1940.
110 SHD AT: 27N69. GQG 2nd Bureau, report, 11 March 1940.
111 SHD AT: 27N69. GQG 2nd Bureau, a soldier of the 214th RI, 8th Army, report, 2 January 1940.
112 Établissement de Communication et de Production Audiovisuelle de la Défense (ECPAD). Journal de Guerre, n. 14, week of 6 January 1940, http://www.ecpad.fr/journal-de-guerre-14-semaine-du-6-janvier-1940/ [accessed 17 April 2017].
113 SHD AT: 27N69. GQG 2nd Bureau, report, 8 October 1939.
114 SHD AT: 27N69. GQG 2nd Bureau, a soldier of the 42nd Colonial RA, 30th DI, 5^h Army, report, 21 December 1939.
115 SHD AT: 27N69. GQG 2nd Bureau, a corporal, 21st BI of the 24th RI, SF B/R, 5th Army, report, 2 February 1940.
116 SHD AT: 27N69. GQG 2nd Bureau, a soldier E.M. and Q. G., 62nd DI, 5th Army, report, 11 March 1940.
117 SHD AT: 27N69. GQG 2nd Bureau, a soldier of the 121st RAL 2nd Group, 9th CA, 4th Army, report, 9 December 1939.
118 SHD AT: 27N69. GQG 2nd Bureau, a soldier of the IInd Génie E. O., 3rd Army, report, 16 December 1939.
119 SHD AT: 27N69. GQG 2nd Bureau, a sergeant in the 109th RI, 47th DI, 8th Army, report, 10 January 1940.
120 SHD AT: 27N69. GQG 2nd Bureau, a soldier of the 302nd RI, 8th Army, report, 6 January 1940.
121 SHD AT: 27N69. GQG 2nd Bureau, a soldier of the 8th Army, report, 24 November 1939.
122 Crémieux-Brilhac, *Les Français de l'an 40*, Vol. 2, pp. 463–464.
123 Ibid., pp. 468–469.
124 Ibid., p. 432.
125 SHD AT: 27N69. GQG 2nd Bureau. A NCO of the 32rd RAC, 7th DI, 4th Army, report, 15 January 1940.
126 Bernard Lefèvre, 'La légende du bromure durant la drôle de guerre', *Arkheia, Revue d'histoire. Histoire, Mémoire du Vingtième siècle en Sud-Ouest*, http://www.arkheia-revue.org/La-legende-du-bromure-durant-la,296.html [accessed 18 April 2017].
127 *Le réveil Beauséjour*, 15 January 1940.
128 Archives départementales de la Meurthe-et-Moselle (AD Meurthe et Moselle), *Le réveil de Beauséjour*, 15 January 1940.
129 SHD AT: 27N69. GQG 2nd Bureau, a soldier of the 75th RA, 9th Army, report, 28 November 1939.
130 Crémieux-Brilhac, *Les Français de l'an 40*, Vol. 2, p. 465.
131 Archives Pathé-Gaumont (APG): 4008EJ31725. Gaumont, Journal éclair, 22 February 1940.
132 Journal Officiel de la République Française (JORF), Chambre des députés, 1 March 1940, p. 416, quoted in Crémieux-Brilhac, *Les Français de l'an 40*, Vol. 2, p. 465.
133 SHD AT: 27N69. GQG 2nd Bureau. A soldier of the 155th RIF, 5th Army, report, 10 January 1940.
134 Crémieux-Brilhac, *Les Français de l'an 40*, Vol. 2, p. 470.
135 SHD AT: 27N69. GQG 2nd Bureau, a soldier of the 44th RAM, 8th Army, report, 6 January 1940.
136 Établissement de Communication et de Production Audiovisuelle de la Défense (ECPAD), Journal de guerre, n. 5, week of 20 October 1939, http://www.ecpad.fr/journal-de-guerre-5-semaine-du-20-octobre-1939/ [accessed 18 April 2017].

137 François Cochet, '1914-1918: L'alcool aux armées. Représentations et essai de typologie', *Guerres Mondiales et Conflits Contemporains*, 222 (2006) 2, pp. 19–32.
138 SHD AT: 27N69. GQG 2nd Bureau, a soldier of the 34th RIF, SF Bas-Rhin 8th Army, report, 21 December 1939.
139 SHD AT: 27N69. GQG 2nd Bureau, report, April 1940.
140 Crémieux-Brilhac, *Les Français de l'an 40*, Vol. 2, p. 471.
141 Ibid., p. 474.
142 Ibid., p. 475.
143 Rapport Parisot, cité dans: Crémieux-Brilhac, *Les Français de l'an 40*, Vol. 2, pp. 472–473.
144 Ibid., p. 473.
145 Ibid.
146 SHD AT: 27N69. GQG 2nd Bureau, an engineer of the 18th Génie, 42nd Cie Radio, 42nd DI, 3rd Army, report, 23 February 1940.
147 SHD AT: 27N69. GQG 2nd Bureau, a soldier of the 85th RI, 45th DI, 4th Army, report, 28 December 1939.
148 SHD AT: 27N69. GQG 2nd Bureau, an officer of the 220th RI, 67th DI, 8th Army, report, 2 January 1939.
149 SHD AT: 27N69. GQG 2nd Bureau, a soldier of the 174th RAIP, SD Sarre, 4th Army, report, 29 January 1940.
150 SHD AT: 27N69. GQG 2nd Bureau, a senior doctor, E.O.C.A. 12th CA, 5th Army, report, 21 February 1940.
151 SHD AT: 27N69. GQG 2nd Bureau, a soldier of the 22nd Brigade, 5th Army, report, 9 December 1939; a soldier of the 32nd RI, 23rd DI, 5th Army, report, 21 December 1939.
152 SHD AT: 27N69. GQG 2nd Bureau, a soldier of the 78th RI, 34th DI, 4th Army, report, 15 January 1940.
153 SHD AT: 27N69. GQG 2nd Bureau, a soldier of the 45th, 4th DI, 3rd Army, report, 21 December 1939; a soldier of the 334th RI, 48th DI, 3rd Army, report, 28 December 1939.
154 SHD AT: 27N69. GQG 2nd Bureau, a soldier of the 57th battalion of machine gunners, SF Boulay, 3rd Army, report, 20 November 1939.
155 SHD AT: 27N69. GQG 2nd Bureau, a soldier of the 334th RI, 58th DI, 3rd Army, report, 28 December 1939.
156 SHD AT: 27N69. GQG 2nd Bureau, a soldier of the sanitary group attached to the SF Vosges, 5th Army, report, 6 January 1940.
157 SHD AT: 27N69. GQG 2nd Bureau, report, 17 March 1940.
158 SHD AT: 27N69. GQG 2nd Bureau, a soldier of the 24th DI, 4th Army, report, 15 January 1940.
159 SHD AT: 27N69. GQG 2nd Bureau, a soldier of the 418th Pionniers, 8th Army, report, 15 January 1940.
160 SHD AT: 27N69. GQG 2nd Bureau, a soldier of the 160th RIF, 3rd Army, report, 6 January 1940; Soldier of the 100th RI, 47th DI, 8th Army, report, 10 January 1940.
161 SHD AT: 27N69. GQG 2nd Bureau, a soldier of the 334th RI, 58th DI, 3rd Army, report, 2 March 1940.
162 Sophie Delaporte, 'Névroses de guerre', in: Stéphane Audoin-Rouzeau and Jean-Jacques Becker (eds), *Encyclopédie de la Grande Guerre* (Paris, 2014), pp. 357–365.
163 SHD AT: 27N69. GQG 2nd Bureau, an officer of the 28th GRDI, 24th DI, 4th Army, report, 15 January 1940.
164 SHD AT: 27N69. GQG 2nd Bureau, a soldier of the 3rd Army, report, 14 October 1939.
165 SHD AT: 27N69. GQG 2nd Bureau, a soldier of the 174th RMIF, SD Sarre, 4th Army and Soldier of the 100th RI, 47th DI, 8th Army, report, 2 March 1940.

166 SHD AT: 27N69. GQG 2nd Bureau, a soldier of the 169th RIF, SF Thionville, report, 3 December 1939.
167 Ibid.
168 Bruge, *Faites sauter la ligne Maginot !*, p. 70.
169 Ibid.
170 Mary and Hohnadel, *Hommes et Ouvrages*, Vol. 3, p. 32.
171 SHD AT: 27N69. GQG 2nd Bureau, report, 31 March 1940.
172 SHD AT: 27N69. GQG 2nd Bureau, a soldier of the 5th Army, report, 20 November 1939.
173 SHD AT: 27N69. GQG 2nd Bureau, a medical doctor, report, 24 November 1939.
174 SHD AT: 27N69. GQG 2nd Bureau, a soldier of the 306th RI, 3rd Army, report, 9 February 1940.
175 SHD AT: 27N69. GQG 2nd Bureau, a soldier of the 68th RAL, 70th DI, 5th Army, report, 3 December 1939.
176 SHD AT: 27N69. GQG 2nd Bureau, a soldier of the 5th Army, report, 28 December 1939.
177 SHD AT: 27N69. GQG 2nd Bureau, a nurse of hospital 21 in the zone of the 5th Army, report, 20 November 1939.
178 SHD AT: 27N69. GQG 2nd Bureau, a soldier of the sanitary group, SF Vosges, 5th Army, report, 6 January 1940.
179 SHD AT: 27N69. GQG 2nd Bureau, a soldier of the 255th RAL, 45th DI, 4th Army, report, 28 December 1939.
180 SHD AT: 27N69. GQG 2nd Bureau, a soldier of the 82nd RIF, SF Sarre, 4th Army, report, 24 November 1939.
181 SHD AT: 27N69. GQG 2nd Bureau, report, 12 April 1940.
182 Bernard Wilkin and René Wilkin, *Fighting for Napoleon: French Soldiers' Letters 1799–1815* (Barnsley, 2015).
183 On the topic, see among others Robert Doughty, *Pyrrhic Victory: French Strategy and Operations in the Great War* (Harvard, 2005).

2 Inaction and demoralisation

The morale of French soldiers was a continuing preoccupation during the Phoney War. The État-Major (EM) cared deeply about the mood in the army and traced its evolution using countless reports. After the defeat, the state of mind within the French Army was considered as one of the main reasons for the disaster by most military leaders. General Gamelin, the Head of the Army during the Phoney War, declared that French soldiers had 'not received the morale and patriotic education needed to face this drama' and were 'too accustomed to an easy life'.[1] The political world was also denounced. According to many superior officers, communists, socialists and members of the Government of the Third Republic were responsible for the demoralisation of French soldiers. The Supreme Court even stated that 'we only had to discipline a handful of agitators to guarantee the cohesion of France, manufacture weapons and reinforce the will to fight the enemy'.[2] Newspapers and diaries published immediately after the Phoney War also reflected this position.[3]

This harsh view was typical of the 1940s but simplified complex changes of mood on the frontline. It is necessary to put this outdated explanation aside and offer a new and thorough analysis of French soldiers' morale on the Franco-German front. When looking at the morale situation, we must turn to the history of the lower ranks, their lives and mental attitudes, to understand the experience of this complex period. Using sources from the EM, reports from the CP and private papers belonging to soldiers, we can offer a balanced picture of the mood on the frontline. When doing this, we must remember living conditions, examined in the previous chapter, as well as individual and external preoccupations. Two French historians, François Cochet[4] and Jean-Louis Crémieux-Brilhac, have already looked briefly at French morale from September 1939 to May 1940. Using Headquarters' reports and personal papers, Crémieux-Brilhac described a three-step evolution: the mobilisation and the first two months of the war, then the winter months and finally a third period from March to May 1940.[5] Our own analysis, while nuancing this interpretation, concurs with Crémieux-Brilhac's timeline.

Mobilisation and inaction

When the Germans invaded Poland on 1 September 1939, France mobilised its army. It was the first general mobilisation since the Great War although there had been four partial mobilisations from 1936.[6] The first two followed the remilitarisation of the Rhineland (March 1936) and the Sudetenland crisis (September 1938).[7] The French learned valuable lessons during these episodes. After the 1938 mobilisation, the EM realised that material conditions were far from optimal.[8] The Sudetenland crisis also demonstrated the necessity to draw a 'red zone' in front of the Maginot Line and to rethink the evacuation plans of 1936.[9] It became equally clear that the media and channels of information needed to be controlled in times of crisis.[10] The partial mobilisations of March and August 1939 were seen as warning signals by the French people, who suddenly realised that the Munich agreement of 1938 was threatened. When border reservists were recalled on 24 August 1939, civilians had the distinct feeling that conflict was impeding.[11] The declaration of war on 3 September 1939 was to shatter all hopes of a peaceful settlement with Germany.[12]

What was the state of mind of the French military in September 1939? Clues can be found by looking at the desertion rate and the number of refractory soldiers during this period. Comparing conflicts is also useful. At the beginning of the First World War, 0.018% of the French army deserted.[13] In 1939, being absent without leave remained uncommon; 4,454 deserters (0.099% of all mobilised soldiers), 3,068 in mainland France and 1,386 in the colonies, were tried by military courts.[14] Looking at the rate for the end of 1939 was equally telling: 310 men deserted in October, 230 in November and 180 in December.[15] It is always useful to compare France with its main ally. In the British Expeditionary Force (BEF), an army of volunteers, 49 soldiers were tried as deserters.[16] The British, according to two prominent French historians, greeted the 'declaration of war with calm, without enthusiasm or jubilation [...] but were convinced that the war was necessary'.[17] British soldiers returned to French soil with a feeling of déjà-vu, with the previous war in mind.[18] Overall, the rate of desertion from the French Army seems to suggest that the war against Germany was accepted by most. As we have seen in the previous chapter, physical conditions were not perfect, but were still better than during the partial mobilisations of 1938.[19] 4,564,000 men, including 725,000 colonial soldiers, were conscripted.[20] The youngest soldiers were still doing their national service while the oldest were veterans of the First World War.[21]

Daladier read numerous reports about the army's morale, which he described as 'excellent'.[22] This statement has been debated over the last seventy years. Historians, comparing the mobilisations of 1914 and 1939, saw 'determination' at the beginning of the first conflict and 'resignation' at the dawn of the second.[23] Other specialists disputed this theory and argued that 'there was no enthusiasm in 1914 or in 1939, only firm resignation'.[24] A third group of historians stated that 'a feeling of determination, impossible the previous spring, was noticeable in 1939'.[25] What can be made of these competing theories? Can we reconcile them? The answer lies in a chronological analysis: in both World Wars, the feeling of resignation turned into determination.[26]

The soldiers of 1939 were not eager to go to war, they were as unenthusiastic as their fathers had been in 1914.[27] They were nonetheless resigned to fight after having witnessed Hitler's behaviour during the Rhineland militarisation (1936), the Anschluss (March 1938), the Sudetenland crisis (1938–1939), and the invasion of Poland (1939). According to an IFOP (the *Institut Français d'Opinion Publique*)[28] poll conducted in August 1939, 76% people supported a robust reaction in the event of a German invasion of Poland.[29] A few months earlier, 70% had declared that it was time to resist Hitler.[30] Pacifist feelings, strong until 1936, soon evaporated.[31] By September 1939, most pacifists supported the mobilisation order.[32] This does not mean that war was universally accepted. The far-right newspaper *Je suis partout* and left-wing pacifists, such as Paul Faure, were prominent voices preaching the cause of peace. Communists were also against the war but were reduced to silence when their newspapers, such as *L'Humanité* and *Le Soir*, were banned following the signing of the Molotov-Ribbentrop pact (23 August 1939). On 17 September 1939, the Communist Party was banned after the invasion of Poland by the USSR.[33] The Chairman of the Communist Party, Maurice Thorez, deserted the French military and left for Moscow to 'lead communist militants who are stalked and hunted'.[34] Famous intellectuals also denounced the war and even wrote a leaflet titled 'immediate Peace'. This was signed by more than forty personalities, including the famous philosopher Alain and the writer Jean Giono.[35] Despite their efforts, the pacifists failed to convince the French in 1939. French soldiers were convinced that war was a necessity, having witnessed how negotiation with Hitler had failed. There was an ambivalent feeling, 'one between determination and resignation'.[36] The mobilisation of 1939, just like the one of 1914, did not trigger many displays of enthusiasm[37] but future soldiers showed great 'determination'.[38] The French went to war to end, once and for all, the threat to peace that Hitler posed. As André Maurois summarised:

> We have had enough. We love life, indeed, but want to live in a world where we can raise our children, build something, have great and noble projects without being torn twice a year from everything we love to satisfy the wishes of an insatiable monster.[39]

In an article, Maurois explained why he wanted to fight: to secure peace and 'prevent our children from experiencing such moments'.[40] The exact same sentence was found in several war diaries[41] and soldiers' letters.[42] For example, a letter by a soldier of the IIIrd Army, written at the beginning of December 1939, stated:

> The main goal is to avoid anxiety. We must enjoy good times, do our duty. We must accept our situation. And what do you want? You are a man, you need to do your duty without fearing the other side. They are also made of bones and flesh and, therefore, no stronger than you... And when everything is over, we will come home and we will not fear this uncertainty which we have experienced for years, always waiting to go. This is not a life and we have to say it: if we are here, it is because Hitler wanted it and it is time to stop him because, later, this game will become even harder.[43]

Here, we have to disagree with Jean-Jacques Becker's arguments. The French soldiers of 1939 were as determined to do their duty as the men of 1914. They consented to fight to 'avoid doing it all over again in 6 months'[44] and, above all, to 'secure peace'.[45] Hitler's peace speech, on 6 October 1939, failed to convince. Like Daladier and Halifax, French soldiers were not willing to compromise with Germany or seek peace at all cost. Prefects'[46] reports were clear: 'morale is good. War is accepted, without enthusiasm, but knowing how serious the situation is.'[47] In September 1939, the French left for the frontline, realising that 1914–1918 had not been the *Der des Ders* (*Dernière des Dernières* – a famous French nickname for the Great War), but firmly convinced that this new conflict would be the last.

Despite being sure that they were doing 'the right thing', the men did not leave without anxiety.[48] They feared death, physical and psychological pain, and isolation. The population, especially veterans, knew too well what it meant to go to war. After all, the death toll of the previous conflict was still in everybody's mind. Too many were old enough to remember the carnage of 1914–1918. Fear was on everybody's face, especially when waiting for the train taking the conscripts to the frontline. In stations, the atmosphere was calm, 'not a scream, not a song, almost not a word. Dead silence' wrote Georges Sadoul in his war diary.[49] The same eerie feeling was encountered during the journey to the front:

> We reached Blois station. [...] Morale is excellent, a few families came with us. Sadness was painted on most faces. Then, we had to leave and said goodbye. Tears were visible. It is 10 in the morning, handkerchiefs are waved. At Beaugency, women, young girls bring drinks and their pretty smiles but the train moves and this sweet sight goes away.[50]

This kind of farewell was common in France,[51] but contradicted expected clichés. During the interwar period, it had become widely believed that, in the previous conflict, passionate crowds had given enthusiastic patriotic send-offs to those heading for the front. In other words, the myth of the *fleur au fusil* was very much alive.[52] The conscripts of 1939 expected such treatment and complained when it did not materialise.[53]

The journey to the front was a phase of transition between the civilian and the military world. Officers were sometimes allowed to travel by car, but this privilege was not common. Jean Zay was one of them and, despite suffering mechanical breakdown, had a 'very good journey'. He even slept in an 'excellent hotel' before reaching his final destination.[54] More commonly, the train journey lasted a few hours for those leaving from Paris-Est[55] or a few days for the men departing from the South of France.[56] The trains were far from pleasant or comfortable, even if the SNCF did its best to accommodate soldiers.[57] Nights were especially difficult:

> The night came and our torture resumed. We must sleep on a space 4 by 2 metres, some lie down to sleep, others stay seated. Thrown left and right, we wake up those sleeping on the floor at midnight to allow those who were seated to swap. When the night is over, we are all totally exhausted.[58]

The lack of comfort was a taste of what war was really about. However, many did not feel that they were involved in a conflict. Some believed it was a false alarm, a mobilisation similar to the one of 1938.[59] Others took it more seriously, knowing perfectly well how dangerous the situation could become. The mood was dark and many wondered if they would survive the war.[60] Trains were seen going in the opposite direction. They were usually filled with old people, women and children evacuated from the border region and heading for the South-West of France:

> In front of us, a long cattle train is filled with refugees from Bitche and Saint-Avold. There is a group of pretty girls who smile and laugh. In other wagons, we see nuns standing still. We can only see their faces and their hats. Through the window, we see two old people's faces, standing still, framed by the black wood of the wagon as a very sinister and old family portrait. Elsewhere, children sleep on a pile of straw.[61]

Witnessing such scenes was usually enough to sadden soldiers. Once the train reached its destination, the journey to the regiment was not over.[62] The men still had to board motor transport or march:

> 3 in the morning and we reached Wasselonne, Bas-Rhin. We are exhausted and have to carry our equipment. The bag is heavy on my shoulders, we are knackered, 7 km to do on foot. After two pauses, we reach the little village of Nordheim, where we will be based. Streets are muddy and dirty, our group stays in a two-room flat on the 1st floor. It is there that we can shed our equipment and rest. Sleeping is almost irresistible.[63]

The terms used to describe the first few days in the army, such as fatigue, uncertainty and fear, were telling. This 'world of war', as Sartre called it when reaching Marmoutier, was a militarised universe deprived of freedom or individuality.[64] However, the armed force reassured civilian populations. A report from the *Institut d'Etudes Européennes de Strasbourg* described the mood on mobilisation day:

> The population of the Rhine departments experienced hope, sorrow and expectation. Proximity with the border justified this apprehension. It is only fair to highlight that the Alsatian population displayed the best mood possible. It was never possible to notice any lack of spirit. [...] In a small town like Rosheim, in the Bas-Rhin, there are more soldiers than civilians. More than two thousand men sleep in the farms and the houses, and the local people welcome them generously. The mass of military men brings hope. We were able to notice that faith in the future was proportional to the size of our garrison.[65]

Once deployed on the frontline, soldiers were quick to adopt daily gestures and military routines. The enjoyable weather of September 1939 made transition between civilian and military life smoother.[66] We must make a distinction between two sectors of the front: the Alsatian front following the Rhine and the front of Lorraine facing the Sarre and the Palatinate.[67] In Alsace, the situation remained quiet during the whole Phoney War. On the other hand, French soldiers fought more frequently in Lorraine and even took part in the Sarre offensive.

On 7 September 1939, the 4th Army of General Requin and the 3rd Army of General Condé launched the Sarre offensive. This operation was primarily conducted to investigate the other side: 'we need to see how the Germans are implemented. [...] We need to take key points to prepare objective number 3, the engagement of French forces'.[68] The 2nd DI (the Iron Division) crossed the Sarre and the 21st DIM of General Pigeaud took the hills north of the Blies, the wood of Saint Arnuald and the forest of Warndt.[69] During their progression, the men encountered field mines in evacuated enemy villages. They were to prove lethal during the days and months to come. At the beginning of October 1939, one soldier serving in the 45th DI wrote the following:

> We have not suffered many casualties so far. Most were caused by mines in German territory. Example: a soldier picks the kepi of a Hun officer, a mine explodes. He picks an apple, a mine explodes; a hare lies dead on the ground, he drags it, a mine explodes. The most dangerous mines have a fuse which delays the explosion. They are buried in the villages we occupy.[70]

Combats during the offensive were violent and were even reminiscent of the Great War. Corporal-chief Armand Petitjean, who served in a *corps franc* (an elite unit), explained:

> Three days under mortar fire. We took refuge in a water pipe, 80 cm below ground and had to stay knee deep in the mud the whole night. If the ceiling collapses, we are stuck. Impossible to go out and take a piss. The day arrives and we see the first wounded, the first dead.[71]

It is in this context that Petitjean saw his wounded friends, struck by shrapnel, losing their minds while being evacuated.[72] Examples like this were common[73] and went beyond the French operation. On 12 September, the Sarre offensive was brought to a standstill. Two days later, General Prételat ordered his men to settle in the occupied zone.[74] Fewer soldiers were lost but local skirmishes were common:

> Yesterday, we were bombarded by 77 and 105 cannons. Shells fell no more than 30 metres from us. We had to dig. I do not know if we hurt them, but we did not have any casualties. Aviators are the most scary.[75]

On 30 September, the generals commanding the 3rd, 4th and 5th Armies met. Having been informed that German troops were being brought back from Poland to the Western front, they decided to look for the safety of the Maginot

Line.[76] The French army fell back before 4 October but the first line fought until the final retreat on 17 October.[77] Immediately after the evacuation of the Sarre, the Germans attempted a small incursion and forced the French to flood the coal mine of Petite-Rosselle.[78] This minor move allowed the Wehrmacht to occupy a small piece of French territory. According to General Réquin, the French lost 98 officers, 178 non-commissioned officers and 1,578 soldiers during the Sarre offensive.[79]

During these weeks, French morale was deemed 'good' by the EM.[80] Unsurprisingly, soldiers were afraid of dying:

> Of course, my dear, we have to defend until the end, but you might change your mind when you see soldiers returning from the first line. You will wonder if we have the right to inflict such suffering to these poor guys who suffer greatly and are not responsible.[81]

Such feelings were inherent to the life of a soldier on the frontline, especially when facing death. Meanwhile, men deployed along the Rhine and on the Maginot Line were leading a more peaceful life. Witnessing no violence, many asked 'where the war was?'.[82] Soldiers who served during the Sarre offensive experienced routine by mid-October 1939, the others faced it from mid-September 1939. This differentiation highlights how dangerous it is to summarise too quickly the French experience during the Phoney War.

Routine and the winter crisis of 1939–1940

The Phoney War's unique nature became clear during the middle of September 1939. Jean-Paul Sartre, based 40 km from enemy lines in Alsace, explained his perplexity in his diary:

> A ghost war. A Kafkaesque war. I cannot *feel* it, it is fleeing me. Military dispatches say nothing of our losses. Wounded men are nowhere to be seen. Sergeant Naudin talked about gassed men, but others contradict him. A few spare fragments of news. The Germans are not on our soil, no bombardment of the rear. Military operations are localised on a very narrow sector. Soldiers in the Marmoutier sector have greater freedom, they are like civilians. To feel this war, I need to receive Castor's letters [Simone de Beauvoir]. Castor is at war, not me. I imagine that this feeling is common to many. [...] When I left Castor, on 2 September, I was ready for more and for better than this quiet mediocrity. Now, I am infected, rotten.[83]

Like many other soldiers, Sartre was disillusioned. The men had hoped to fight a short war before going home, but the lack of action suggested a long adventure to come.[84] The feeling of being involved in an unconventional war spread within the ranks of the French army in a matter of weeks. The term *drôle de guerre* [the French equivalent of Phoney War] was popularised by Roland Dorgelès[85] in

October but was already commonly used on the frontline.[86] Routine became the norm on the North-East front in October 1939 and the first signs of morale weakness appeared soon after.

From October 1939 to February 1940, French soldiers were hit by a form of winter depression. In November, the CP reported that morale had 'gone down quite a bit'[87] and was 'seriously worse'.[88] Morale had gone from 'excellent' in September to 'very good' at the beginning of October and 'good' at the end of the month.[89] At the beginning of 1940, a general report highlighted the main reasons for the morale decline in the army. It stated that 'the troops were passive, lacked enthusiasm and motivation'.[90] Inaction and life conditions were blamed; the absence of German atrocities on French soil was also pointed at. The commander of the 5th Army explained:

> Officers and men accept the war without enthusiasm but with gravity. They feel its complexity, which is more difficult to understand than in 1914–1918, because the national territory is not occupied. Civilian populations were not subjected to collective massacres, capture, deportations, systematic destructions and penalties. But frontline soldiers are resolved to fight to stop the instability which is taking them away from their homes regularly, compromising their material situation and threatening to ruin their families. They are willing to sacrifice themselves. A German assault would probably strengthen their morale.[91]

German inaction on the French front was indeed difficult to accept as the men were eager to fight and wanted to feel useful. Inaction triggered depression and led to what the CP called 'spleen', a term coined by Baudelaire.[92] French soldiers preferred the term *cafard* [cockroach].[93] Mental illness was a clear threat, a fact stated in several letters:

> If you knew how depressed I am. Sometimes, we think we are becoming mad, we would welcome mass-killing to end this. I cannot stand this anymore and many of my comrades are like me. Yesterday, a poor guy had a terrible crisis: he was calling for his wife, his child, and was really an unfortunate sight.[94]

The nervous tension led to a high rate of suicides.[95] Self-inflicted deaths were usually deeply disturbing:

> Our group of non-commissioned officers faced a tragedy. Someone was lost to the *cafard*. He put a bullet in his head after coming back from furlough and did not miss. Losing one of us felt really bizarre. He should have waited a bit or try to get killed cleanly by the Huns.[96]

Suicide accounted for 3.8% of all French losses during the Phoney War..[97] In their letters, soldiers often expressed their desire to take part in a major offensive:

'I am so tired of this fucking life. Why cannot we have a real fight, GOD? If we have to die, at least it will be over and we will not talk about it anymore.'[98]

Writing to family members was a good way to fight demoralisation but also triggered serious problems. At the beginning of September 1939, between 15 and 60 percent of the letters sent to relatives gave away classified information. In a few regiments, the proportion was even higher. For example, 90% of the soldiers serving in the GRDI of the 18th DI 4th Army mentioned the name Guenviller, the place where they were deployed.[99] To fight this breach of confidentiality, the GQG and the government issued warnings reminding troops to be careful about their letters' content.[100] Later, furloughs were cancelled to send a stronger signal,[101] a good way to 'considerably diminish the number of indiscretions'.[102] By January 1940, problems were reported in fewer than 15% of the letters, a figure which dropped to 10% in May 1940.[103]

The presence of wives and fiancées in the army zone was another disciplinary issue.[104] This phenomenon was well-documented and happened everywhere. Sartre, for example, remembered a sergeant's wife who 'slept illegally in this Alsatian hole's only inn' in September 1939.[105] He himself welcomed Simone de Beauvoir at the beginning of November 1939.[106] Most officers knew about this but tolerated women as long as they did not cause problems.[107]

The third disciplinary problem was probably the most difficult to accept. As we have already seen in the previous chapter, evacuated villages and towns were pillaged between September and October 1939. It became common knowledge in November 1939, when illegal trips to the forbidden zone were organised.[108] In the penal code of 2 September 1939, pillage was punished by death.[109] However, guilty soldiers were usually placed in isolation or forced to endure extra duties only.[110] Most soldiers were never tried and could count on their superiors, who saw these 'illegal requisitions' as a way to make life better.[111]

These three common acts of indiscipline worried the government, especially considering that other problems were reported, such the lack of respect toward officers or a poor appearance while on leave.[112] The lack of order betrayed morale problems within the army without revealing the causes. What where they?

Morale was particularly low during the winter of 1939–1940. The previous chapter highlighted how difficult living conditions were, but it is clear that other factors weighed in. In most regiments, soldiers' duties aggravated an already difficult situation. Indeed, French military units adhered to a tedious routine made of administrative tasks and unstimulating assignments. Once again, we must make a distinction between different parts of the front. Jean-Paul Sartre, serving in a weather station, did not experience the same war as radio operator Georges Sadoul or Jean Zay, working for the train service. Likewise, men deployed in front of the Maginot Line witnessed a different conflict. Lieutenant Jean Zay led the following life:

> We wake up at 6 or 6.30. My help comes, cleans my shoes and comes back to clean the bedroom once I leave. At the mess, breakfast is served at 7, lunch at 13.00 and dinner at 20.00. The rest of the time, I am at my office or on the road. I will probably travel more in the future and it is suiting me

perfectly. After dinner, at around 21.30, we go back to the office. We work for a while if something new has happened. From 22.00 to midnight, officers play cards. Personally, I go for a walk in the dark and then go to sleep, because my colleagues play bridge and I do not know how to play. I will learn this game soon.[113]

Georges Sadoul, deployed near Nancy, experienced a different war. Having served briefly as a nurse, he was transferred to a radio unit in an Alsatian town near the Maginot Line.[114] His main task was to copy reports, a role that he found difficult to accept.[115] Routine was also the ruling principle on the Maginot Line. Fortification soldiers were subject to the following schedule:

6.00–6.30: shower/breakfast
6.30–7.30: maintain the rooms and weapons
7.30–8.15: physical training
8.30–11.30: instruction
11.30–14.00: duties, meal, free time
14.00–17.00: instruction
17.00–18.00: dinner
18.00–21.00: free time
21.00: end of the day[116]

Underground soldiers rarely saw the light of day and moved very little, a stark contrast with men like Jean Zay or Georges Sadoul. Moreover, it was always about 'the monotonous life in a concrete block',[117] the same tasks repeated again and again. 'The most difficult things here are not the Huns or the shells and bullets, but boredom. It ruins our morale.'[118] This feeling of boredom was widespread in the French army:

Days go by, long and empty, without the shadow of a thing to do, without any other obligation than being called during the morning and at lunch time. The evenings are acceptable. [...] We drink beer and schnapps. We joke. [...] But the afternoons are sinister. [...] We cannot always play cards, drink, write to our wives. We stay on the straw and yawn, we embrace *cafard* and idleness. We wash less and less, we do not shave, we do not have the courage to clean, to clear the table after eating. Spilled wine, old crusts, dried soup, bones. Filth comes with boredom.[119]

In forward posts, idleness was less problematic but soldiers were nonetheless disoriented by the lack of action. Their physical life was more intense as they were tasked with maintaining fortifications, the digging of new trenches, etc. Jean Malaquais, serving in a pioneer unit, wrote that 'the military profession was to load and unload things, dig trenches, etc. No danger but a lot of tiredness' to André Gide.[120] Many other pioneers complained about the 'harshness of their work and the distance needed to reach it'.[121] Long marches and exercise were recurrent problems making life harder: 'We just walked 54 km; this was a real mess, men were exhausted; they stayed on the side of the road, in barns, everywhere.'[122]

Boredom should not hide the fact that soldiers also fought, even if violence was far more uncommon than during the previous war.[123] Several first-line soldiers wrote about isolated German actions and French counter-actions:

> Yesterday, I told you in my letter that we were forced to retreat because the Germans were close to the factory. Our *corps francs* went there this morning and made them retreat by 1,500 metres. But the poor devils, they lost a few, not dead but wounded. They took 12 prisoners, it is really a strange job. Poor devils, they are really brave.[124]
>
> A squadron of 125 men protects 5 km of border. We guard the roads while the rest is free. As a result, German patrols come at night and attack us ... As soon as the night came, we heard the Huns cutting barbwire and we feared while waiting. I can assure you that sometimes our mouth was dry. Now, we are getting used to this.[125]

These two extracts, picked from among many others, show how different life in forward bases was from the rest of the front. Fear triggered nervous problems:

> This tiredness was caused by our duty on the frontline that some found too long (18 to 22 days). A lieutenant serving in the 107th RI wrote: for more than 22 days, we have fought and they do not even tell us when we will be relieved. This wait is quick to erode morale and exhaust men.[126]

Fighting soldiers unanimously wished to be relieved.[127] The same can be said of the men who had served during the Sarre offensive in October.[128] The postal control for the 4th Army noted:

> They were expecting a period of rest very far from the line (behind Nancy) and they were disappointed to be so close to the front, in a region lacking civilians, after a month on the frontline. 'We would like to breathe fresh air'; 'We suffered a lot, because of the enemy, but also because of the noise, the rain, the mud' (lieutenant, 31st RI).[129]

Frontline men could not help but notice that other soldiers were less exposed to danger. This disparity triggered a feeling of unfairness:[130]

> We are currently the most exposed unit in the French Army. I really have the feeling that our great leaders do not realise how tired our men are and how unfair this is. They are aged between 30 and 35 and are very surprised to be here while their younger comrades have never seen a Hun.[131]

The EM was in fact in agreement with this principle, finally adopted in April 1940.[132] Younger conscripts were sent to the frontline while units were rotated faster between forward zones and the Maginot Line.[133] These measures came too late to fight the feeling of injustice. The age difference was not the only issue between men. The clash between rural and urban population became a source of concern. Those coming from the cities were far from being used to the realities of the countryside:

> Temperature was between -20 and -25 for a month. The weather has been better for the last three days. The road/main street is reddish and smells foul. Now that the snow is melting, manure piled in front of the houses by the noble people of Lorraine (the nicer the house, the bigger the pile of manure), is fermenting and pouring down the street.[134]

This extract, taken from a letter written by Malaquais to André Gide, highlighted how urban soldiers clashed with the rural world. Most men came from the city, a major difference to the First World War, as we can see in the following census table of France.

Table 2.1 Urban and rural population in France (1901–1936)[135]

Year of census	Total population in millions	Distribution in %	
		Rural population	Urban population
1901	40,7	59	41
1921	39,1	55,9	46,4
1926	40,4	51	49
1931	41,5	48,8	51,2
1936	40,5	47,6	52,4

Urban Frenchmen became the dominant group in 1931. This was still true in 1939. The conscript of the Phoney War was therefore typically used to the comfort of the city and was very far from the rural life or the Spartan comfort found in the army. The contrast between pre-conscription and war conditions was sometimes violent but the army offered temporary answers to appease the men. Furlough was a much coveted luxury and a real obsession among soldiers.[136] *Permissions* were introduced at the beginning of November 1939 and immediately triggered 'unanimous joy'.[137] In February 1940, a second round of furlough caused 'deep satisfaction'.[138] The first soldiers left at the end of November 1939,[139] far earlier than during the First World War. Indeed, the first soldiers who were allowed to go home for a short break left in 1915, sometimes at the beginning of 1916.[140] Not all soldiers were allowed to go home in November 1939. Those who stayed behind were eagerly waiting for their turn:

> This is really disgusting and shameful to be given a rest but being refused to go home. Those from Nancy are always granted furlough, those from further

away must stay... My head hurts, it revolts me, I have no more taste for anything ... We will lose our sense of patriotism. They are mocking us.[141]

Frontline soldiers were indeed given between 24 and 48 hours to meet their families, fetch clothes, buy food or simply rest.[142] However, furlough was often delayed or cancelled, making soldiers extremely unhappy.[143] For those who were allowed to see loved ones, the way home was often plagued by cold train carriages.[144] Returning from home was also difficult, especially considering the clash between life on the home front and in the army:

> Soldiers on leave told us that life on the home front was hard: morale was not as good as before, draft dodgers were everywhere and 'greasers' (especially found in commercial activities) shocked normal families. But this had various consequences. Some (older soldiers or those who were probably depressed when they left) came back even more depressed or bitter. By contrast, younger soldiers and those with friends returned without much regret and with better morale. They enjoyed their leave, brought back good memories, mocked or pitied the rear, but are happy to see their pals. They wait for 'the next one' and 'are not worried'. But this is only a first impression, we will need to check later.[145]

Just a week later, the CP was able to confirm the above-mentioned statement:

> French people from the rear are met with incomprehension, indifference, or contempt. They fail to understand the current war and ignore what the fighters endure (rain, cold, mud, night alarms, family separation). Instead of admiring and expressing their gratitude to those who are back from the front, they look at them as an inconvenience or as idiots who failed to find a safe place.[146]

Furlough was heavily debated by the Government and the GQG. They knew that interactions between the front and the rear were dangerous and might threaten national cohesion. When soldiers denounced the home front, they often talked about men who had escaped military duty. In a few cases, soldiers on authorised leave of absence had brawls with men of the rear who had dared to talk about life on the frontline. This was deemed unacceptable, 'draft-dodgers' who lacked the 'decency to shut up'.[147] Military men were more tolerant toward women. They were supposed to have emotional connexions with their husbands and children and were linked to the reality of the frontline by their correspondence. Negative feelings toward the rear were quickly spread by returning soldiers, who talked about life outside the army. Tales were irremediably tainted with sadness and anger, as shown in the following extract:

> A few friends came back and are totally disgusted by how they were treated in Paris. Civilians almost reproached them the fact that they had not been

killed or wounded. According to the rear, this is not a war, there is no shell, no bomb, no battle, soldiers are happy and are not cold and there is no rain. It is 1914 all over again. The rear is selfish because it does not understand the conflict. It will have to; we are determined to make them respect us because they lack common decency and accuse us of being intruders. There are, fortunately, a few exceptions.[148]

Incomprehension between the frontline and the rear was very much present until January 1940.[149] But was the rear so biased? And why? It seems that civilians were indeed in the dark when it came to representing the conflict. The press was partly to blame for this situation. With a few exceptions,[150] journalists gave a false picture of the Maginot Line.[151] Soldiers were unanimously angered by the media:

> And what can we do? There is nothing on the Maginot Line! Ooh la la, newspaper pictures are so nice. If one of our cute photographers liked it so much here, I would happily trade my place with him.[152]

Soldiers serving in forward posts were even angrier at journalists than those based on the Maginot Line. The fact that military actions were either badly explained or not reported at all was upsetting.[153] In the French press, the Franco-German front was described as a quiet sector where little happened. Official dispatches did nothing to help. For example, the newspapers talked about 'a quiet night on the whole front' for the first day of the Sarre offensive.[154] Vague articles about 'quiet days'[155] during which 'nothing significant happened'[156] were common. The press painted a positive portrait of life in the army to reassure civilians: soldiers were well fed and equipped, slept comfortably, fought little or not at all, and worked with farmers.[157] Nothing suggested violent encounters between opposing armies.[158] In winter, not a word was said about the cold on the frontline. One soldier was outraged:

> I have never suffered that much before ... Nothing is comparable to those hours spent with a backpack during the cold night. Many of us dropped like flies. Frozen feet, cold, exhaustion (because we had to walk so much) are very problematic ... What the newspapers are saying about soldiers' well-being is false ... It is the truth, we are determined to spread it.[159]

Parallels with First World War propaganda, the infamous *bourrage de crâne*, were easily drawn.[160] It was only in February 1940 that newsreels began to mention living conditions and violent episodes on the Maginot Line.[161] Becoming more accurate than newspapers, newsreels explained that the lack of detailed information did not mean an absence of danger on the frontline.[162] We should also note that sounds of artillery explosions were added in studio to highlight the dangerous nature of war.[163] Soldiers were presented as heroes, a difficult task when the press was portraying the frontline as a quiet and idle place.

The French press was misleading when reporting on evacuated villages of Alsace and Lorraine. Pillaged houses did not feature in the newspapers. In fact, the Tharaud brothers,[164] who worked for *Paris-Soir*, explained how well soldiers looked after civilian houses.[165] Likewise, politicians like Daladier[166] and Chautemps[167] lied about the topic in their speeches. Frontline soldiers denounced[168] and mocked[169] these attempts to hide the truth.

The authorities were equally embarrassed by soldiers from Alsace and Lorraine, whose relatives had been evacuated to the south of France. Life was difficult for refugees, who lacked private spaces, money and social interactions.[170] Frontline soldiers on authorised leave of absence were furious to see how badly their parents were treated: 'Have you already had a furlough? I went to see my parents in Charente, their state is so miserable that I was unable to find a space to sleep with my wife.'[171] The authorities wanted to avoid this precise reaction,[172] but soldiers were nonetheless shocked and their morale suffered greatly.

The Government wanted to protect civilians' morale but forgot that frontline soldiers also read newspapers. General Bourret, commanding the 5th Army, asked that

> the press and the radio stop minimising soldiers' efforts in order to appease the rear. They must stop describing the front as a quiet place and should emphasise the patience and the courage of men constantly working or fighting, men who are ready for the task ahead.[173]

Special duty workers, civil servants, commanding officers, and even the British, were disliked.[174] Indeed, jealousy was widespread in the French army. Soldiers particularly hated those too important to be conscripted.[175] Factory workers were criticised by farmers, who felt that they also had work to do back home:

> I am back from furlough. Here, nothing to do. There, so much work. I have not planted a single seed. I will be ruined and there is nothing I can do to escape this.[176]

Special duty workers were heavily discussed by the Government and were a major cause of protest on the frontline. If it was clear that factory workers were needed, other sectors applying for the special status were not considered as necessary for the war effort. Offices, companies and religious institutions all asked for special workers in great numbers. In January 1940, 13,000 of these workers were sent back to the front, but 50,000 men were removed from the army the next month to work in various places.[177] Jealousy was widespread:

> I am deeply depressed and I think constantly about those who have no worries, these cowards who came home to swipe offices and factory courtyards. We are nearly forty years old and are still there. It is shameful to see this.[178]

As can be seen in this extract, there was also a conflict between generations. Older soldiers complained about the presence of younger men in factories.[179] Likewise, younger generations denounced the demobilisation of older *classes* (1909 to 1911) and the departure of the last *classes* of the Great War (1916 to 1918) for units serving far from the frontline.[180]

There were still more reasons to complain. Salary differences between soldiers of various ranks and military status were great. Conscripts complained about their lesser salary, reserve non-commissioned officers did not understand why they received less than active duty non-commissioned officers while doing the same job.[181] A soldier serving in the Vth Army explained :

> It is clear that Gil is accumulating money. He holds the rank of *adjudant* and must be well paid. These guys hope that the war will last, they are not really bothered. They are really mocking us and then they say 'Liberty, Equality, Fraternity'. The Government should really know that if we are all defending the fatherland, we should be paid the same. Pay nobody or everybody better. When this is over, the civil servant will still have his job but I will have lost my customers.[182]

In fact, everybody complained about something or someone, always finding more privileged people. Inactivity was partly responsible for this situation. The lack of action made soldiers believe that their presence at the front was not needed. Worse, their military duty sometimes had financial consequences:

> Our duty is not desirable. A soldier earns 0,70 per day. They tell us that factory workers work 60 hours per week without a pay rise. This is shameful and I believe that it would be normal to consider factory workers as conscripted. They should receive only food indemnities.[183]

For many soldiers, the main preoccupation was to provide for the family, which was difficult with the amount received on the frontline. The CP recorded several protests in January 1940:

> Frontline conscripts, separated from families with little or no means to survive, have worries. They appreciate gestures of solidarity from their officers and their comrades, but complain about the violation of their rights. Their salary does not seem fair, is not always paid or not regularly. Frontline soldiers compare their situation to the life of those special workers, who have high salaries and live comfortably.[184]

It is essential to remember that the cost of life rose by 17% for most goods and by 30% for food during the winter of 1939–1940.[185] Mobilised soldiers' families faced difficult times. Soldiers felt this inflation but were not as deeply affected as the rear since they were fed by the army. The military salary, between 7 and 8 francs per day and an extra 4.5 francs per child/day, was not indexed to match the market.[186] Soldiers felt unable to do anything to help their families, despite their cry for help. This was too much for many: 'It is a pity to realise that we are losing everything and that we are not given the means to feed our wives and children.'[187]

The link between the rear and the frontline was never severed. Letters from family and friends were sent during the whole Phoney War and were reinforced by furlough. The post, however, was not always reliable. In October 1939, the CP warned about the speed and the erratic nature of mail distribution: 'It is becoming urgent to make things better because it is going to have an impact on morale, so far quite high.'[188] In this report, the CP complained about the number of unnecessary letters and even talked about 'postal incontinence'.[189] This remark seems to suggest that there was a disconnection between the EM and the men. From the frontline to the rear, letters took 3 to 5 days. In the opposite direction, 8 to 15 days were necessary.[190] The situation, however, became better. In November 1939, fewer and fewer soldiers complained, except sporadic outbursts in a few sectors.[191] Improving mail distribution was vital to guarantee this connection between soldiers and families, especially considering the lack of action. After all, writing letters was a good way to kill time.

Spring returns

The end of February 1940 was a turning point in terms of soldiers' morale.[192] The situation did not change overnight but the mood improved drastically. The return of mild temperatures played a huge part. After the autumnal rains and the harsh winter, the weather became warmer, making life on the frontline considerably easier. Soldier Folcher said that from mid-February it 'became a bit warmer', 'snow is melting' ; at the end of February it was 'very nice' and in March 'walking was a pleasure', 'the month of April is really nice'.[193] Gabriel Girard, serving in the 211st RI of the 6th company, talked about a 'nice spring weather'.[194]

However, this also meant the return of unpleasant tasks: digging trenches, installing new electric and phone wires, building new bunkers.[195] These physical efforts, as well as long marches, were better accepted than during winter.[196] The weather also allowed skirmishes in the Sarre and Palatinate sectors. From February 1940, the number of small scale actions rose sharply along the border. Units belonging to the 2nd, 4th and 5th Armies were ambushed[197] and bombed by the Germans:

> On 22 February, it is still fresh at 15h30, but while we were cutting trees in the forest near the first line, we were bombed by the Germans. The first shell fell 10 metres away from me and got closer and closer. Three of them fell less than two metres away from me. I was trying to get cover behind a tree. I do not know how I was saved. There is no doubt that Our Lord intervened. One of my pals, lying 1m50 from me, was cut in two and died without a sound. Another, even closer, had his ribs broken and his belly

opened by shrapnel. His state is very serious and we doubt that he will survive. A guy from Rhône, who was lying next to me, was not hurt. We were both safe. A few times, shrapnel came close to our helmets. What an awful time. In twelve minutes, sixty shells of 105 fell on us. Such was the summary of this sad evening: 2 dead and 5 seriously injured, 2 lightly wounded. Today, while writing this letter six days after this event, I still cry when thinking about this horrible carnage and the horrifying screams heard after the bombing.[198]

This sobering account from a *chasseur* of the 31st BCP of the 14th DI (4th Army) shows that the relatively low number of casualties hid traumatising scenes. But the French were not only passive actors. They also attacked German positions, hoping to take prisoners[199] and gather intelligence:

We have arrived at a more agitated place in the forest of Warndt between Forbach and Saint-Avold. You should stay there because those from the 10th *Génie* could trade their place. They blew up an observation tower last week. You can be sure that these guys have guts. They failed twice but succeeded the third time after three hours of work. I do not understand how they managed. We patrol, ambush, explore, and have been 5 km from their forward bases to gather information. As you can imagine, this was not done without violence but, thank God, we have not lost anybody. A few have been hit by small shrapnel because they tried to be clever.[200]

Such missions were dangerous but kept the troops occupied. Routine was still a frustrating factor on the frontline but was less ordinary than behind the Maginot Line. With the arrival of spring, the situation changed little for those posted in the quieter sector, who realised that 'it was still quiet'.[201] Once again, boredom[202] triggered alcoholism,[203] considered by CP to be 'the only remaining problem' when it came to soldiers' morale.[204] Several letters described appalling scenes of physical violence, shots and wounds triggered by alcohol: 'I see all around me nice guys drowning their boredom in red wine and, for a few, it gets ugly. Last week, one fell, cracked his skull and had to be brought to the hospital.'[205]

Farmers were the most vocal about the lack of action. Not only were they bored and feeling useless, but they were desperate to go home to attend to their farms. All were wondering how their families would survive if nobody was there to work.[206] Farmers serving in non-combatant units far from the Maginot Line were allowed 30 days to work their properties but those deployed on the front-line did not have that luxury. Anger was high:

Once again, I have noticed that I cannot be granted a furlough to work the field because I am on the frontline. Those who are inside the country will be allowed to go home for a month. We are not happy because it is always the same here. Many serving inside the country are lazy, jobless people, but they will get everything and we will lose everything.[207]

Farmers on the Franco-German border also resented the rear.[208] As a result, they sometimes refused to use their expertise on the frontline: 'I am like you. I have not been granted an authorised leave of absence to take care of my farm. They asked me to work the fields in the evacuated region but I refused.'[209]

At the end of February 1940, a second round of furlough was awarded. Farmers were the first to leave, to the great dissatisfaction of others, but were nonetheless unhappy. Having a few days was just not enough to take care of the farm.[210] At the end of April 1940, all furloughs were cancelled but the great majority of soldiers believed that this measure was only temporary.[211] According to CP, this alert, caused by the invasion of Norway and Denmark, 'excited the soldiers, who regained their patriotism and their fighting spirit. They all found it normal to stay at the front.'[212] Even if this decision was justified, it was a blow to morale.[213] Moreover, the situation remained the same on the Franco-German border: the enemy was still desperately quiet. Soldiers were finally allowed to go home for a break, but this decision was also to damage morale. Sadoul, for example, visited Paris at the beginning of April 1940 and wrote that 'Paris at war is horrible. It depresses me.'[214] However, relations between fighting men and civilians improved at the beginning of April. So far, both sides had had little understanding for each other but with the arrival of spring, everybody believed in an offensive. This perspective was welcomed by the men, as explained by this cavalry officer of the 4th Army :

> Our state of mind can be understood by looking at the last days: we were told that we would probably face an assault and this was enough to make us happy. It is not a taste for danger but we just hope that our lives will have a meaning after eight months of waiting. If this continues for a little while longer, I will become neurasthenic. This closed circuit with our artillery and our observatory is becoming unbearable. I admire my comrades who can endure it. I have not told you that I have volunteered to go to Finland. If they ask for it, I will volunteer for Norway. I would go anywhere as long as I can move.[215]

This determination to gamble everything was common: 'If we have to face an offensive, may it happen once and for all. We will die or come back, but this monotonous uncertainty needs to stop as soon as possible. It is a general desire, I believe …'.[216] Those who came back from the frontline also complained about this half-rest and did not feel at ease, even describing haunting 'bad thoughts'.[217]

External operations were heavily scrutinised by French soldiers. The USSR had launched an offensive against Finland on 30 November 1939. During the winter of 1939–1940, Franco-British authorities designed strategies to help Finland but also to stop Sweden from providing iron ore to Germany. On 5 February 1940, the Allies agreed to rescue Finland through Norway and Sweden. They created a French Expeditionary Corps in Scandinavia (*Corps Expéditionnaire français en Scandinavie*) led by General Audet on 16 February 1940.[218] However, the signature of the Finnish-Soviet treaty on 12 March delayed its departure.[219] For frontline soldiers, this defeat left a 'painful feeling':[220]

> Finland's submission, despite what they tell us, is not going to make us look good on the world stage. It is a catastrophic event because it throws Scandinavia to the Huns and gives them Swedish iron ore, which is as essential as fuel.[221]

This defeat had direct consequences on the French political world. Daladier, who had failed to aid Finland, had to resign and was replaced by Paul Reynaud on 22 March 1940. The new President of the Council, who was also the War Minister, organised a new Scandinavian expedition at the beginning of April. The transport of iron ore from Sweden to Germany was against the principle of neutrality but the landing of German soldiers in Norwegian ports and in Denmark was an even better reason to intervene.[222] On 9 April, the French and the British decided to move: 'the war for iron is declared'.[223] This operation made the headlines in France for ten days in a row. 'The Reich brought war to Scandinavia', 'France and Great Britain will help Oslo',[224] 'The Narvik victory is a strategically important victory',[225] 'New Allied troops and lots of supplies sent to Norway'[226] were the headlines of *L'Œuvre* during this period. Moreover, Paul Reynaud gave lots of speeches about Norway to keep the nation motivated.[227] This intervention was welcomed by the population and by the army, who felt that something was finally happening.[228] CP reported:

> Most soldiers are optimistic. Finally the war began ; we are leaving stagnation behind ; we hope that the operations will be led by the French and the British with energy and resolution, and that this will happen outside the border. Hitler will not be 'crazy enough' to attack the Maginot Line and if he did, he would be stung ; France will not be the battlefield, and a victorious peace is close.[229]

This optimism, helped by good progress on the ground by allied soldiers, delighted the rear and the military.[230] However, the subsequent failures brought 'bitter deception'.[231] Soldiers were worried about the rear's morale[232] and lost their enthusiasm.[233] Georges Sadoul's diary demonstrated how little civilians and soldiers knew about what was happening in Norway. Reading the French press, they believed either that the Allies or the Germans had won. On 1 May, Sadoul and his unit realised that Norway was lost when Namos was captured: 'This evening, we read the newspapers. It is clear that we are routed.'[234] The British fleet and Franco-Polish units captured Narvik on 28 May 1940, but the battle of France eclipsed this success. Anyhow, the troops left Scandinavia between 1 and 8 June 1940.

Despite the setback in Norway, the CP reported that morale was good between 25 April and 10 May. It never collapsed like it had during the winter of 1939:

Morale is surviving the Norwegian crisis, stabilised, improved in a way. There is no debate about an early peace, a 'white peace'. It is clear that the army will find its fighting spirit when the time comes.[235]

This extract, sent to Generals Georges and Doumenc, suggested that French soldiers needed extra stimulation to be ready for combat. If morale improved after February, the winter experience, permanent problems and inaction left traces. Jean-Louis Crémieux-Brilhac highlighted that French morale was good enough to survive the Phoney War but might not have been high enough to survive the general offensive of 10 May 1940.[236]

Conclusion

This chapter has argued that the French soldiers agreed with the mobilisation order and were willing to fight the Germans. The men did not seek glory and were not enthusiastic but wanted to secure peace for the next generation. They saw their time as a civic duty but remained concerned citizens of the Republic. Leaving for the army was often a shock. Most Frenchmen were used to the comfort of the city and were unhappy in their new environment. Urban soldiers disliked the countryside and had generational problems within the military. The lack of action compromised morale on the frontline, especially during winter. Several cases of depression, even suicides, were reported. Alcoholism and aggressive behaviour were also common. The EM looked for new strategies to ease the pain. Letters and furloughs were widely employed to satisfy the men but contacts with the rear were not always positive. The lack of civilian understanding for the reality of war frustrated French soldiers. Likewise, media personalities were denounced as professional propagandists by the army. The arrival of spring brought a relief. With the warmer weather came physical activities and the return of violence. On the frontline, limited actions brought casualties but also gave a purpose to the Phoney War. News of a Scandinavian offensive was seen as a step in the right direction but the outcome was to worry many men. As this chapter hinted, soldiers' morale might have been irremediably damaged during the winter of 1939–1940. Was it really the case? And were the authorities trying to use propaganda to curtail the crisis in the army?

Notes

1 Archives Nationales (AN): 74AP/22. Fonds Reynaud, quoted in: Crémieux-Brilhac Jean-Louis, *Les Français de l'an 40*, Vol. 2, *Ouvriers et soldats* (Paris, 1990), p. 363.

2 Henri Michel, *Le Procès de Riom* (Paris, 1979), p. 235.

3 Passera François, 'Premiers témoignages publiés de la guerre 1939–1940. Des histoires vraies cousues de fil blanc ?', in : Bertrand Fonk and Amable Sablon du Corail (eds), 1940, *l'empreinte de la défaite: Témoignages et archives* (Rennes, 2014), pp. 179–199.

4 François Cochet, *Les soldats de la drôle de guerre* (Paris, 2004).

5 Crémieux-Brilhac, *Les Français de l'an 40*, Vol. 2, p. 365.

6 The French Army usually recalled those who had finished their military duty less than three years ago. Reserve units, mainly from the border, were sometimes reactivated.

7 Four partial mobilisations happened between 1919 and 1939: April 1936, September 1938, March 1939 and August 1939.

8 SHD AT: 7N4034. EMA, 3rd Bureau, report, 1938.

9 Nicholas Williams, 'Les évacuations de 1939 en Moselle et en Sarre : cadres et plans stratégiques pour la prise en charge des populations civiles', *Vingtième Siècle. Revue d'histoire*, 128 (2015), pp. 91–104.

10 AN: 72AJ580. Service Général d'information. L'enseignement de la crise du mois de septembre 1938, 18 November 1938.

11 Cochet, *Les soldats de la drôle de guerre*, p. 30.

12 Letter dated Sunday 3 September 1930, 13h, Paris, in: Christian Melchior-Bonnet, *Lettres du temps de guerre : 1939–1942* (Paris, 1999), p. 19.

13 Jean-Jacques Becker mentioned 1,600 cases of desertion or insubordination between August and December 1914. Jean-Jacques Becker, *1914: Comment les Français sont entrés dans la guerre, contribution à l'étude de l'opinion publique, printemps-été 1914* (Paris, 1977), p. 258. In Great Britain, 0,061% of the soldiers (1,169 in 1914). Christoph Jahr, *Gewöhnliche Soldaten* (Göttingen, 1998), p. 56.

14 Cochet, *Les soldats de la drôle de guerre*, p. 47.

15 Crémieux-Brilhac, *Les Français de l'an 40*, Vol. 2, p. 428.

16 30,740 desertions were recorded in the British army for the whole war. Edward Smalley, 'In the Courts or Off the Records : Discipline in the British Expeditionary Force, September 1939 – June 1940', *University of Sussex Journal of Contemporary History*, 16 (2015), pp. 75–91.

17 Bruno Cabanes and Édouard Husson (eds), *Les sociétés en guerre: 1911–1946* (Paris, 2003), p. 39.

18 Ibid.

19 Fabrice Grenard, *La drôle de guerre : L'entrée en guerre des Français: Septembre 1939–mai 1940* (Paris, 2015), p. 90.

20 Grenard, *La drôle de guerre*, p. 91.

21 Ibid.

22 Comité international d'histoire de la Deuxième Guerre mondiale, *Français et Britanniques dans la drôle de guerre : actes* (Paris, 1979), p. 8.

23 Cabanes and Husson, *Les sociétés en guerre: 1911–1946*, p. 33.

24 Cochet, *Les soldats de la drôle de guerre*, p. 43. This idea was also found in Becker, *1914 : Comment les Français sont entrés dans la guerre*, p. 297.

25 Crémieux-Brilhac, *Les Français de l'an 40*, p. 426.

26 Becker, *1914 : Comment les Français sont entrés dans la guerre*, p. 258.

27 Ibid., p. 146–248.

28 IFOP was founded in 1938. It was the first French poll organisation created in the country.

29 Cochet, *Les soldats de la drôle de guerre*, p. 43.

30 Christian Delporte, *La Troisième République, 1919–1940. De Poincaré À Paul Reynaud* (Paris, 1998), p. 388.

31 Maurice Vaïsse, 'Der Pazifismus Und Die Sicherheit Frankreichs 1930–1939', *Vierteljahrshefte Für Zeitgeschichte*, 33 (1985), pp. 590–616.

32 Delporte, *La Troisième République*, p. 391.

33 Vaïsse Maurice, 'Der Pazifismus und die Sicherheit Frankreichs 1930–1939', *Vierteljahrshefte Für Zeitgeschichte*, 33 (1985), pp. 590–616, p. 607; Serge Berstein and Pierre Milza, *Histoire de la France au XXe siècle*, Vol. 2, *1930–1958–* (Paris, 2009), pp. 302–303.

34 Christian Melchior-Bonnet, *Lettres du temps de guerre : 1939–1942* (Paris, 1999), p. 16.

35 Berstein and Milza, *Histoire de la France au XXe siècle*, Vol. 2, p. 303.

36 Jean-Louis Crémieux-Brilhac, *Les Français de L'an 40*, Vol. 1, *La Guerre, Oui Ou Non* ? (Paris, 1990), p. 57.
37 Becker, *1914: Comment les Français sont entrés dans la guerre*, pp. 323–324.
38 Comité international d'histoire de la Deuxième Guerre mondiale (ed.), *Français et Britanniques dans la drôle de guerre*, (Paris, 1979), p. 6.
39 *Le Figaro*, 2 September 1939.
40 SHD AT: 27N69. A soldier of the 8th Army, report, 12 October 1939.
41 Jean-Paul Sartre, *Carnets de la drôle de guerre : septembre 1939–mars 1940* (Paris, 1995), p. 51.
42 SHD AT: 27N69. Report, 12 October 1939. We have found 321 other extracts expressing the same opinion.
43 SHD AT: 27N69. CP, report, 9 December 1939.
44 SHD AT: 27N69. A soldier of the 5th DIC, 3rd Army, report, 8 October 1939.
45 Louis Gillet, 'Pourquoi te bas-tu ?', quoted in: Pierre-Frédéric Charpentier, *La drôle de guerre des intellectuels français* (Lavauzelle, 2008), p. 275.
46 We must remember that France was divided in *Départements*, each headed by a *préfet*.
47 AN: Fonds Moscou 20010216/0229. Commission du contrôle postal d'Annecy, quoted in: Grenard, *La drôle de guerre*, p. 98.
48 Crémieux-Brilhac, *Les Français de l'an*, Vol. 2, p. 426.
49 Georges Sadoul, *Journal de guerre: 2 septembre 1939–20 juillet 1940* (Paris, 1977), p. 16.
50 Eric Deroo and Pierre de Taillac, *Carnets de déroute 1939–1940 : Lettres et récits inédits* (Paris, 2010), p. 24.
51 Sadoul, *Journal de guerre*, p. 14.
52 Becker, *1914: Comment les Français sont entrés dans la guerre*, pp. 324–328.
53 Deroo and de Taillac, *Carnets de déroute*, p. 21.
54 Jean Zay, *Lettres de la Drôle de Guerre* (Paris, 2015), p. 20.
55 Sadoul, *Journal de guerre*, pp. 14–15 ; Sartre, *Carnets de la drôle de guerre*, p. 35.
56 Deroo and de Taillac, *Carnets de déroute*, p. 24 ; Paul Nizan, *Intellectuel communiste*, Vol. 2 (Paris, 1970), p. 253.
57 Grenard, *La drôle de guerre*, p. 91.
58 Deroo and de Taillac, *Carnets de déroute*, p. 24.
59 Sadoul, *Journal de guerre*, pp. 16–17.
60 Ibid., pp. 14–15 ; Sartre, *Carnets de la drôle de guerre*, pp. 20–21.
61 Sadoul, *Journal de guerre*, pp. 17.
62 Gustave Folcher, *Les carnets de guerre de Gustave Folcher, paysan languedocien, 1939–1945* (Paris, 2000), p. 30.
63 Deroo and de Taillac, *Carnets de déroute*, p. 26.
64 Sartre, *Carnets de la drôle de guerre*, pp. 21–23.
65 ADBR: 98AL490. IEE, La situation en Alsace à la veille de la mobilisation, 1 September 1939.
66 Zay, *Lettres de la Drôle de Guerre*, pp. 26–27.
67 See chapter 1 for a map.
68 Cochet, *Les soldats de la drôle de guerre*, p. 165.
69 For an overview of military actions on a daily basis, see: Henri Hiegel, *Ils disent drôle de guerre ceux qui n'y étaient pas … Tome 1, 3 septembre 1939–10 mai 1940* (Sarreguemines, 1983), pp. 219–254.
70 SHD AT: 27N69. A soldier of the 45th DI, 4th Army, report, 12 October 1939.
71 Armand Petitjean, 'Journal de guerre', *La Nouvelle Revue française*, 10 mai 1940, p. 602, quoted in: Charpentier, *La drôle de guerre des intellectuels français*, p. 58
72 Ibid.
73 Paul Tuffrau, *De la 'drôle de guerre' à la libération de Paris (1939–1944) : Lettres et Carnets* (Paris, 2002), p. 16.

74 See Figure 1.4.
75 SHD AT: 27N69. 4th RI 15th DI, report, 4 October 1939.
76 Hiegel, *Ils disent drôle de guerre ceux qui n'y étaient pas*, p. 240.
77 Ibid., pp. 246–254.
78 Bruge, *Faites sauter la ligne Maginot !*, pp. 62–63.
79 Ibid., pp. 61–62.
80 SHD AT: 27N69. CP, report, 7 October 1939.
81 SHD AT: 27N69. A soldier from the SF Rohrbach, report, 14 October 1939.
82 Jean Malaquais, *Journal de guerre, journal du Métèque (1939–1942)* (Paris, 1997), p. 3.
83 Sartre, *Carnets de la drôle de guerre*, pp. 35–36.
84 Ibid., p. 45.
85 *Gringoire*, 26 October 1939.
86 Charpentier, *La drôle de guerre des intellectuels français*, p. 268.
87 SHD AT: 27N69. CP, report, 16 December 1939.
88 SHD AT: 27N69. CP, report, 21 December 1939.
89 SHD AT: 27N69. CP, report, 2 January 1940.
90 SHD AT: 27N69. EM, 3rd Bureau to the War Minister, morale, 25 March 1940.
91 SHD AT: 27N69. Commander of the 5th Army to the Commander of the infantry, 14 January 1940.
92 Charles Baudelaire, *Les Fleurs du mal* (Paris, 1857).
93 SHD AT: 27N69. Report, 12 October 1939.
94 SHD AT: 27N69. CP, a soldier of the 172nd RIF SF Bas-Rhin, report, 21 December 1939.
95 SHD AT: 27N69. Report, 17 October 1939.
96 SHD AT: 27N69. CP, NCO, 23 GR Rec 13rd CA 8th Army to his brother, report, 29 January 1940.
97 Jean Quellien, Françoise Passera, Jean-Luc Leleu, and Michel Daeffler (eds), *La France pendant La Seconde Guerre mondiale: Atlas historique* (Fayard, 2010), p. 37.
98 SHD AT: 27N69. CP, Brigadier 22nd RIF, SF of Haguenau, report, 15 January 1940.
99 SHD AT: 27N69SHD. Report, 8 December 1939.
100 SHD AT: 27N69SHD. GQG 2nd Bureau, N. 5.315/FTCE of 22 October, 09 November 1939.
101 Crémieux-Brilhac, *Les Français de l'an 40*, Vol. 2, p. 440.
102 SHD AT: 27N69. Report, 15 January 1940.
103 SHD AT: 27N69–70. Report.
104 Jean-Yves Le Naour, *Misères et tourments de la chair durant la Grande Guerre. Les mœurs sexuelles des Français, 1914–1918* (Paris, 2002), pp. 360–380.
105 Sartre, *Carnets de la drôle de guerre*, p. 66.
106 Simone de Beauvoir, *La force de l'âge* (Paris, 2000), pp. 480–483.
107 Cochet, *Les soldats de la drôle de guerre*, p. 130.
108 Maude Williams, *Kommunikation in Kriegsgesellschaften am Beispiel der Evakuierung der Deutsch-Französischen Grenzregion, 1939/40* (PhD Thesis: Tübingen/Sorbonne Université 2016), pp. 323–422.
109 *Journal officiel de la République Française (JORF)*, 'Décret réprimant le pillage en temps de guerre', 2 September 1939, p. 10974.
110 ADBR: 98AL283. Rapport de M.M. Charles Saint-Venant et Paul Sion, Députés, Visite du Département du Haut-Rhin.
111 SHD AT: 27N69. CP, report, 20 November 1939.
112 Crémieux-Brilhac, *Les Français de l'an 40*, Vol. 2, p. 439.
113 Zay, *Lettres de la Drôle de Guerre*, p. 25.
114 Sadoul, *Journal de guerre*, p. 72.

115 Ibid., p. 79.
116 Gérard Giuliano, quoted in: Cochet, *Les soldats de la drôle de guerre*, p. 89.
117 SHD AT: 27N69. CP, SF of Boulay 3rd Army, report, 16 December 1939.
118 SHD AT: 27N69. CP, Corporal 153rd RIF 5th Army, report, 10 January 1940.
119 Sadoul, *Journal de guerre*, pp. 86–87.
120 André Gide and Jean Malaquais, *Correspondance: 1935–1950...* (Paris, 2000), p. 91.
121 SHD AT: 27N69. CP, report, 4 November 1939.
122 SHD AT: 27N69. CP, Soldier of the 5th DINA, report, 21 December 1939.
123 At sea and in the air, the fight was often more intense. See: Cochet, *Les soldats de la drôle de guerre*, pp. 161–184.
124 SHD AT: 27N69. CP, a soldier of the 609th pioneers Region of Forbach 9th CA, report, 9 December 1939.
125 SHD AT: 27N69. CP, a *maréchal-des-logis* GRDI 28th DI 5th Army, report, 9 December 1939.
126 SHD AT: 27N69. CP, report, 7 October 1939.
127 SHD AT: 27N69. CP, a lieutenant of the 32nd RI, report, 7 October 1939.
128 SHD AT: 27N69. CP, report, 7 October 1939.
129 SHD AT: 27N69. CP, report, 4 November 1939.
130 SHD AT: 27N69. CP, a soldier of the 327th RI 23rd DI 5th Army, report, 21 December 1939; a soldier of the 307th RI 62nd DI and soldier of the 223rd RI 70th DI 5th Army, report, 29 January 1940.
131 SHD AT: 27N69. CP, a lieutenant of the 24th GRCA 12th CA 5th Army, report, 28 December 1939.
132 Bruge, *Faites sauter la ligne Maginot !*, p. 66.
133 SHD AT: 27N69. GQG 2nd Bureau, report, 1 November 1939.
134 Gide and Malaquais, *Correspondance*, p. 124.
135 Conférence Universitaire de Démographie et d'Étude des Populations, La population de la France, 2005 ; http://cudep.u-bordeaux4.fr/sites/cudep/IMG/pdf/La_population_de_la_France-2.pdf [accessed 11 July 2017]
136 SHD AT: 27N69. CP, report, 12 October 1939.
137 SHD AT: 27N69. CP, report, 1 November 1939.
138 SHD AT: 27N69. CP, report, 23 February 1940.
139 SHD AT: 27N69. GQG, report on morale, 26 November 1939.
140 Cochet, *Les soldats de la drôle de guerre*, p. 90.
141 SHD AT: 27N69. CP, a soldier 2nd DI 8th RAD 4th Army, report, 16 December 1939.
142 SHD AT: 27N69. CP, report, 9 February 1940.
143 SHD AT: 27N69. CP, a soldier of the 223rd RI 70th DI 5th Army, report, 3 December 1939 and 2 January 1940.
144 SHD AT: 27N69. CP, a soldier of the 15th Génie 3rd Army, report, 21 February 1939; a soldier of the 146th RIF 4th Army, 9 February 1940; a soldier to his wife, SD Sarre 4th Army, report, 28 December 1939.
145 SHD AT: 27N69. CP, report, 16 December 1939.
146 SHD AT: 27N69. CP, report, 21 December 1939.
147 SHD AT: 27N69. CP, a sergeant of the 154th RIF 5th Army, report, 6 January 1940.
148 SHD AT: 27N69. CP, a sergeant of SF Bas-Rhin 5th Army, report, 21 December 1939.
149 SHD AT: 27N69. CP, report, 6 January 1940.
150 *Paris-Soir*, 12 December 1939.
151 AGP: PJ 1940.538. Newsreel, Gaumont, 29 February 1940; 3952GJ00017, Gaumont, Journal Gaumont, 28 December 1939; Jérome et Jean Tharaud, *Paris-Soir*, 22 October 1939.
152 SHD AT: 27N69. CP, a soldier of the 162nd RIF 3rd Army to a friend, report, 15 January 1940.

153 SHD AT: 27N69. CP, report, 24 November 1939.
154 *Paris-Soir*, Communiqué n° 17, 13 September 1939. War scenes are more visible in newsreels. See: AGP: PJ1939.517, 29 September 1939; PJ1939.518, 12 October 1939.
155 *Paris-Soir*, Communiqué n°180, 4 December 1939.
156 *Paris-Soir*, Communiqué n° 163, 25 November 1939.
157 AGP: PJ 1939.521.9. Newsreel, 1 November 1939.
158 *Paris-Soir*, 29 November 1939.
159 SHD AT: 27N69. CP, a soldier of the 3rd RIA 29th DI 4th Army to his parents, report, 9 February 1940.
160 Sartre, *Carnets de la drôle de guerre*, p. 151.
161 AGP: PJ 1940.535.14. Newsreel, 8 February 1940.
162 AGP: PJ1940.539.15. Newsreel, 7 March 1940.
163 AGP: PJ1940.539.15. Newsreel, 7 March 1940; PJ 1940.535.14. Newsreel, 8 February 1940; PJ1939.517. Newsreel, 29 September 1939; PJ1939.518. Newsreel, 12 October 1939.
164 Many soldiers denounced these two journalists. See: Tuffrau, *De la 'drôle de guerre' à la libération*, p. 24.
165 *Paris-Soir*, 19–20 October 1939.
166 *L'œuvre*, 25 December 1939.
167 *Strasbourg en Périgord*, 12 November 1939.
168 SHD AT: 27N69. A soldier of the 68th RAD 5th Army, report, 1 November 1939.
169 SHD AT: 27N69. CP, report, 18 January 1940.
170 On refugees, see: Laird Boswell, 'Fissures dans la nation française : Les réfugiés alsaciens et lorrains en 1939 – 1940', in: Max Lagarrigue (ed.), *1940. La France du repli, l'Europe de la défaite* (Toulouse, 2001), pp. 197–208.
171 SHD AT: 27N69. CP, an Alsatian soldier of the 5th Army, report, 11 March 1940.
172 ADBR: 98AL651. IEE of Strasbourg. The problem with furlough, 11 November 1939.
173 SHD AT: 27N69. Army General Bourret, commander of the 5th Army, to the General-in-Chief, 14 January 1940.
174 On Franco-British relations, see chapter 5.
175 See chapter 1.
176 SHD AT: 27N69. A soldier of the 5th Army to his brother, report, 28 December 1939.
177 Cochet, *Les soldats de la drôle de guerre*, p. 136
178 SHD AT: 27N69. A maréchal des Logis of the 58th RA 27th DI, report, 10 January 1940.
179 SHD AT: 27N69. A soldier of the 5th Army, report, 16 December 1939.
180 Cochet, *Les soldats de la drôle de guerre*, p. 137.
181 SHD AT: 27N69. A non-commissioned officer of the 17th CA 5th Army, report, 10 January 1940.
182 SHD AT: 27N69. A soldier of the GRCA n. 17 5th Army, report, 10 January 1940.
183 SHD AT: 27N69. A soldier of the 172nd RIF SF Bas-Rhin, 2 January 1940.
184 SHD AT: 27N69. 5th Army, report about morale, 14 January 1939.
185 Cochet, *Les soldats de la drôle de guerre*, p. 133.
186 Ibid., p. 134.
187 SHD AT: 27N69. A non-commissioned officer 23rd GRDI 31st DI 5th Army, report, 21 February 1940.
188 SHD AT: 27N69. Report, 17 October 1939.
189 Ibid.

190 SHD AT: 27N69. Report, 5 October 1939.
191 SHD AT: 27N69. CP, report, 15 January 1940.
192 SHD AT: 27N69. CP, report, 15 February 1940 and 23 February 1940.
193 Folcher, *Les carnets de guerre*, p. 62.
194 Deroo and de Taillac, *Carnets de déroute*, p. 108.
195 Ibid., pp. 148–153.
196 Ibid., p. 108.
197 SHD AT: 27N69. A soldier of the 31st DCP 14th DI 4th Army, report, April 1940.
198 SHD AT: 27N69. A chasseur of the 31st BCP 14th DI 4th Army, report, 11 March 1940.
199 SHD AT: 27N69. A Brigadier-chef 304th RAD 14th DI 4th Army, report, April 1940.
200 SHD AT: 27N69. An Alsatian soldier 44th RI 2nd BCF 47th DI 4th Army, report, 25 March 1940.
201 SHD AT: 27N69. A soldier 10th RIF SF Mulhouse 8th Army, report, 30 April 1940.
202 SHD AT: 27N69. A lieutenant 268th RAL 70th DI 5th Army, report, 30 April 1940.
203 SHD AT: 27N69. 45th DI 4th Army and 3rd RIC 4th DIC 5th Army; report, April 1940.
204 SHD AT: 27N69. Report, 30 April 1940.
205 SHD AT: 27N69. A soldier of the 109th RI 47th DI 4th Army, report, 30 April 1940.
206 SHD AT: 27N69. Report, 17 March 1940.
207 SHD AT: 27N69. A gunner 12th RAC 4th DIC 5th Army, report, 11 March 1940.
208 SHD AT: 27N69. 3rd Army 2nd bureau, study on soldiers' morale, March 1940.
209 SHD AT: 27N69. A soldier of the 168th RIF SF Thionville 3rd Army, report, 30 April 1940.
210 SHD AT: 27N69. Report, 17 March 1940.
211 Folcher, *Les carnets de guerre*, p. 62 ; Cochet, *Les soldats de la drôle de guerre*, p. 210.
212 SHD AT: 27N69. Report, 30 April 1940.
213 SHD AT: 27N69. Report, April 1940.
214 Sadoul, *Journal de guerre*, p. 173.
215 SHD AT: 27N69. A chef d'escadron 49th RAMP Sarre sector 4th Army, 30 April 1940.
216 SHD AT: 27N69. CP, 23th BCC 4th Army, report, 23 February 1940.
217 SHD AT: 27N69. CP, a corporal of the 2nd RTM 1st DM 3rd Army, report, 23 February 1940.
218 See: ECPAD, Nicolas Férard, 'La campagne de Norvège. 9 avril – 13 juin 1940, dossier n°1 : la campagne vue du côté français'. http://archives.ecpad.fr/wp-con tent/uploads/2010/06/norvege.pdf [accessed 25 November 2017]
219 On the campaign of Norway, John Kiszely, *Anatomy of a Campaign: The British Fiasco in Norway, 1940* (Cambridge, New York, 2017); François Kersaudy, *Norway 1940* (Lincoln, 1998) ; T. Derry, *The Campaign in Norway* (London, 1995).
220 Sartre, *Carnets de la drôle de guerre*, p. 593.
221 Tuffrau, *De la 'drôle de guerre' à la libération*, p. 41.
222 Alf Johansson, 'La Neutralité Suédoise et Les Puissances Occidentales Entre 1939 et 1945', *Revue d'histoire de La Deuxième Guerre mondiale*, 28 (1978), pp. 9–31.
223 *L'Œuvre*, 12 April 1940.
224 *L'Œuvre*, 10 April 1940.
225 *L'Œuvre*, 15 April 1940.
226 *L'Œuvre*, 17 April 1940.
227 Speeches made on 9, 10 and 16 April 1940.
228 Tuffrau, *De la 'drôle de guerre' à la libération*, p. 50.

229 SHD AT: 27N69. Report, April 1940.
230 Sadoul, *Journal de guerre*, p. 181 ; SHD AT: 27N69. Report, 30 April 1940.
231 Georges Pernot, *Journal de guerre, 1940–1941* (Franche-Comté, 1971), p. 58.
232 Sadoul, *Journal de guerre*, p. 187.
233 SHD AT: 27N69. Report, 30 April 1940.
234 Sadoul, *Journal de guerre*, p. 187.
235 Crémieux-Brilhac, *Les Français de l'an 40*, Vol. 2, p. 519.
236 Ibid., p. 522.

3   The struggle against *cafard*

In 1939, mandatory military duty was already a long French tradition, having first appeared with the Jourdan law of 1798.[1] Motivating conscripts proved difficult in the various wars of the 19th century, but the generalisation of propaganda in 1914–1918 made the management of conscripted soldiers even more complex. By then, morale had become a central issue as well as the target of new dedicated units.[2] With the Phoney War came a different type of warfare, a fact understood by the French and the Germans. Indeed, the sluggish nature of the conflict was an unexpected novelty and a rupture with the Great War. The struggle against low morale in the army became a priority at the very beginning of the conflict. This chapter will look at various strategies and forms of entertainment adopted by the military and the Government to keep soldiers' morale high.

Soldiers' morale: a priority

As soon as the war started, the État-Major (EM) saw the management of soldiers' morale as an essential issue.[3] The First World War had demonstrated that victory was impossible without looking after soldiers, both mentally and physically. In his diary, soldier Tuffrau wrote down an opinion shared by many on the frontline:

> Hitler's best weapon is this lethargic state that he has spread, helped by the communists and other pacifists. He will use it to launch a big offensive. This, he has always done openly: demoralise first, attack next.[4]

To prevent a morale collapse, the EM studied various strategies. At the beginning of the war, the CP, a First World War creation, was revived.[5] In 1939, the EM saw it first and foremost as a mirror reflecting the state of mind on the frontline. This service was composed of various commissions spread between military regions. They were split into sub-commissions with different tasks: the international commission looked at foreign mail, the prisoner of war commission examined communication aimed at captured soldiers, a third one looked at letters within the French *départements*, and the last commission targeted specific units.[6] In various places, such as Marseille, Dijon, Chambéry, Bordeaux and Lille, translation sections were also at work. If needed, letters were sent to a scientific laboratory to be inspected chemically or by ultraviolet light. Commission reports were sent to the president of the *commission interministérielle* of the CP based in Paris, the 2nd Bureau of the GQG and the generals in charge of military regions.[7]

CP reports were complemented by additional information provided by the EM. In December 1939, the head of the French Army ordered the redaction of reports on 'officers' and soldiers' morale'.[8] Those were written by 'commanders and unit leaders'.[9] Reports were written at each level of the hierarchy up to the *corps de troupe*. The objective was to gather enough information to complete existing reports. As the EM stated:

> Due to the nature of the war, it is important for the EM to understand:
> What the troops think (officers and men),
> What are the factors affecting the men's state of mind,
> How to react. [...]
> This will be valid only if reports are written freely and honestly, leaving aside any attempt to 'please' the higher authority.[10]

This note clearly shows that the EM understood the Phoney War's exceptional nature. It was essential to adapt to a new form of warfare led on a psychological level. This point was also found in previous observations made in November 1939:

> This war has seen few military actions but we need to prepare for the trials to come. The country's morale is an essential factor to resist and be victorious.[11]

On 24 November 1939, the Ministry of National Education created an 'army unit to provide readings, arts and leisure', which was to 'coordinate and control all initiatives aimed at supporting intellectually and distracting troops within the army zones and inside the country with the help of military authorities'.[12] Georges Duhamel, a writer and a member of the French Academy, was made director while Julien Cain, General Administrator for the National Library, was brought onto the directing committee.[13] This service was divided in three sections: '1. Reading, 2. Music and 3. Leisure and games'.[14] The first section opened libraries and loaned books, 'taking into account the cultural level of our readers, trying to distract but also instruct, and even satisfy the intellectual curiosity of a minority'.[15] The second section was to distribute music records and organise concerts. The last section supplied board games and other distractions. During the following months, front-line entertainment became more diverse. In January 1940, a sport section was created to keep soldiers busy.[16]

On 25 April 1940, the French Government created a Morale Section to monitor the army.[17] The unit's goal was to centralise information far spread between various sections of the EM, a problem for those wanting 'to know easily and quickly how troops felt'.[18] This new unit, belonging to the 3rd Bureau of the EM, was supposed to: [19]

1. Gather information about morale.
2. Lead the way, coordinate and control operations aimed at improving soldiers' morale [...].
3. Link with other departments.
4. Prepare notes and instructions, check the execution of orders by different offices and services concerned with the spirit of the army.[20]

This Morale Section had its own liaison officers in constant contact with all offices involved. Moreover, other officers were asked to fulfil specific missions, like Captain Lebrun who was, among other things, studying morale among soldiers from North Africa.[21] The new unit had to 'study problems, build plans of action, gather ideas and interesting experiences, make useful suggestions, follow tenaciously those agreed upon'.[22]

Gathering data allowed the military and the Government to deploy different strategies to fight low morale. Two broad categories can be distinguished: initiatives to instruct soldiers and make them work and, on the other hand, attempts to divert men using games and leisure.

Fighting boredom through action, instruction and work

When inaction became the norm in October 1939, measures were taken to break the monotony. The CP noticed that busy men were far less affected by boredom: occupations like 'exercise, shooting, fortification work, agriculture, keep the men busy'.[23] The EM defined three courses of action: the rotation of troops, instruction time and manual work.

In October 1939, the EM ordered a faster rotation on the North-East frontline. This was designed to 'train troops but also to identify poor commanders as well as units lacking instruction or training'.[24] This measure was not entirely effective. Until 10 May 1940, only a third of all divisions was sent to the frontline.[25] As can be expected, those concerned found this situation unfair and denounced it loudly.[26] Moreover, harsh conditions on the frontline meant that the rotation process tired a great number of men.[27] Fortress soldiers were not sent to rest all at once but in separate groups.[28] From 19 September 1939, these men were replaced by quarters. In a note written in November 1939, General Gamelin wrote that it was important to 'keep soldiers serving on the fortified line in good physical and mental shape'.[29] In the same report, he detailed the most effective methods of rotation to keep the men fit. This method involved instruction centres, close to the Maginot Line, used to teach new military methods in fortified sectors. Theoretically, a quarter of the men were supposed to be replaced every twelve days. Soldiers sent to the instruction centres would rest, learn new warfare techniques and remain physically and mentally fit.[30] This rotation cycle was evaluated in various reports sent by sector commanders of the 5th Army in Spring 1940. General Lescanne, commanding the 43rd Army Corps, was optimistic: the quarter system let him 'send a quarter of the crews to rest in the instruction centre of Oberbronn. This quarter was replaced by an equal fraction coming from the instruction centre, which allowed the fortresses to dispose of a fifth quarter.'[31] In other fortified sectors, such as Haguenau (12th Army Corps) or Bas-Rhin (17th Army Corps), rotation worked but encountered difficulties. The 17th CA, for example, was unable to follow this rhythm, lacking men in the instruction centre.[32] On the other hand, the *bataillons d'intervalle* were able to follow the rotation in both Army Corps: 15 days of rest for 30 days on the frontline. The situation remained precarious and units were sometimes forced to adapt.[33] While resting, soldiers lived in instruction centres, in cities behind the Maginot Line or evacuated towns, although this last solution was not ideal because the towns lacked the necessary comfort and entertainment.[34]

The French EM followed another path to fight boredom: military education. This route was not only a way to fight low morale but also a method to keep the army efficient, especially considering that a large number of soldiers came from the reserve and had a mere 18 months or less of military duty.[35] During the Phoney War, the lack of experience on the North-East front was a major problem:

> Many reservists did not know how to shoot. The lack of training was depressing for those who did not feel ready for the role that they might have to play later.[36]

The lack of action was detrimental to the army's morale but also made men less efficient. Gamelin had ordered that 'all divisions acquire the same fighting value by spring' but this objective was not reached and gaps between active duty and reserve units became wider.[37] In fortified positions, motorised units, artillery crews and elite formations, soldiers were regularly trained. The Moiry bunker, for example, followed six hours of training daily and an hour and a half of physical exercise.[38] In the military zone, there was but a handful of training camps, all located in flat and empty landscapes, a far cry from what the men faced in real conditions. Despite this issue, the EM was afraid to send troops further away as it might break units.[39] As a result, reserve troops remained passive and lacked the necessary knowledge to fight the war. The case of the 55th division illustrated this problem; in eight months, two of its regiments spent two weeks in various training centres. Its artillery only went for a day.[40] Strangely, those who would have benefitted the most from further training were the most neglected.

Soldiers did not welcome physical exercise and military education. Long marches and training sessions in the woods were exhausting and failed to convince the men.[41] Many wrote in their letters or private diaries observations such as: 'Why are we training for war, instead of doing it?'[42] Moreover, they voiced their anger at how exercises were organised, like the time when a working section was asked to come 'with weapons and helmets'.[43]

The EM put in place a third course of action to fight boredom: work. Soldiers were asked to improve the Maginot Line or take care of the crops. These activities started as soon as September 1939 but slowed down with the arrival of winter before stopping entirely with the snow.[44] Most soldiers hated them and saw them as a burden.[45] From December to February 1940, physical activities were therefore restricted. However, the arrival of spring encouraged the EM to resume physical work, leading to nine to ten hour working days.[46] The commander of GA n°2, for example, wanted to 'wake up' his men and take them out of this winter lethargy:

> The French soldier fights well, but if he knows how to shoot his weapon, he is far less keen on using tools. We need to act vigorously against physical laziness, which triggers melancholy and discouragement. We need to make the men understand that each hole dug, each pile of concrete poured, is a life saved.[47]

To do so, the general did not offer anything else but agricultural and construction work on the Maginot Line. Conditions were poor because the ground was flooded by melting snow.[48] Soldiers working on fortified structures were primarily asked to excavate, pour concrete, reinforce defensive lines with antitank pits and install new barbed wire. Most units lacked equipment and were rarely supported by engineers, mostly sent to 'rectify antitank pits already dug'.[49] Soldiers were asked to improvise with whatever equipment was available but, often, tools were falling apart and rain made any type of work complicated.[50] Moreover, the soldiers of 1939 were not those of the First World War; many of them came from cities and had no experience with manual work. It must be remembered that in 1936, 52% of the French population came from an urban environment.[51] Many soldiers, unable to cope with the physical strain, complained about their wartime service. Intellectuals, including Jean Malaquais, often believed that they would be better employed in propaganda departments:

> A few days ago, Galy saw Jean Paulhan, who told him that I would be far more useful in another regiment than the pioneers. He was to talk to Giraudoux. Indeed, I would have been in a better mood if I had not been asked to do manual work. It is deplorable that I have to work with a pickaxe, doing this kind of work, when I can speak English, German, Russian, Polish, and have very good references. I can also use a radio, a typewriter, know how to work as an accountant, drive a car, a motorbike, a lorry, and I am not stupid.[52]

Officers found it hard to order their men to do tasks in which they did not believe. Commander Raymond voiced his scepticism after witnessing the chaos surrounding excavation work linked to the defensive plan:

> It is the third time in fifteen days that the battalion has to dig elsewhere. [...] As a result, the ground is filled with holes, but nothing is finished. Men shovelled thousands of cubic metres of soil but as soon as something takes shape, it is abandoned to start something new by order of someone who has a degree and personal ideas to test. [...] This type of leadership is showing chaotic intellectual gaps. Everybody wants to win the argument without looking at what has been done and previous orders are branded stupid.[53]

This incoherence was a major source of anxiety. In March 1940, soldiers tasked with perfecting telegraphic lines between various forts noticed the lack of vision. Georges Sadoul denounced:

> If they wanted us to install a definitive line, it would have been logical to put it below ground. […] It is very likely that they are ordering us to do this to keep us busy, to avoid demoralisation. But demoralisation increases when you work for nothing.[54]

The lack of material and the overall dissatisfaction with having to work on pointless jobs made the fight for a better morale inefficient. If men were not bored, they were busy doing useless tasks.

Farm work did not improve this situation. In Alsace, soldiers helped with the culture of beet, grown for sugar production in factories.[55] According to a March 1940 report by representative André Dupont, the beet harvest was saved by soldiers, who managed to increase production by 30 to 40%.[56] In autumn 1939, the army also helped with the grape harvest and even saved that year's wine production.[57] From March 1940, soldiers worked the fields in the area located in front of the Maginot Line. On 5 March 1940, the National Assembly had a major debate on whether to use the army for agricultural work. Highlighting the lack of manpower, the agricultural commission asked to 'apply to other classes of the second reserve measures taken for the farmers of classes 1912, 1913, 1914 and 1915'.[58] This meant temporary transfers and agricultural holidays. These had already been authorised but were rarely applied, as representative Dupont regretted and proved by showing several soldiers' letters.[59] The fault lay with the EM and its unwillingness to release mobilised men. Mobilised farmers did not understand why they were asked to do agricultural work far from home in a potential fighting zone, while their land was left abandoned:[60]

> To think that we have to cultivate the land here while everything is left untouched at home.[61]

Cultivating the land so close to the frontline was badly perceived by many men, who wondered what kind of war allowed this. At the beginning of April 1940, the new Agriculture Minister, Paul Thellier, a left-wing republican, visited the frontline.[62] This appearance failed to impress:

> Really, we wonder if this is a war, because our friends cultivate the land next to the lines. It is weird to grow potatoes so close to the Germans.

> The new Agriculture Minister came to see us. He was there to look at the agricultural fields in front of the Maginot Line. Artillerymen are doing this. This is really a very weird war.

I do not understand anything. We are told that this is war but, arriving here, I plant potatoes.[63]

The French population was given a different view of the situation. Newspapers and newsreels showed eager soldiers employed in farms and factories. Homefront newspapers reproduced pictures of men working the fields and picking grapes.[64] One of these pictures was described as such:

The farmer-soldier does not drive the cart for the first time in his life. You can be sure that furrows are straight. [...] Strong and masculine shoulders [...] do a job that women could not accomplish. The female farmer, wearing manly trousers and carrying a fork in her hands, is pleased to see such hard work being done.[65]

The gendered captions ignored frontline polemics to gather the country around the military and the government. 'Goodwill' was enough for France to 'feed itself'.[66] This positive message was recycled in April 1940, as it can be seen in the *Illustration*, when the picture of a French soldier-farmer was reproduced alongside an article praising the devotion of the French army.[67]

Entertaining the army

In October 1939, the President of the Council, backed by the EM, passed a decree allowing military clubs for officers, non-commissioned officers and soldiers.[68] These clubs, as well as army libraries, were not a first for the French military.[69] During the First World War, the universal committee of the YMC and its general secretary, a Frenchman called Emmanuel Stautter, created the *Foyers du soldat*.[70] In 1916, the War Minister encouraged this initiative which 'protected young recruits against the dangers of alcoholism and venereal dangers by offering healthy distractions and drinks'.[71] The creation of new clubs was actively supported by the French authorities, especially after the mutinies of May–June 1917. In August, the French-American cooperation, including the association *Union franco-américaine*, financed many of these clubs.[72] By February 1919, there were 1,452 *Foyers du soldat*.[73]

In 1939, the French Government set the legal background to revive this form of entertainment. The 23 October 1939 decree authorised privately-funded clubs, as long as they were controlled by military authorities. They were allowed to hire civilians, including women serving as nurses and cooks.[74] This decree distinguished three types of clubs aimed respectively at officers, non-commissioned officers and soldiers. The one for soldiers was named *Foyer militaire* while the others were titled *cercles*, a terminology already used during the Great War. They included 'one or more shops, meeting and playing rooms, one library and reading room, one or more hairdressing station, etc.'.[75] An officer served as director but a consultative commission made of soldiers was allowed. Paul Truffau, serving on the Belgian border, was named manager of several *Foyers* in February 1940. He travelled regularly to 'advise, lead and [...] check the accounting books of 35 *Foyers* spread on a given territory'.[76] In spring 1940, he was asked to standardise the price of food and drinks to match local shops. Benefits were given to the poorest soldiers.[77] It should be highlighted that the *Foyer* was not unique to the French military as the Swiss army created a section called *Armée et Foyer* in September 1939.[78]

By February 1940, 1,110 *Foyers* were already open while 500 were planned and another 300 were managed by private companies.[79] The design varied greatly from one place to another.[80] Some were described as comfortable and attractive places:

> At Chambley, our *foyer* was inaugurated a week ago – a room decorated with flags. A piano was brought from Metz. There were 2 or 3 colonels, a baroness, several officers. A piano teacher from Metz played Chopin. A guy from the 402nd (who won the 1st prize at *Radio-Cité*) sang twice. We were given chocolate and listened to a speech. Since that day, the *Foyer* is open every day; there is a reading room, a place to eat, to read the mail, to listen to the radio, etc. Since yesterday, we have a movie on Sundays.[81]

Others were less convincing. Georges Sadoul, serving in the evacuated region, described his local *foyer*:

> It is a pitiful schoolroom. A board used as a counter. On dirty old benches, soldiers sit, not knowing where to put their long legs. They drink red wine in filthy glasses. The mess does not manage to cover the noise made by the radio. A dim light, grey ceilings, muddy floors. . . We want to run away.[82]

The GQG did all it could to provide the *Foyers* with various distractions. Colonel Gaucher, leading the 2nd Bureau of the GQG launched a press appeal to collect 'balls, pins, cards, various games, etc.'.[83] Despite the significant number of clubs, not all units had access to a *Foyer*.[84] Sporadic complaints were voiced until April 1940, especially around the fortified sector of Thionville, where the lack of games, reading material or radio equipment was felt.[85] Fortress soldiers, who had little access to the outside or games, desperately needed entertainment.

In these conditions, the press proved useful. At the beginning of the Phoney war, civilian newspapers reached the frontline with difficulty. On 25 September 1939, General Gamelin announced that the distribution of the main Parisian titles was 'being organised'.[86] A month later, this was still not successfully managed.[87] In order to make newspapers more widely available, Colonel Gaucher authorised alternative methods of distribution. He used military liaison staff to deliver the main titles. As with most other services, the *Fedération Nationale des journaux français* was working at a slower pace and was unable to cover army territories.[88]

French soldiers also wrote and read frontline newspapers. This type of reading material had appeared for the first time at the end of 1914. For the First World War, Stéphane Audoin-Rouzeau identified 400 titles, of which 169 were preserved in the archives.[89] There is no similar study for the Phoney War but primary sources make it clear that frontline newspapers were widespread. On 30

October 1939, the 'General-in-chief authorised the creation of unit newspapers, inspired by the last war. A maximum of one newspaper per unit forming an army corps is allowed'.[90] Colonial troops were also authorised to write their own newspapers. The *Aiglon. Journal humoristico-sérieux du 3ᵉ RTM* was published between April and May 1940 while *La Chikaïa. Journal Officiel du 7ᵉ RTM* was printed first in April 1940.[91] In Alger, the newspaper *Ya Allah! Illustré, mensuel des militaires musulmans nord-africains*, was printed in September 1939; others were written in Tunisia and Madagascar.[92] On 24 March 1940, a report sent to the Commandant-in-Chief stated that 200 frontline newspapers existed.[93]

At first, this type of press circulated freely between the rear and the army zone. Several soldiers sent them to their families to illustrate life in the French military.[94] The authorities also forwarded them to the Parisian press to fuel propaganda.[95] However, leaks of military secrets forced the EM to restrict their distribution to the frontline in March 1940.[96] Frontline newspapers did not escape censorship. The 2nd Bureau controlled the content and established new censorship rules:

> Any information that can help the enemy know more about the French army is strictly forbidden. [...] Anything that damages the prestige and the morale of the Army is strictly forbidden.[97]

Frontline newspapers were censored by specialised officers before being sent to the Press department of the Army and the 2nd Bureau of the GQG. They were also transferred to the CGI of Jean Giraudoux.[98] Titles giving away confidential information could be banned temporarily or indefinitely.[99] Despite this strict process, frontline newspapers were popular among soldiers. Army General Bourret, encouraged by this popularity, ordered the redaction of a military almanac for the 5th Army:

> Aside from the calendar, recipes and advice, which make the basis for an almanac, a lot of space will be dedicated to songs, tales, legends, anecdotes, war stories, texts, popular pictures, in other words anything on which Alsatian Army folklore rests. Dialects of our provinces will be allowed.[100]

This project was organised as a contest. Soldiers were allowed to contribute until 20 February 1940, the best submissions being granted a prize.[101] Other initiatives saw the light of day on the frontline, including the creation of an association called *La Presse du Front* in the 3rd Army. It stated that soldiers were allowed to express their unhappiness through the newspaper *Le Front*. This was quickly banned by the EM.[102]

The content, the reception and the effects raise interesting questions. Frontline newspaper did not talk much about politics or the military situation. In fact, they mostly printed anecdotes, amusing stories, caricatures mocking Nazi leaders, satirical songs, fake soldiers' letters and games such as crosswords. Their stated goal was to 'fight an enemy more dangerous than the Hun, the *cafard*'.[103] They offered a light-hearted vision of the front, one making fun of the daily routine, as shown in Figure 3.1.

UN... DEUX... UN... DEUX... Exercice journalier pour pieds gelés.....

Figure 3.1 Fighting frozen feet[104]

Frontline newspapers were designed to be funny but also contained serious articles. Most titles reproduced practical advice about furlough or hygiene.[105] Officers also used them to talk to their men.[106] Quality varied greatly between titles, depending on the editorial team. Some were built around pictures, others only reproduced texts. Regular contests were organised to find new content.[107] For example, the *Le poilu du 6-9* announced a 'great humoristic drawing contest' in March 1940:

> Open to all our readers on the topic 'civilians'. Drawings need to be inked and have a title. [...] Selected drawings will be published in the newspaper. Prizes will be given to the ten best submissions following their publication. Among the prizes, boxes of beer from Vézelise, wine, alcohol, tobacco, cigarettes, pipes, chocolate, knives and other goods.[108]

In several reports, censorship units made it clear that these activities were useful and improved morale.[109]

Radio was a significant novelty on the frontline. Becoming popular after the First World War, it was used by more than half of the population in 1939.[110] France had a good network as well as public and private broadcasters.[111] Unsurprisingly, it became one of the favourite means of communication during the Phoney War. In December 1939, tens of millions of francs were spent on buying radios.[112] These sets were delivered by the *Arts, lectures et loisirs* department led by Georges Duhamel and Alfred Cordot.[113] Soon before Christmas, the President of the Council sent 8,000 radios to the frontline. This action had an aim:

> Giving away radios will entertain soldiers. We strongly recommend the bi-daily show (11.45 to 12.00 and 18.30 to 18.45) *Quart d'heure du soldat*, produced by the GQG with the CGI.[114]

This show first appeared at the end of November 1939 and was played by all channels except Radio Paris.[115] Army Press Officers wrote to the show and addressed the following topics: furlough, salaries, advice to the soldiers' wives.[116] This show was described as too intellectual and not entertaining enough by many soldiers.[117] In fact, the lack of music encouraged many men to listen to German channels.[118]

Live shows were not forgotten. Before the French Revolution, the Swiss Army already had *loustics*, men who used humour to preserve morale.[119] During the First World War, short shows and funny songs, the famous *café-concert* of the Belle Époque, were played by and for soldiers.[120] They appeared for the first time in 1915 before being taken over by the army and the rear. The *théâtre des armées* was created by Emile Fabre, the administrator of the *Comédie Française*, while the *théâtre du front* was organised by the painter Emile Scot. Both appeared on the frontline in 1916. One brought artists from the *Comédie Française* to play classic plays. The other, sponsored by the EMA, used movable stages for a more modern form of entertainment.[121] Music, selected by Alfred Cordot, also played a part in the *théâtre des armées.*[122]

The experience of the First World War was copied during the Phoney War but took time to materialise. At the end of November 1939, General Condé, commanding the 3rd Army, complained about the blurry status of the *théâtre des armées*. In doubt, he imposed the following rules:

> You cannot contact directly an artist or an association. Do not accept any direct offer. If you are approached, redirect them toward the *Direction Générale des Beaux-Arts*, where offers are centralised. Unit commanders are free to organise shows if they use their own resources. Moreover, theatre plays are organised by the GQG.[123]

The *théâtre aux armées*, civilian artists supervised by the military, should not be confused with frontline theatres made up of soldiers. Homefront theatres were closed to the army, except for charity shows organised by the Red Cross or if they were to 'maintain good relations between civilians and local people living in the area'.[124] Moreover, artists belonging to the civilian world, unless invited, were not allowed on the frontline until March 1940.[125] This fragmentation between civilians and soldiers had an impact on how frontline theatres were organised. The *Direction Générale des Beaux-Arts*, which managed the *théâtre aux armées*, employed civilians under military supervision. Artists, approved by the GQG, 'visited regularly major centres according to the schedule made by the army'.[126] Famous celebrities did not travel much to the territories controlled by the army. Joséphine Baker and Maurice Chevalier went once in November to the areas around Metz, Thionville and other places which were kept secret.[127] This tour was advertised widely by the media.[128] Maurice Chevalier, singing his song *Ça fait d'excellents français!* caught the French spirit.[129] As Jean-Paul Sartre wrote in his diary, it reflected the mentality of the frontline.[130] French soldiers were not pictured as heroes but as normal people such as employees, workers, bakers, etc.[131] Other famous artists, sent by the *théâtre des armées*, brought joy to the frontline:

> The *théâtre aux armées* came fifteen days ago. Georgius and Nadia Dauty were there. We wish for more shows like this and more often. It was a transformation and gave us hope.[132]

The *théâtre aux armées*, despite not always sending celebrities, was a major success among ordinary soldiers. Officers, however, did not always enjoy the 'rude language used in the shows'.[133] Intellectuals were also sceptical. As Pierre-Frédéric Charpentier explained in his study, Georges Bonnefoy, Robert Desnos, Jean-Paul Sartre and Antoine de Saint-Exupéry complained that 'despite a sense of solidarity born out of a common fate, intellectuals mocked or looked sceptically at the crowd's enthusiasm'.[134]

Frontline theatres, run by the military with the help of Red Cross members or civilians approved by the army, were more common.[135] Unit commanders were allowed to 'pick among their men a few mobilised artists to have them perform around their sector'.[136] This type of entertainment was not always to the highest standard but was nonetheless popular:

> The *théâtre aux armées* that came was not the famous one. No civilian among the actors. Only soldiers. Some were professionals, others were amateurs. When I say actors, I should say musicians because most of the show was made of a jazz band with 18 instruments. As usual, this happened in our *Foyer*. For the occasion, a stage was built. [...] The show lasted three hours. Jazz, songs from Montmartre, imitators, Russian dancers, we saw everything. Good fun and [word erased]. The crowd was pleased, you should have seen this. I think that this kind of entertainment is very good for the morale of our troops. Of course, it triggered memories and brought the *cafard*. This is not a bad thing.[137]

Many voiced their satisfaction while actors were pleased to see the public, 'these big boys, [...] agitated, laughing loudly'.[138] On 9 January 1940, General Condé authorised the creation of a '3rd Army theatre', made of soldiers 'loaned by the Corps to the Army'.[139] Generals were responsible for the stage and security.[140]

However, many soldiers were unable to see the show. Indeed, theatres were unable to travel everywhere and there was a limited number of seats:

> There is a show 8 km from here. You must have heard of these theatres in the newspapers. We were looking forward to it but were disappointed. We thought that we could all go to the show, but no, they selected a non-commissioned officer and a man per section, who will tell us what they saw. This is our pleasure.[141]

The CP recorded 200 similar complaints. In most cases, the lack of seats was pointed at.[142] Understanding this, the EM tried to make things better by creating the so-called 'light tours (3 or 4 artists)'.[143] Other shows, however, were reserved for officers and non-commissioned officers, triggering protests:

> [...] A ball was supposed to follow the evening. Unfortunately, it was announced that the night was only for non-commissioned officers and officers as soon as the curtain closed. A huge disappointment for many of us, who wanted to dance despite having walked 25 km in the morning. But this is what we call equality [...] Today, we talk about this insult. The poor soldier will always be last. The soldier is not a man, he is a beast.[144]

This anger should not hide the fact that organised shows remained a major success to the credit of the EM.

Playing movies on the frontline was another great novelty. Not unlike theatre plays, cinema was largely dependent on unit commanders and the availability of equipment, either given by the EM or by private groups. The 3rd Army had a specialist, Sergeant Jean Mercier, who built an improvised cinema. The projector, a Pathé Nathan 175, was loaned by a priest but had not served since March 1939.[145] Jean Mercier managed to make it work and was even able to play movies four times a day.[146] According to our primary sources, there was no imposed schedule. Movies were sometimes played during the week in the afternoon, others on Saturdays, Sundays or during the evenings.[147] Soldiers were not free to choose what they wanted to watch. Each movie was strictly controlled and had to bear the censorship mark of the *Service Cinématographique de l'Armée*.[148] Moreover, soldiers were not allowed to visit cinemas intended for civilians.

Different types of movies were allowed on the frontline: documentaries, newsreels and the *Journal de guerre* of the army. This weekly newsreel, made by the *Service Cinématographique des Armées*, explained what had happened on the frontline.[149] Usually, it showed movements of troops as well as politicians and superior officers visiting military regions. These twenty-minute long movies were supposed to reflect the truth but propaganda was always present, sometimes with unfortunate consequences. For example, soldiers of the 3rd Army 'recognised themselves and laughed when they saw a movie in which sounds of automatic weapons had been added'.[150] This was not the only problem. Movies were sometimes delayed and soldiers were even offered news from the 'previous month'.[151] The army seems to have taken the whole experience as an entertaining curiosity.[152] Despite these issues, cinema had a positive impact as it offered a form of escapism: 'tonight, we go to the movies [...] We forget our miserable life during the show.'[153] 'Tonight, we went to the movies and it was rather good, it is a nice way to gather your thoughts.'[154]

Sport was perceived as a fundamental way to keep the body busy while cooperating with fellow soldiers. Officially instituted in January 1940, sport as a leisure activity had in fact appeared the previous autumn. On the Maginot Line, stronghold crews, who rarely saw daylight, were ordered to play outside.[155] For those trapped in concrete structures, this had a hugely positive psychological impact.[156] In other units, many initiatives appeared as soon as November 1939. Regiments bought or received balls and played against other regiments.[157] However, sport really became a State priority when the weather improved in March 1940. Leagues and competitions were even created.[158] Soldiers took part in various sports and activities: gymnastics, rugby, boxing, skiing, poaching, fishing and above all football.[159] In March 1940, Captain Fouret, the press officer for Army Group 3, detailed which sport investments were agreed by the State:

> 4,500 balls were delivered. This was done by the 3rd bureau and the balloons were given to 35 divisions, first to those coming back from the frontline. In the next 3 to 4 months, we hope to give another 15,000 balls (1 per company or battery). A credit of 3 million was agreed for various fees (field, equipment, etc.); it will be spread between Corps commanders, who will spend this budget in local or military shops.[160]

Money also came from private donations. At the beginning of 1940, a British citizen 'offered 2,000 balls to the French Army. [...] The first were given to General Requin, commander of the 4th Army, who was joined by a British superior officer'.[161] Therefore, most soldiers were given the possibility to practise a sport, football being the favourite.

These initiatives were welcomed by the men. Soldiers, as well as frontline newspapers, talked a lot about matches between teams. For example, the *Rose Maginot* created a dedicated space for a football championship between battalions:

> Two official matches were held at Easter. I cannot say that the five hundred people who saw the match, all wearing khaki uniforms for a good reason, witnessed scientific or academic football. But all of us were encouraging the players and were delighted to see this. Some players, having used shovels for too long, had almost entirely lost the ability to use their feet for anything else than marches. Despite this, and after a few minutes, the game became quite attractive.[162]

Tournaments were numerous. When spring arrived, matches were even organised between French and British teams. According to the CP, these matches 'are always popular and help maintain good relations between allies'.[163] The EM was supportive but wanted to control sportive activities:

> There is no need for sports officers. Tournaments should be kept to a minimum and at Division level, with the agreement of the general in charge. Sportive activities cannot go against normal duties and should not lead to the selection of specific players. They should be organised in coordination with the 3rd and 1st Bureaux.[164]

The above-mentioned activities were not created solely to entertain soldiers but also to trigger a sense of comradeship and encourage patriotism. This was especially visible in movies, songs and newspapers. Symbols were equally important. Many men were brought to the Maginot Line to witness the power of the French Army. This was visibly effective:

> Day of rest. I go with the officers of my company to the fort of Métrich, one of the most important on the line. I spent two hours and was amazed. It is a real factory and has lifts, a railway running around the corridors and bringing men and ammunitions. It has towers and formidable weaponry. They can live without external communication for three months.[165]

According to the CP, visits on the Maginot Line had a 'formidable and very reassuring effect'.[166] Moreover, other visits were organised in factories and in other industrial places to witness the power of the French economy. This worked: 'I can swear that it is reassuring to see the *Défense nationale* at work.'[167] Cultural places were also picked, such as the monastery of Sainte-Odile, the protector of Alsace.[168] This important religious place was located in the Bas-Rhin region, on top of a mount. It was already a popular Catholic pilgrimage before the conflict.

Following the same desire to mix entertainment and national duty, the EM organised a competition to fight espionage. In November 1939, the War Minister released a 'note about counter-espionage in the army' in which an artistic contest was announced:

> Our counter-espionage campaign must be lively, attractive, convincing. It must be conceived to educate our men, who rarely understand the danger. We need short recommendations made of slogans and caricatures. It would be beneficial to involve our men.[169]

This competition targeted artists serving in the army but was also looking for new ideas to be used in talks, movies, etc.[170] There were two objectives: to educate soldiers and to entertain the army.[171] Participants were allowed various mediums: drawing, songs, etc. Prizes ranging from 50 to 200 francs were given.[172]

Propaganda and entertainment, as already stated above, were often combined. A cycle of conferences was ordered by the EM. At the beginning of the conflict, the EM also wanted to use individual propaganda, targeting 'non-commissioned

officers and officers, puzzled by the unusual nature of the conflict'.[173] The
following was ordered:

> Corps commanders will use personal actions (one to one meetings, direct
> contact) to address anything that looks like a lack of spirit or
> determination.[174]

This order came with a set of instructions from the 2nd Bureau. It gave typical
arguments to use such as the fact that the stagnation on the frontline was
'political' and linked to 'the specific nature of a coalition war'. The Phoney War
was advantageous to the allies, who had superior human and economic resources.
Germany was also hurt by the blockade.[175] Moreover, soldiers lacking determination were to be told that the current conflict was essential to defend civilisation
and would be led 'until final victory, whatever the duration or the cost'.[176]

In November 1939, the 2nd Bureau studied a new type of conferences based on
the 1917 model. These talks would target soldiers about to go on holiday to make
sure that interactions between the rear and the front had 'positive effects'.[177]
Varying advice was given on how to talk about the Maginot Line or denounce
German propaganda.[178] At the end of the month, the EM suggested the designation of unofficial 'morale specialists' among officers, non-commissioned officers
and soldiers. The operation was supposed to remain discreet to 'avoid accusations
of interference'.[179] This seems to have failed, as Georges Sadoul revealed:

> Since the end of November, top secret reports have been revealed. The 2nd
> Bureau is visibly concerned about the army's morale. They ask [...] for
> motivational speeches, activities and a group of people is tasked with main-
> taining morale.[180]

In the report, it was suggested to organise 'broad conferences of vulgarisation'
to explain major current themes or the history of Alsace. Other topics included 'the
origins of war', 'Hitler's lies' or talks about the war at sea or Great Britain.[181]
Realising that soldiers were on the look-out for propaganda, the 2nd Bureau asked
for these conferences to be 'empty of the propaganda spirit' and stated that they
should be accessible as well as 'lively, clear, without any technicality or
abstraction'.[182] In December, the order was given to find speakers in each unit
and possible topics, which needed to be sent for approval by the EM before 20
December 1939.[183]

In fact, conferences on topics such as 'the current war and Hitler' had already
appeared in November 1939.[184] Georges Sadoul reported that talks about 'the
dreadful internal situation of Germany', looking mostly at the economy, back-
fired as French soldiers knew that their country suffered similar problems.[185]
Intellectuals were also asked to address the troops: Marc Bloch talked about the
British while Georges Bonnefoy looked at Hitler.[186] Jean Zay (4th Army) was
ordered to explore topics such as 'Why are we at war? Why is the war taking this
shape.'[187] In other units, officers talked on a daily basis.[188] In March 1940, a

special round of conferences on 'morale, social and family questions' was organised by the Commandant en chef (CEC) of the 3rd Army.[189]

Conferences were entertaining and kept the men busy for a few hours but they
do not seem to have had a profound impact. The nature of the Phoney War, this
'psychological war', demanded a more profound form of help. Paul Nizan
understood this paradox, seeing a fundamental difference between material
distractions and the essential preoccupations:

> The EM looks after the army's morale. He offers healthy distractions but
> does not suspect that he should take care of the metaphysical side of the
> army. Even a farmer understands this struggle, this fight against the void,
> feels the mystery of time as Kafka would. There is no remedy and no *foyers
> du soldat* can fight against this feeling of oblivion.[190]

It is not an accident that many writers compared the Phoney War to Franz
Kafka and that Jean-Paul Sartre wrote his masterpiece *l'Être et le Néant* during
that time.

Metaphysical questions were not entirely absent from the frontline as religion
played an important role. During the First World War, Catholics, Jews and
Protestants had military priests, rabbis and pastors. This was guaranteed by the
law of 8 July 1880 and was confirmed by the law on the separation of the church
and the state of 9 December 1905.[191] However, the organisation had failed and
several units had been without a chaplain.[192] By the end of the conflict, there
were only 46 rabbis, 68 pastors and nearly 500 Catholic priests.[193] During the
Phoney War, chaplains were 'attached to the divisions' and CA's headquarters
and not to the *service de santé* as during the previous conflict.[194] The army called
older religious men to serve behind the frontline and younger chaplains to
integrate forward units. By contrast with the First World War, Imams were also
recruited to assist colonial troops.[195] Religious men had various roles depending
on the religion but all talked with soldiers and brought psychological help. We
lack primary sources for Jewish, Muslim or Protestant men. Fortunately, Catholic
priests, the largest group by far, left many letters:

> I take care of the spirit in the fortress. The chaplain of the sub-sector, Abbot
> Claude, the priest of Saint-Laurent, Epinal, is very happy about it because he
> has too much work. On Sunday: 2 masses and confessions. The attendance
> of the officers and the men (80% of Alsatians) is spectacular.[196]

To perform this religious duty, various objects were needed. Priests managed
to find them more or less officially, sometimes taking in abandoned parishes
what they could not get elsewhere. They also asked the hierarchy for portable
altars.[197] Both chaplains and soldiers noticed the regain of interest for religion.
Most men found in a priest a friendly ear and a psychological relief.[198] Without
surprise, this regain of interest for spiritual matters pleased those who believed
in God:

I am in charge of a machine gun section made of good guys, as are all our soldiers. On this Christian ground of Lorraine, facing danger and suffering, our Frenchmen have rediscovered their souls. On Sunday, it is a beautiful sight to see our churches filled with praying men.[199]

This extract is obviously the reflection of a practising Catholic but there is little doubt that religion was popular on the frontline. Protestants, having little access to their own denomination, sometimes went to Catholic masses. The masses of Christmas 1939 and Easter 1940, as well as elaborated meals, became special moments in the life of a soldier and had positive effects.[200] The church, understanding the potential benefits, organised several campaigns to help the French army.[201] Muslim soldiers also tried to celebrate important days. One of them explained:

We celebrated Eid: food, dances and other distractions. We will hold the frontline because our duty is more important than any pain. We will come back honoured and ready to celebrate.[202]

Religion was an important topic in colonial soldiers' letters. Muslims from Morocco often saw their presence in France as God's will.[203] For them, religion was a familiar beacon in a foreign land:

As for myself, I prefer my country to any other. God always. God protects us and will bring peace forever ... It rains, thanks to God and it is destiny. We always pray to God and ask him to protect us and bring a good peace to bring us home to our family.[204]

Other colonial soldiers expressed similar thoughts.[205]

If the soul was satisfied, the flesh desperately needed attention. Despite everything, the lack of women was really difficult to accept. Both married men and single soldiers found the situation almost impossible to bear. A poem from the frontline newspaper *La Rose Maginot* expressed the need to meet women. Many articles and soldiers' letters also talked about them. However, women were sometimes present illegally on the frontline. As we already mentioned in chapter 2, Simone de Beauvoir stayed with Jean-Paul Sartre from 31 October to 5 November 1939. In her memoirs, she explained:

Brumath. I arrive on the empty platform. I follow people. When I reach the exit, I am left alone. There are a few soldiers but they do not stop me. [...] Here is the *Taverne du Cerf* where, according to his letters, he eats his breakfast.[206]

After a night in a hotel, she met Sartre the next day. At the beginning of her stay, she felt 'observed' and was uneasy, but the population helped her and only the gendarmes were feared.[207] She managed to get a permit, pretending to visit a cousin, and ate regularly with Sartre. In her diary, she described the strange atmosphere in this Alsatian town, filled with soldiers and local civilians.

Simone de Beauvoir was far from an exception. Other testimonies confirm the presence of women, mostly wives of officers and non-commissioned officers.[208] In fact, this phenomenon was so common that the EM was forced to fight against it. In February 1940, General Bourret (5th Army) released an order stating that 'women, legitimate wives or not, must be removed from the front as their presence harms soldiers' morale'.[209] Actions followed. At the end of February, soldiers were punished for bringing women into the army zone:

> I saw punishments aimed at officers. There are two of them: one for a commander and one for a captain who brought their wives. Can you imagine? I know that you have never seriously contemplated the idea of coming here but I tell you nonetheless.[210]

This issue was obviously linked with the management of sexual desires. 'Women are the warrior's entertainment said Napoleon and he was bloody right!'[211] This rather enlightening thought was written by a soldier in his war diary. He had not seen women for a long time and was complaining openly. Prostitution on the frontline is still an obscure topic. However, clues suggest that it was treated differently than during the First World War. In 1914–1918, the EM allowed prostitutes forward before creating on 13 March 1918 the *Bordels Militaires de Campagne.*[212] During the Phoney War, the EM studied the question in January 1940. The 1st Bureau of the EM recommended that brothels should be forbidden. Another note, written on 26 February 1940, explained the current rules:

> Prostitution in the army zone is a matter for the local councils. The commander, who is in charge of public order and army safety, must enforce whatever is decided by the local authorities. This control must make sure that the health system is good (sanitary measures) and army safety is guaranteed (general police measures).[213]

As can be seen, brothels were allowed by local councils but were heavily scrutinised by the military. The commander also checked isolated and illegal prostitutes, in coordination with the police.[214] From a sanitary perspective, civilian and military authorities worked together to avoid sexual diseases. Moreover, brothels were monitored to avoid spies.[215]

In April, the 2nd Bureau changed its mind about brothels. New houses were advised 'exceptionally' in the army zone to answer 'necessities'.[216] It seems that the question was not settled when the Germans launched the May offensive but sources suggest that the French army was moving in the same tolerant direction as during the First World War.

The initial reticence can be explained by the fact that during the 1920s and 1930s, there was a trend against prostitution. In Strasburg and Mulhouse, brothels had been closed to fight sexual diseases.[217] In January 1940, the authorities were debating:

> The soldier is waiting for the arrival of spring. He thinks that the offensive will start at the end of February or at the beginning of March. Inaction is difficult to accept. He does not like to exercise. [...] However, fortress soldiers coming to Mulhouse complain about the 'lack of a certain type of distraction'. A move was taken a few years ago to abolish prostitution. I am studying the matter and am looking at ways to regulate it. Meanwhile, I ordered the very strict surveillance of prostitutes.[218]

As can be seen, attempts were made to relax the rules. It is not sure that new brothels were opened before the Germans attacked. Organising this would have been difficult in such a short time. More research on the topic would be very useful.

The lack of brothels was not the only consideration. Another problem was mentioned by the commander of the VIIth military region. In a report, he stated that it was needed to open prostitution houses for 'indigenous soldiers' made only of 'indigenous staff'.[219] The reasons for this request were inspired by racism and colonialism:

> It seems indeed that in order to maintain the prestige of France, we need to avoid as much as possible sexual relations between indigenous soldiers and French women, even prostitutes. We also noticed that most rapes of French women in North Africa were committed by indigenous soldiers who stayed for a time in France and had encounters with white women. If we want to avoid the mistakes of the previous war, we need to take the necessary measures to suppress contact between colonial soldiers and white women.[220]

The idea was suggested to 'create brothels staffed exclusively with indigenous women and equipped with transportation to go where North-African units were resting'.[221] A similar service was already in place for a long time in North Africa and Syria and, according to the commander, was 'working' and had never been 'a problem'.[222] On 10 April 1940, the Commander-in-Chief gave his approval to open new establishments and looked to the Police prefecture of Paris to recruit prostitutes.[223] Considering the date, it is likely that this project never saw the light of day.

Conclusion

This chapter has highlighted the legacy of the First World War. In 1939–1940, the authorities studied the conduct of the morale war during the previous conflict. Using the same monitoring tools, they also copied various forms of entertainment such as military clubs, brothels, theatres, etc. In this respect, the EMA, the GQG and the Government followed hard-learned lessons on victory and morale. They believed that a positive state of mind on the frontline was crucial to win against Germany. Looking at previous experiences did not mean that the authorities were unwilling to adopt new technologies. Indeed, radio and cinema were common tools of military propaganda during the Phoney War. These various attempts to offer mental relief proved partly successful. Most soldiers enjoyed the range of activities designed to keep them both mentally and physically happy. Colonial troops, despite racial considerations, also appreciated the efforts deployed to accommodate their religious or sexual needs. Sport and social events clearly helped but never replaced what soldiers cherished above all. Indeed, the separation with the family or the rupture with the civilian life proved difficult to accept. The lack of action was also hard to overcome. However, this did not mean that soldiers were unwilling to fight. As we have seen in the previous chapters, the French were determined to endure hardship to secure peace. We must also remember that missing one's relatives was not specific to the French. Soldiers have always suffered when deployed and still find it hard today. In the next chapter, we will address a fundamental and controversial part of the Phoney War: German propaganda.

Notes

1 This issue is explained in detail in: Bernard Wilkin and René Wilkin, *Fighting for Napoleon: Soldiers' Letters 1799–1815* (Barnsley, 2015).
2 On the matter, see for example Bernard Wilkin, *Aerial propaganda and the Wartime Occupation of France, 1914–1918* (London, 2017).
3 SHD AT: 2N224. Conseil Supérieur de la Défense, confidential report, 15 September 1939.
4 Paul Tuffrau, *De la 'drôle de guerre' à la libération de Paris (1939–1944): Lettres et Carnets* (Paris, 2002), p. 30.
5 The phone and the telegraph were also controlled. Jean-Noël Jeanneney, 'L'opinion Publique En France Pendant La Première Guerre Mondiale', *Publications de l'École Française de Rome*, 54 (1984), pp. 209–227.
6 SHD AT: 31N102. Note for the Government, 25 January 1934.
7 SHD AT: 31N102. Commission interministérielle de contrôle postal de Paris, Note for the postal commission of Vesoul, 22 April 1940. They also reached the commanding officer of the CP (EMA 5th Bureau), the commission archives and the colonel coordinating the sub-sections of the North-East (Besançon).
8 SHD AT: 27N69. GQG, 3rd Bureau, report on morale, 18 December 1939.
9 Ibid.
10 Ibid.
11 SHD AT: 27N69. GQG, EMG, 2nd Bureau, report on morale, 25 November 1939.
12 *Journal Officiel de la République Française (JORF)*, 24 November 1939, p. 13349.
13 From March 1940, Julien Cain served as *secrétaire général de l'Information*.
14 Decree of 24 November 1939, *Journal Officiel de la République Française*, p. 13349.
15 Martine Poulain, *Livres pillés, lectures surveillées* (Paris, 2013), p. 213.
16 *Paris-Soir*, 9 January 1940.
17 SHD AT: 27N178. CEC of the North-East front, EM, 3rd Bureau, morale, 20 April 1940.
18 Ibid.
19 Ibid.

20 Ibid.
21 SHD AT: 27N178. CEC of the North-East front, EM, 3rd Bureau, Section -M-, internal organisation, 25 April 1940.
22 Ibid.
23 SHD AT: 27N69. Note for the commander, 12 October 1939.
24 François Cochet, *Les soldats de la drôle de guerre* (Paris, 2004), p. 149.
25 Jean-Louis Crémieux-Brilhac, *Les Français de l'an 40*, Vol. 2 (Paris, 1990), p. 450.
26 See Chapter 2.
27 SHD AT: 28N13. Officer's report, 1 April 1940.
28 SHD AT: 29N290. Gamelin to the generals commanding Army Groups, 27 November 1939.
29 Ibid.
30 Ibid.
31 SHD AT: 29N290. General Lescanne to the General commanding the 5th Army, 1 March 1940.
32 SHD AT: 29N290. General Dentz, commander of the 12th Corps to the Army General commanding the 5th Army, 5 March 1940.
33 SHD AT: 29N290. General Noël, commanding the 17th Army Corps to the general commanding the Vth Army, 5 March 1940; SHD AT: 29N290. General Dentz, commanding the 12th Army Corps to the general commanding the 5th Army, 5 March 1940.
34 SHD AT: 29N290. General Dentz, commanding the 12th Army Corps to the Commander of the 5th Army, 5 March 1940.
35 Cochet, *Les soldats de la drôle de guerre*, p. 38.
36 SHD AT: 29N259. 4th Army, direction des étapes, Etat-Major, 3rd bureau. General Oppermann to the general commanding the 4th Army, 9 January 1940.
37 Crémieux-Brilhac, *Les Français de l'an 40*, Vol. 2, p. 449.
38 Cochet, *Les soldats de la drôle de guerre*, p. 89.
39 Ibid., p. 450.
40 Ibid.
41 Eric Deroo and Pierre de Taillac, *Carnets de déroute 1939–1940: Lettres et récits inédits* (Paris, 2010), p. 28.
42 Georges Sadoul, *Journal de guerre: 2 septembre 1939–20 juillet 1940* (Paris, 1977), p. 87.
43 Deroo and de Taillac, *Carnets de déroute 1939–1940*, p. 28.
44 Crémieux-Brilhac, *Les Français de l'an 40*, Vol. 2, p. 453.
45 See chapter 2.
46 Crémieux-Brilhac, *Les Français de l'an 40*, Vol. 2, p. 453.
47 SHD AT: 27N178. Army group 2, 3rd bureau, instructions for the men and the officers, 16 February 1940.
48 SHD AT: 27N69. Report for the commander, 21 February 1940.
49 Crémieux-Brilhac, *Les Français de l'an 40*, Vol. 2, p. 453.
50 Ibid., p. 452.
51 Jean Molinier, 'L'évolution de la population agricole du XVIIIe siècle à nos jours', *Economie et statistique*, 91 (1977) 1, pp. 79–84.
52 André Gide and Jean Malaquais, *Correspondance: 1935–1950* (Paris, 2000), pp. 91–92.
53 Deroo and de Taillac, *Carnets de déroute 1939–1940*, p. 36.
54 Sadoul, *Journal de guerre*, p. 152.
55 Luise Stein, Grenzlandschicksale – Unternehmen evakuieren in Deutschland und Frankreich, 1939/1940 (PhD Thesis: Ruhr-Universität Bochum, 2017).
56 *JORF*, 5 March 1940, p. 436.
57 ECPAD. Journal de guerre, n. 10, week of 29 November 1939. http://www.ecpad.fr/journal-de-guerre-10-semaine-du-29-novembre-1939/ [accessed 12 November 2017].

58 *Journal officiel de la République française*, 5 March 1940, p. 436.
59 SHD AT: 27N69. A soldier of the 168th RIF, SF Thionville, 3rd Army, April 1940.
60 SHD AT: 27N69. A soldier of the 121st RAL, 9th CA, 4th Army, report to the commander, 12 April 1940.
61 SHD AT: 27N69. A soldier of the 63rd GRDI, 56th DI, 3rd Army, report, 12 April 1940.
62 Paul Thellier (1899–1944) was the Agriculture Minister from March to June 1940. He had already occupied this position from January to June 1936.
63 SHD AT: 27N69. Letters of soldiers from the 63rd GRDI, 56th DI, 3rd Army, report, 12 April 1940.
64 ECPAD. War diary n° 10, week of 29 November 1939; *Le Miroir*, 15 October 1939.
65 Ibid.
66 *Le Miroir*, 15 October 1939.
67 *L'Illustration*, 27 April 1940.
68 *JORF*, 23 October 1939, p. 12582.
69 They first appeared during the 19th century. Decree of 12 July 1886 and decree of 5 February 1887.
70 A Christian organisation founded by Georges Williams in 1844 and based in Geneva from 1894. See: François Cochet, *Première Guerre mondiale: dates, thèmes, noms* (Quétigny, 2001), pp. 76–78.
71 Ibid.
72 Timothy Dowling, *Personal Perspectives: World War I* (California, 2006), p. 236.
73 Ibid.
74 It should be highlighted that the British Expeditionary Force employed far more women.
75 *JORF*, 23 October 1939, p. 12582.
76 Tuffrau Paul, *De la 'drôle de guerre' à la libération de Paris (1939–1944): Lettres et Carnets (Paris, 2002)*, p. 36.
77 Ibid.
78 André Lasserre, 'En Suisse, aux frontières de la politique et du militaire: "armée et foyer" 1939–1945', *Revue d'histoire de la Deuxième Guerre mondiale et des conflits contemporains*, 130 (1983) 33, pp. 77–89.
79 Crémieux-Brilhac, *Les Français de l'an 40*, Vol. 2, pp. 454–455.
80 Tuffrau, *De la 'drôle de guerre' à la libération de Paris*, p. 36 ; Crémieux Brilhac, *Les Français de l'an 40*, Vol. 2, p. 454.
81 SHD AT: 27N69. CP. Non-commissioned officer to his friends, 402nd DCA, 5th Group, 3rd Army, report, 13 November 1939.
82 Sadoul, *Journal de guerre*, p. 149.
83 AN: F/41/979. Grand Quartier Général, information for the press, 20 October 1939.
84 SHD AT: 27N69. cP. A soldier of the 164th RIF, SF Thionville, 3rd Army, Note for the High Command, April 1940.
85 Ibid.
86 SHD AT: 27N65. Gamelin to the Army commanders, 25 September 1939.
87 SHD AT: 27N65. GQG, EM General, 2nd Bureau, army report, 31 October 1939.
88 SHD AT: 27N65. GQG, EM General, 2nd Bureau, army report, 31 October 1939.
89 Stéphane Audoin-Rouzeau, 'Les soldats français et la Nation de 1914 à 1918 d'après les journaux de tranchées', *Revue d'Histoire Moderne & Contemporaine*, 34 (1987), pp. 66–86.
90 SHD: 29N130. 3rd Army, EM, 2nd bureau, 30 October 1939.
91 Olivier Blazy, 'La presse militaire française à destination des troupes indigènes issues des différents territoires de l'Empire puis de l'Union française', *Revue historique des armées*, 271 (2013), pp. 51–59.

92   *AKANI, Micro journal à tendance bi-mensuelle édité par les médecins, pharmaciens, dentistes et vétérinaires du 6ᵉ RTS* and *Madagascar aux armées.*

93   The following titles have been discovered in the archives for the front of Lorraine: *Terre à cheval, Et avec ça ?; L'Hirondelle ; La cage à douille ; La nation ; Le poilu du 6-9 ; Le poilu lorrain ; Le réveil de Beauséjour ; Lorraine Gironde ; Secteur postal ; Cambronne ; Coup de Bambi ; CQ; Hausse 400 ; Je passe partout ; l'Isard de Metz ; La rose Maginot ; La voix de la voir de 60 ; Le cheval Vapeur ; Le chic à nied ; Le cri du béton, Le pied lourd ; Rouge vert.* There is little doubt that there were many more titles.

94   SHD: AT 27N69. CP, 155th RAP, 5th Army, report for the commander, 16 November 1939.

95   SHD: AT 29N130. Commander-in-chief, report on the publication of frontline newspapers, 31 March 1940.

96   Ibid.

97   SHD AT: 29N130. The Commander-in-Chief, rules to follow for the censorship of army newspapers, 24 March 1940.

98   SHD AT: 29N130. 3rd Army, EM, 2nd Bureau, report, 30 December 1939.

99   Ibid.

100   SHD AT: 29N269. 5th Army, EM, 2nd Bureau, report, 3 February 1940.

101   This almanac is unfortunately not preserved in the archives.

102   SHD AT: 29N130. 3rd Army, EM, 2nd Bureau, report, 18 April 1940.

103   *L'Isard de Metz*, 15 December 1939.

104   Ibid.

105   Ibid.

106   *Je passe partout*, 1 December 1939.

107   *L'Hirondelle*, 15 March 1940 ; *Et avec ça ?*, 15 May 1940, *Je passe partout*, 15 December 1939.

108   *Le poilu du 6-9*, April 1940.

109   SHD AT: 27N69. Report for the commander, 29 January 1940.

110   Cécile Méadel, 'Programme en masse, programmes de masse ? La diffusion de la radio en France pendant les années trente', in: Régine Robin (ed.), *Masses et culture de masse dans les années trente* (Paris, 1991), pp. 51–68, p. 56.

111   Ibid., p. 53.

112   Crémieux-Brilhac, *Les Français de l'an 40*, Vol. 2, p. 455.

113   François Anselmini, 'Alfred Cortot et la mobilisation des musiciens français pendant la Première Guerre mondiale', *Vingtième Siècle. Revue d'histoire*, 118 (2013), pp. 147–157.

114   SHD AT: 30N59. GQG, 2nd bureau, report to the army, 29 December 1939.

115   Paris Soir, Émissions du centre d'informations, 5 December 1939.

116   SHD AT: 28N52. GA n°3, EM, 2nd bureau, report about the press officers' meeting, 30 March 1940.

117   Hélène Eck, *La guerre des ondes : histoire des radios de langue française pendant la Deuxième Guerre mondiale* (Paris, 1985), p. 21.

118   See Chapter 4.

119   Anonymous, *Dictionnaire d'anecdotes suisses* (1823), pp. 186–187.

120   Hervé Jovelin, 'Poilu's Park (1914–1919) Un parc d'attractions pour soldats sur le front', *Guerres mondiales et conflits contemporains*, 183 (1996), p. 111–123.

121   Ibid., p. 115.

122   Anselmini, 'Alfred Cortot et la mobilisation des musiciens', p. 151.

123   SHD AT: 29N130. 3rd Army, General Condé, report, 20 November 1939.

124   SHD AT: 29N130. Army General Condé, 3rd Army, report, 28 March 1940.

125   SHD AT: 28N52. Army Group 3, EM, report to the GQG 2nd Bureau, 30 March 1940.

126 SHD AT: 29N130. Army General Condé, 3rd Army, report, 28 March 1940.

127 Hervé Boterf, *Le Théâtre en uniforme: le spectacle aux armées, de la drôle de guerre aux accords d'Évian* (Paris, 1973), p. 46.

128 ECPAD, 3rd Army, Journal de guerre, n. 7, week of 11 November 1939, http://www.ecpad.fr/journal-de-guerre-7-semaine-du-11-novembre-1939/ [accessed 5 January 2018] ; *Le Miroir*, 26 November 1939.

129 See the annex.

130 Jean-Paul Sartre, *Carnets de la Drôle de Guerre: Septembre 1939–Mars 1940*, ed. by Arlette Elkaïm-Sartre (Paris, 1995), p. 533.

131 Ibid.

132 SHD AT: 27N69. CP, Maréchal des logis, Parc de réparation d'artillerie d'armée, 505th RI, 5th Army, Note for the High Command, 21.12.1939. Georgius was a very famous artist. In 1945, he was banned for a year by the *Comité National d'Epuration du Spectacle* for collaboration. Arrêté du Ministre de l'Education Nationale, 11 January 1945. Nadia Dauty was also a famous singer of the 1930s.

133 SHD AT: 28N52. Army Group n°3, EM, 2nd bureau, meeting with press officers, 30 March 1940.

134 Pierre-Frédéric Charpentier, *La drôle de guerre des intellectuels français* (Paris, 2008), p. 66.

135 SHD AT: 29N130. General Condé, 3rd Army, entertainment, 8 March 1940.

136 Ibid.

137 Deroo and Taillac, *Carnets de déroute 1939–1940*, pp. 97–98.

138 SHD AT: 27N69. CP, a lieutenant to his wife, 21st RI 13rd DI, 8th Army, report, 9 December 1939.

139 SHD AT: 29N130. Army General Condé, 3rd Army, 8 March 1940.

140 Ibid.

141 SHD AT:27N69. CP, report, 28 December 1939.

142 SHD AT: 27N69. CP, report, 21 February 1940.

143 SHD AT: 28N52. Army Group n°3, EM, 2nd bureau, 30 March 1940.

144 SHD AT: 27N69. CP, a soldier of the 156th RI, 43rd DI, 4th Army, report, April 1940.

145 This was enough for an audience of 100 people. *Catalogue Tiranty*, 1934, pp. 336–337. http://www.cinematheque.fr/fr/catalogues/appareils/collection/projecteur-de-film-17-5-mm-sonorecnc-ap-96-130.html [accessed 15 January 2018].

146 Jean-Pierre Duhard, *Écrits de guerre et de captivité* (Paris, 2015), pp. 25–26.

147 Charpentier, *La drôle de guerre des intellectuels français*, p. 64 ; SHD AT: 27N69. CP, canonnier 103rd RAL, EOCA 6, 3rd Army, report, 25 March 1940.

148 SHD AT: 29N130. Army General Condé, 3rd Army, 8 March 1940.

149 Violaine Challéat, 'Le Cinéma Au Service de La Défense, 1915–2008', *Revue Historique des Armées*, 252 (2008), pp. 3–15. ECPAD. http://www.ecpad.fr/tag/journal-de-guerre/ [accessed 6 January 2018].

150 SHD AT: 28N52. Army Group 3, EM, 2nd Bureau, 30 March 1940.

151 Duhard, *Écrits de guerre et de captivité*, p. 32.

152 Charpentier, *La drôle de guerre des intellectuels français*, p. 64.

153 SHD AT: 27N69. CP, canonnier 103rd RAL, EOCA 6, 3rd Army, report, 25 March 1940.

154 SHD AT: 27N69. CP, a soldier of the 256th company A.O., EOCA 21, 3rd Army, report, 11 March 1940.

155 SHD AT: 29N290. General Gamelin, CEC, to the generals commanding Army Groups, 27 November 1939.

156 See chapter 2.

157 SHD AT: 27N69. CP, a soldier of the 31st DI, 8th Army, report, 16 November 1939.

158 SHD AT: 27N69. CP, a non-commissioned officer, PGRF 3rd Army, report, 21 February 1940.
159 SHD AT: 27N69. CP, a lieutenant to a non-commissioned officer, report, 13 November 1939; AD Moselle: 5R628. *Le Chic à Nied*, Le sport, Pâques 1940, 25 March 1940 ; SHD AT: 27N69. A soldier of the GR, tanks 501 – 31st Btn E.A., 5th Army, report, 9 February 1940; Duhard, *Écrits de guerre et de captivité*, p. 34; AD Meurthe-et-Moselle. *Le réveil de Beauséjour*, Concours de pêche aux Martigues, 1 February 1940.
160 SHD AT: 28N52. Army Group 3, EM, 2nd Bureau, 30 March 1940.
161 Jacques Marseille and Daniel Lefeuvre, *1940 au jour le jour* (Paris, 1989), p. 40.
162 *La rose Maginot*, 13 April 1940.
163 SHD AT: 27N69. Report, 12 April 1940.
164 SHD AT: 28N52. Army Group 3, EM, 2nd Bureau, 30 March 1940.
165 Deroo and de Taillac, *Carnets de déroute 1939–1940*, p. 29.
166 SHD AT: 27N69. CP, GRDI, 56th DI, 3rd Army, report, 15 April 1940.
167 SHD AT: 27N69. CP, a soldier of the 48th RAD, 56th DI, report, 12 April 1940.
168 SHD AT: 27N69. CP, report, April 1940.
169 SHD AT: 29N269. Ministry of Defence, report, 16 November 1939.
170 Ibid.
171 Ibid.
172 SHD AT: 29N198. 4th Army, EM, 2nd Bureau, report, 8 April 1940.
173 SHD AT: 27N69. GQG, EM, report by General Bineau about morale, 25 September 1939.
174 Ibid.
175 SHD AT: 27N69. EM of Argenlieu to the 2nd Bureau, 30 September 1939.
176 Ibid.
177 SHD AT: 27N69. GQG, EMG, 2nd Bureau, report on morale, 25 November 1939.
178 Ibid.
179 SHD AT:27N69. GQG, EMG, 2nd Bureau, report, 30 November 1939.
180 Sadoul, *Journal de guerre*, p. 90.
181 SH AT: 27N69. GQG, EMG, 2nd Bureau, report, 30 November 1939.
182 Ibid.
183 SHD AT: 27N69. GQG, EM, 2nd Bureau, 3 December 1939.
184 SHD AT: 27N69. Report, 9 November 1939.
185 Sadoul, *Journal de guerre*, pp. 90–91.
186 Chapentier, *La Drôle de guerre des intellectuels*, pp. 66–67.
187 Jean Zay, *Lettres de la Drôle de Guerre* (Paris, 2015), p. 109.
188 SHD AT: 27N69. CP, a soldier of the Gr. Btn tanks 501, 31 Btn E.A., 5th Army, report, 9 February 1940.
189 SHD AT: 29N130. The Commander-in-chief to the 3rd Army, 28 March 1940.
190 Letter of Paul Nizan to Henriette Nizan, 9 January 1940. In Paul Nizan and Jean-Jacques Brochier, *Paul Nizan, Intellectuel Communiste, 1926–1940. Articles et Correspondance Inédite* (Paris, 1967), p. 269.
191 Xavier Boniface, 'Les aumoniers militaires', in: Robert Vandenbussche (ed.), *De Georges Clemenceau à Jacques Chirac: L'état et la pratique de la loi de Séparation* (Lille, 2012), pp. 131-47.
192 Xavier Boniface, 'Au service de la nation et de l'armée: Les aumôniers militaires français de 1914 à 1962', *Guerres Mondiales et Conflits Contemporains*, 187 (1997), pp. 103–113.
193 Philippe-Efraïm Landau, 'La communauté juive de France et la Grande Guerre, Summary', *Annales de démographie historique*, 103 (2002), pp. 91–106.
194 Boniface, 'Au service de la nation et de l'armée', p. 106.
195 Ibid.

196 Archives épiscopales de Strasbourg (AES): Guerre 1939–40. 22nd RIF, 1st CEO, Hochwald, 18 September 1939.
197 AES: Guerre 1939–40. Priest 15, GRDI, EM, 31 October 1939.
198 SHD AT: 27N69. CP, 2nd mountain artillery regiment, 28th DI, 5th Army, report, 9 December 1939.
199 SHD AT: 27N69. CP, a sous-Lieutenant to his friend, 143rd RI, 32nd DI, 3rd Army, report, 24 November 1939.
200 SHD AT: 27N69. CP, report, 12 April 1940 and SHD AT: 27N69. GQG, 2nd Bureau, report, 2 January 1940.
201 Maude Williams, 'La communauté catholique d'Alsace-Lorraine face aux évacuations (septembre 1939–juin 1940)', *Annales de l'Est*, 2 (2014), pp. 203–224.
202 SHD AT: 27N69. CP, 23rd Régiment Tirailleurs Algériens, 4th DINA, 4th Army, report, 3 December 1939.
203 'Allah wanted us to be there'. SHD AT: 27N69. CP, a soldier from 1st DI Morocco, 3rd Army, report, 16 December 1939.
204 SHD AT: 27N69. CP, a north-African soldier, 51st RANA, 4th Army, report, 15 April 1940.
205 'The French and the Arabs will win because Allah is with the French and the Arabs.' SHD AT: 27N69. CP, 47th and 51st Bons, 4th Army, report, 15 April 1940.
206 Simone de Beauvoir, *La force de l'âge* (Paris, 1960), p. 477.
207 Ibid.
208 SHD AT: 27N69. CP, 209th RAD, report, 4 November 1939.
209 SHD AT: 27N69. CP, 5th Army, report, 16 February 1940.
210 SHD AT: 27N69. CP, a lieutenant R.P. SF of Rohrbach, 5th Army, report, 2 March 1940.
211 Deroo and de Taillac, *Carnets de déroute 1939–1940*, p. 44.
212 Jean-Yves Le Naour, 'Épouses, marraines et prostituées. Le repos du guerrier, entre service social et condamnation morale', in: Evelyne Morin-Rotureau (ed.), *Combats de femmes, 1914–1918. Les Françaises, pilier de l'effort de guerre* (Paris, 2014), pp. 63–79.
213 SHD AT: 27N65. Major-General Doumenc to the CEC, 26 February 1940.
214 SHD AT: 27N65. GQG, EMG, 2nd Bureau, report about prostitution, 24 April 1940.
215 Ibid.
216 Ibid.
217 Ibid.; ADBR: 98AL635. Sous-préfecture of Mulhouse, Cabinet, report about the morale, 25 January 1940.
218 ADBR: 98AL635. Sous-préfecture of Mulhouse, Cabinet, report about morale, 25 January 1940.
219 SHD AT: 27N65. CEC, report about brothers for indigenous soldiers, 3 April 1940.
220 Ibid.
221 Ibid.
222 Ibid.
223 SHD AT: 27N65. CEC, 2nd Bureau to the General commanding the 7th region, 10 April 1940.

4   Dealing with German and communist propaganda

The Phoney War was a war of nerves, a psychological conflict in which pictures and speeches complemented traditional forms of combat. At the front, leaflets and slogans were more common than violence. Waiting for an offensive, French soldiers could not help but question their place in such a strange environment. Enemy propagandists sought to exploit these doubts. Both sides, reflecting once again on the experience of the First World War, had prepared for a campaign of demoralization since the 1930s.[1] The French and the Germans not only had large propaganda units, made up of experts and communication specialists, but also financial and political support. At the front, enemy psychological warfare was not the only problem; communism was also a worry for the military and for civilian society. This chapter will evaluate how important these threats really were and how the French government and the army campaigned against them.

Communist propaganda and the army

The signing of the Molotov-Ribbentrop Pact of 23 August 1939, named after Foreign Ministers Joachim von Ribbentrop and Viatcheslav Mikhaïlovitch Molotov, caused great turmoil among French communists. This pact provided a guarantee of non-belligerence but also included a secret protocol dividing territories of Eastern Europe into spheres of influence.[2] In France, leaders and members of the French Communist Party (Parti communiste français – PCF) were taken by surprise. At first, the PCF announced a 'defensive' line, following a parliamentary meeting, and on 25 August released a press communiqué written by First Secretary of the Communist Party Maurice Thorez:[3]

> If Hitler declares war on us, he must know that he will face the people of France, the communists at the forefront, to defend the safety of the country, our freedom and the people's independence.[4]

In their newspaper *L'Humanité*, the PCF also published a declaration. The pact was presented as a USSR initiative to preserve peace.[5] This did not prevent the newspaper, founded by Jean Jaurès thirty-six years before, from being banned the very same day by the government. On 24 August 1939, Interior Minister

Albert Sarraut, Council President Édouard Daladier, Keeper of the Seals Paul Marchandeau and President Albert Lebrun, signed a decree-law which 'allowed the confiscation and suspension of publications damaging the defence of the nation'.[6] On 25 August 1939, the Parisian team printing *L'Humanité* was arrested. Moreover, during the following days communists distributing leaflets supporting the Molotov-Ribbentrop Pact were put in custody.[7]

A month later, the PCF was dissolved. The Soviet invasion of Poland on 17 September 1939 forced the French communists to adapt. The Comintern (Communist International) had stated at the beginning of September that the distinction between 'fascist countries' and 'democratic countries' was obsolete and that the fight against capitalist and imperialist countries was the only important cause, alongside peace.[8] Leaders of the PCF were made aware of this directive in the middle of the month but failed to enforce it entirely, refusing to denounce the 'imperialist war' in their speeches and leaflets.[9] On 26 September, the French government banned the PCF and 'any activity connected directly or indirectly to the Third International' in order to support the Polish government.[10]

The PCF was removed from the official political scene but still played a part in French society. In a matter of days, a clandestine press movement developed and was ready to publish monthly illegal copies of *L'Humanité*. A first underground edition was released on 26 October 1939.[11] The first page, quoting Anatole France, showed the newspaper's total devotion to the USSR: 'they tell us that we die for the country, but we die for bankers, for the capitalists'.[12] Through the newspaper, the PCF enounced its principles: no to the capitalist war, peace now, but also obedience to military duty.[13] It should be underlined that French communist propaganda did not promote desertion, mutiny or fraternisation with enemy soldiers.[14] On the other hand, leaflets were firmer in the event of a war against the USSR:

> Soldiers, if you are asked to fight Soviet workers, refuse to fight the Red Army. [...] Remember the example of André Marty and the sailors of the Black Sea.[15]

This article was a reference to the Odessa mutiny of 1919, when French sailors refused to fight the Russian Revolution.[16] During the Phoney War, communist propaganda remained openly opposed to the conflict, presented as a war between capitalist nations. In October 1939, Thorez said to the *Daily Worker* that 'having men killed for capitalists' bank accounts! No!'[17] This line of conduct was relayed by the clandestine press. In November 1939, the first special issue of *L'Humanité* wrote: 'The French people should not pay for the capitalists of Paris, London and Berlin.'[18] The message was conflictual as the war was rejected but defection was discouraged.

French communists had trouble identifying an enemy and did not know how to reconcile their convictions and the Molotov-Ribbentrop Pact. In October-November 1939, the British, the Germans and the French were all seen as 'warmongers'.[19] From December 1939, two enemies were denounced: the British and the

Daladier government (replaced by Reynaud in April 1940). The British, according to the communists, represented the archetype of imperialism, an argument already used by German propaganda in the occupied territories of France during the First World War.[20] The French government was blamed for following the British and transforming France into an 'English dominion'.[21]

The communists tried to make contact with soldiers. A few copies of *L'Humanité* were found on the frontline while a small group of militants gravitating around Victor Michaud and Danielle Casanova[22] was asked by Benoît Frachon[23] to take care of communist actions in the army.[24] In January 1940, a clandestine newspaper published on a monthly basis and named *Le Trait d'Union des soldats, ouvriers et paysans* was created. Other newspapers, such as the *Lettre aux soldats*, and leaflets were also distributed on the frontline. Most discussed peace and denounced living conditions in the army. Military authorities saw this campaign as a significant threat:

> We need to fight vigorously against this campaign of defeatism led by the ex-communist party. This action of propaganda intensified during the last weeks; on the territory of the 2nd Army, 12 leaflets were found during the month of March, as much as during the period of 1 September–1 March. The confiscated leaflets came almost entirely from Paris. This is where the leaders can be found. We need to make it impossible for them to carry on.[25]

This note, written by General Huntziger, betrayed the EM's anxiety more than a serious danger. Indeed, French communists serving in the army were isolated and disorganised.[26] Leaflets and illegal newspapers were brought by soldiers on an irregular basis, mostly when coming back from visiting their family.[27]

Communist propaganda was uncommon on the frontline in winter but became more frequent during spring 1940. In the 5th Army, leaflets were discovered in the *Foyer du Soldat* of Sarrebourg (Moselle) at the end of February:

> At the end of the afternoon on 24 February 1940, Lieutenant Agosse of the 2nd Company of the 204th RRP, based in Sarrebourg, found small leaflets (7x3 cm) in the *Foyer Militaire* (showroom). These communist-defeatist leaflets had been inserted illegally in a stack of newspapers and magazines on the table. Fifteen other papers were found, glued on the toilets' walls and on the ground floor of the same building. Another six were removed from the toilets the next day, 25 February.[28]

These leaflets were handmade, making the production or diffusion on a large scale impossible.[29] Sending leaflets in the mail or simply writing about communism in correspondence was equally rare. The CP highlighted a few incidents, such as this one:

> Tonight, I received a big envelope. [...] There was a letter from A. Marty to L. Blum. Communist propaganda. Blum was violently attacked as an ally of

Daladier and Chamberlain, a traitor to the working class, etc. etc. It was given to the officer.[30]

In fact, soldiers were far more inclined to talk about patriotism in factories or at the front than to dream of a proletarian revolution:

I do not understand why Paulette fears a French revolution. It seems impossible in my sector, where most men are workers who used to belong to red parties. Despite all our military troubles, dangers, tiredness and family situations, despite everything, their morale is formidable and they believe in the sacred union (many similar letters).[31]

Many soldiers claimed that it was impossible to find even a single communist or a former communist on the frontline.[32] The month of February 1940 was a notable exception as the presence of 'revolutionary propaganda' was mentioned more frequently.[33] A few arrests were also reported.[34] However, communist propaganda was so rare that it never became a distinct category in CP reports. As we have seen in previous chapters, protests were not about politics but living conditions. Seditious songs were heard only four times in the *Théâtres des Opérations Armées du Nord et Nord-Est*.[35] The same can be said of the propaganda material found in the Parisian region or in factories. It rarely reached the Franco-German front.[36] At the beginning of 1940, the Interior Minister estimated that there were around 5,000 active members of the CFP. The 5th Bureau of the EMA considered that there was no notable communist implementation in the army.[37]

The fact that communist propaganda was not commonplace in the army did not mean that the EM was not taking it seriously. The communists and the Germans used similar arguments when trying to discourage French soldiers: the lack of fighting spirit, strong criticism of the government and Britain and the need for an immediate peace. As a result, the EM made it a point to fight communist propaganda in the army zone. During the Riom trial, General Gamelin judged that 'thanks to the commandment's vigilance, all propaganda attempts were stopped in time'.[38]

Tracking revolutionary, communist and defeatist propaganda

The EM, firmly convinced that the communist threat was real, launched a campaign of counter-propaganda in October 1939.[39] The French army kept records, the 'special PR list' (*propagande révolutionnaire*), which provided information 'by decision of the Minister of War, [on] soldiers who were guilty of spreading revolutionary propaganda against the nation, the army or republican institutions'.[40] These lists were managed by the 3rd *Bureau PR* of the Ministry of War.[41] The only person with the power to remove a name from the list was the Minister.[42] The 5th Bureau of the EMG, tasked with centralizing relevant information and managing counter-espionage, led the fight against PR. This action was coordinated with the *Bureau Central de Renseignements* (BCR) in each military region and the 2nd Bureau, made of two commissaries and six inspectors from the *Direction générale de la Sûreté*.[43] Until September 1939, Commander Jacquot led the 3rd Bureau of the War Minister cabinet before becoming the PR officer for the *Quartier Général* in March 1940.

Special PR lists were forwarded to the 2nd Bureau of each army. Corps commanders, helped by an officer holding at least the rank of captain, were given the names of those who were on the list.[44] They were allowed to add names or suggest the removal of someone from the list.[45] In order to add a soldier, the officer had to 'explain the circumstances justifying this measure, the identity of those involved, the steps taken and those proposed. If leaflets have been distributed, a copy must be annexed to the report.'[46] As stated in a secret note sent on 25 October 1937, this report was forwarded directly to the cabinet of the War Minister.[47]

Soldiers registered on the special PR list were watched and excluded from various formations or privileges.[48] Moreover, revolutionary men were spread between regiments to avoid a concentration in a single unit. Other soldiers, not on the list, were sometimes watched by special request of the Army General.[49] In December 1939, *compagnies spéciales de passage* were created to isolate dangerous individuals, mostly criminals but also men deemed politically dangerous.[50]

Despite these measures, checks on those registered on PR lists were not particularly strict.[51] General Henri Marie Auguste Bineau, Major-General of the Armies, declared in a note released on 12 December 1939 that 'revolutionary protests and talks must be punished *immediately*. If needed, a judiciary instruction must be opened.'[52] On the other hand, he also advised caution. False accusations had the potential to trigger a state of psychosis in the army, which would only benefit the enemies of France.[53] This was expressed clearly by Daladier in the 9 March 1940 report. It was stated that 'many denunciations were made by German-Soviet propaganda in order to cast doubt on those who had renounced communism or had never believed in its doctrines in the first place'.[54] Caution was advised when adding names on PR lists but also when dealing with denunciations.

The process of checking on potential revolutionary soldiers was not made easier by subaltern officers, who had direct contacts and plenty of opportunities to debate with suspected communists. They did not find it useful to denounce soldiers who might disagree politically but followed others nonetheless.[55]

The number of suspected soldiers registered on the PR list remained low. Between 1 September 1939 and 9 April 1940, Daladier counted 527 names: '319 communist militants, 125 Trotskyists, revolutionary socialists or libertarians, considered by the PR section as more dangerous, and 65 defeatists or propagandists'.[56] Despite the lack of evidence for a significant communist presence in the army, the fear of propaganda and sabotage was real in the *Étapes*, the regions just behind the frontline.

On 27 October, the case of communist propaganda was investigated by the 4th Army. A 10-page report on the activities of the communist party, the 'most important revolutionary party', was written by officers of the SR.[57] This report explained the perceived strengths and weaknesses of communist networks while arguing that from an ideological perspective, the PCF had lost ground among workers following the German-Soviet Pact and the invasion of Poland. Moreover, the loss of its newspaper, *L'Humanité*, as well as its leaders were important blows. The report warned the Government that 'the communist party will work hard to regain a communication line with workers and will adapt its propaganda to fit the war narrative'.[58] The SR guessed, based on 'past tactics', that the communists were about to launch a significant propaganda campaign. The unit offered different strategies to respond to this. In fact, some of the solutions included in the report were already used by the army. The SR advised the authorities to check on suspected individuals, report them to their officers and transfer them to other units. Finally, it recommended using reliable anti-communist agents to check on communists.

This situation developed in February 1940. A telegram sent by the Interior Minister to the General-in-Chief stated that:

> Communists are considering actions of sabotage or destruction, which could take place soon or whenever the enemy decides to attack. You are advised to do everything in your power to protect our vulnerable points.[59]

The next day, another report explained that 'we must take actions to prevent criminal attacks, planned for the following days by communists'.[60] Particular attention was given to fuel depots, factories working for the war effort, electric power plants and other places playing a vital part in the war economy.[61] This report, relayed in the 20th military region and in the *Étape* of Saint Dié (4th Army), was applied immediately.[62] Individuals considered as 'active and dangerous communists' were placed under surveillance. Inspectors and commissaires in charge of checking on suspects tried to identify leaders and prevent sabotage attempts. In order to do so, they identified notorious pre-war members of the PCF, such as cell leaders, local presidents of the *Jeunes Filles communistes de France*, etc. Investigations often rested on intermediaries, indirect sources and speculation. Reports were systematically vague. For example, the surveillance statement regarding a man called Roquis guessed that 'he could be the real leader of the communists of Saint Dié', while the investigation concerning another individual named Schmitdt said 'there could be a hiding place at his residence'. Another report, on M. Win, highlighted that 'he is a communist cell leader, he might have owned, before the war, a map of the postal office and he might know how to go there by the sewer (information confirmed by three different sources)'.[63] The same report advised the SR to 'gather information on these people and monitor their activities'.[64] In Saint Dié, searches were carried out but produced no significant result.[65]

Pubs, used by communists to meet before the war, were also investigated as potential propaganda centres.[66] In Saint-Michel (Meurthe-et-Moselle), the authorities kept a specific drinking establishment under surveillance but were unable to find a single incriminating element.[67]

The shadow of German propaganda

The EM saw German propaganda as an even bigger danger than communism. Enemy psychological warfare was indeed active on the frontline and took many shapes (radio, leaflets, posters and slogans). The Germans used *Propaganda-kompanien* (PK) on the French-German border. These military units had two tasks: home front propaganda (filming for movies or *Wochenschauen*, photography) and enemy psychological warfare.[68] PK were created between 1936 and 1938.[69] The OKW (*Oberkommando der Wehrmacht*), partly blaming the 1918 defeat on propaganda, worked with Joseph Goebbels and his ministry (*Reichsministerium für Volksaufklärung und Propaganda* – RMVP). They signed an agreement at the end of 1938 to coordinate propaganda efforts in times of war.[70] In April 1939, the *Oberkommando Wehrmacht/Wehrmacht-Propaganda* (OKW/WPr) and the PK became official German army units.[71] These *Propagandakompagnie* were responsible for psychological warfare on the French-German front.

Proximity and the lack of fighting allowed complex propaganda and counter-propaganda actions. French units positioned next to the Rhine saw German soldiers on the other side on a daily basis. As soon as October 1939, this situation was used by the Germans, who installed loudspeakers:[72]

> Nobody shoots, it is forbidden to fire on both sides. Yesterday, at one in the afternoon, the Germans used loudspeakers to play a concert. They played records and, between songs, propaganda in French to make us distrust the English: 'Who would like to transform France into a battlefield? Us? We want to stay at home. You? You want peace. So? When France was on her own, she was loved and respected. Now that she is following English politics, she is exposing herself to grave danger.' While music was playing, German officers were waving their hands or handkerchiefs at us.[73]

This type of propaganda, developed at the end of October 1939, was played by PK 612, 666 and 670 along the frontline.[74]

During this period, peace was a prominent topic. On 6 October, Hitler gave a speech at the Reichstag in which he asked for cessation of hostilities between France and Germany. Extracts of this speech were later borrowed by PK to be played on the frontline:[76]

> Hitler says in his peace speech that: the only thing I wanted for a Franco-German entente was the return of the Saarland. France having resolved this issue loyally, any other German demand was therefore cancelled. There is and will be no other claim of the sort.[77]

In various sectors of the front, loudspeakers were heard on a daily basis. PK followed directives elaborated by the RMVP, the *Auswärtiges Amt* and the OKW/WPr. The strategy was double: a peace campaign until the end of

Figure 4.1 PK loudspeakers[75]

Figure 4.2 PK banner on the Alsatian front[81]

1939,[78] and the exploitation of anti-British feelings. Both themes were explained on gigantic banners, visible from the other side of the Rhine. On these banners, the Germans wrote slogans such as 'why are you fighting?',[79] 'France for the French',[80] or other messages insisting on Hitler's pacific intentions.

PK used several tricks to capture the attention of French soldiers. Music was used to attract the French out of their bunkers. Between songs, PK played pacifist and anti-British slogans while trying to talk with French soldiers to understand how they felt about Germany or the war in general. In PK reports, officers summarised these conversations. The following transcript was written in October 1939:

US [GERMANS] (IN FRENCH): Hi! French soldiers, we want peace.
ANSWER IN FRENCH: Us, French, want peace as well.
US: Tell your President that we want peace.
ANSWER: We will tell him. Tell Hitler that French soldiers want peace. Our commander is strict, we must stay here.[82]

These conversations were common during the Phoney War. Both sides waved or called the other regularly.[83] Shots were uncommon; the French were most likely to answer the Germans or even applaud.[84] PK described these type of reactions as the proof that German propaganda worked, an interpretation that must be taken with caution. Most French soldiers found interactions with enemy propaganda entertaining. When asked about German psychological warfare, French soldiers often stated the following:

> The other night, the Germans placed a banner about 100 metres from us. We could read: 'Us, Germans, do not want to fight this war'. This made us smile.[85]

> The Boches are 200m from us, but everything is quiet. We have been here for 18 days but not a shot has been fired. The Huns wrote a sign 'France for the French' and we wrote 'Poland for the Poles'.[86]

> I will tell you a true story. The Germans put a sign above their line. We could read: 'Men of the north, you are going to fight while the English hit on your women.' The French read it and wrote the following: 'We do not care, we are from the south of France.' Morale is good.[87]

The French found German slogans more amusing than depressing. They mocked them on the frontline, in their letters or in frontline newspapers.

Fraternisation was used by German intelligence to gather information. Cases of French and German soldiers exchanging drinks, cigarettes and news, were reported close to the Rhine or in the no man's land between Moselle and Sarre. Testimonies on both sides are preserved in the archives:

> Every four days, we are on guard duty. The outpost is 90 metres from the Huns and one day they came to see us. They gave us cigarettes and we gave them bread because they have little to eat. We do not trust them too much because they are odd chaps. I think that this must have happened in 1914–1918 as well.[88]

A German soldier confirmed:

> Two French came close to us after a few calls and gestures. Having crossed the barbed wire on their side, they walked on floating wood until they reached the bridge, where we met these two Frenchmen who spoke little German. They were very scared that we might fire at them but became more confident after having been reassured several times. They received two packs of cigarettes. [...] They told us that German-speaking Alsatians were behind the tower. One of them left to fetch a bottle of cognac and his friends. 7–8 men came back. They were old, most were from Alsace. We shook hands and the oldest told us that they were there for another 14 days before being relieved.[89]

The French were cautious toward the Germans, but meetings happened in a relatively friendly atmosphere. It should be remembered that fraternising with the enemy was strictly forbidden on the French side while it was used by the Germans to gather facts. The French realised this but went ahead nonetheless.[90] Whatever new information was communicated was used quickly to feed German propaganda.

Leaflets, already used during the First World War, were dropped above the French lines.[91] They appeared for the first time at the beginning of October. Between October 1939 and May 1940, more than 30 million leaflets were distributed by the Germans.[92] They were designed by the *Auswärtiges Amt* and the RMVP and dropped by Luftwaffe bombers and PK units. The PK imagined various methods to send them. The *Deutsche Propaganda-Atelier* of Berlin had invented new technologies to fire hollow shells, the *Rot-Weiss-Geschoss*,[93] but improved tools, such as bottles or balloons, were equally employed.[94]

Figure 4.3 PK man sending propaganda leaflets[95]

Figure 4.4 PK dropping a bottle with leaflets[96]

Figure 4.5 PK sending propaganda balloons[97]

Balloons were not favoured by the Ministry of Propaganda as the wind on the Western front blew East, bringing back propaganda on German territory.[98] As with other forms of psychological warfare, leaflets were designed around the peace campaign and strong anti-British feelings. Anglophobic material used historical arguments, mostly past Franco-British wars. In the leaflet *Toujours la même chose* (always the same thing),[99] the Burghers of Calais, Joan of Arc, Napoleon and French soldiers on the Maginot Line were represented.[100] These leaflets also denounced British imperialism and capitalism. This was a major argument of German propaganda and was reproduced on many leaflets, such as the one named *En avant, pour le triomphe*, showing a British soldier in a chariot pulled by a French soldier and men from various British colonies.[101] The Germans also denounced the lack of British soldiers on the frontline. They systematically highlighted the fact that the French were fighting while the British were behind, flirting with French soldiers' wives. In May 1940, five versions of a leaflet called *Où le Tommy est-il resté?* were distributed on the frontline.[102] They showed French soldiers, caught in the barbed wire, and in the background British soldiers flirting with French women.

Anti-British propaganda was perceived as a clear attempt to demoralise French soldiers and a way to divide the Allies:

> I have just received a leaflet sent by a German plane. It is always the same. They try to divide us. If our Allies have sometimes been careless or selfish, many of their men died here between 1914 and 1918. I do not think that German propaganda will manage to separate us.[103]

> It is stupid but funny.[104]

> The sector is quiet. German planes throw leaflets. We do not care anymore.[105]

Various reactions were reported. Some found German leaflets pointless, mocked them or condemned them, a few collected them as 'war souvenirs'[106] but others saw them as 'partly true'.[107] It is true that the British Expeditionary Force (BEF) was not deployed on the Franco-German line. A few British units were sent to the Moselle front in November 1939, but stayed clear of the forward posts.[108] Many French people found this situation unacceptable but it needs to be highlighted that enemy leaflets did not create this feeling. Rather, German propaganda reinforced real frustrations, as the following letters demonstrated:

> Yesterday, the Germans dropped leaflets from a plane. There was a lot of bullshit but a few things were true.[109]

> What they do is obvious but there is an underlying truth. We have not seen a single English soldier. It is said that they can be found in the Metz barracks, while we sleep on straw.[110]

This 'underlying truth' was well-understood by the Germans. As the list of the leaflets for this period demonstrates, anti-British leaflets targeted units far from the BEF.[111]

The Germans also designed propaganda leaflets aimed at colonial troops. The main objective was to encourage desertion, as can be seen in this April 1940 leaflet:

Muslims, it is time to act. You can create your own justice. It is time to make France pay for a century of colonisation and tyranny. It is a once in a lifetime opportunity. [...] Germany does not want to harm you. Her enemy is your enemy and the holy companions of the prophet said that those defending another religion will be punished by God. Come to the Germans, who have never harmed the Muslims. Many of your brothers, who escaped the French inferno, are here, in better living conditions. Come and join them, you will not regret this. May those who can read this, read it to the others.[112]

This campaign of subversion carried on during the German offensive. In June 1940, another leaflet aimed at 'coloured soldiers' denounced the presence of African soldiers in France.[113]

The Germans did not neglect modern technologies such as radio in 1939–1940. This recent type of communication had become prominent during the interwar period and had a central place in German propaganda.[114] The *Auswärtiges Amt*, the RMVP and the Wehrmacht were all involved in the conception and diffusion of various radio shows. Different tricks were used to attract a French audience. 'Black radio' was passing as French while 'white radio' was openly German but spoken in French.

Among French soldiers, the most popular broadcast was without a doubt Radio Stuttgart. From 20 August 1939, Radio Stuttgart aired André Obrecht, nicknamed 'Saint Germain', a French 'third-rate' actor.[115] In 1940, the French still had no idea who this 'Stuttgart traitor' was but suspected Paul Ferdonnet, who was in fact the show's writer. Ferdonnet and Obrecht were sentenced to death in March 1940 and again in 1945. Obrecht managed to escape but Ferdonnet was executed.[116]

At the beginning of the war, Radio Stuttgart aired six shows on a daily basis, including two on shortwave frequencies at 20.45–20.55 and 22.45–23.00 for soldiers only.[117] This was later increased to 9 shows per day.[118] The Germans, unlike the French, broadcast songs and 'tendentious news' the whole day.[119] French soldiers at the front listened mainly to German radio.[120]

Radio Stuttgart gave news of the war, criticised the French government and attacked the British. As explained before, this last topic was the most effective among French troops. The arguments were the same as those found in other forms of communication (anti-capitalism, anti-imperialism, absence of British soldiers on the frontline, etc.):

> Tonight, we heard the German radio in French. They still say bad things about the English, but you know, we have never seen one here. They must be in Paris with soldiers' wives.[121]

Others refused to believe this campaign of Anglophobia but there is enough evidence to conclude that the French were uneasy about the British.

From October 1939, German propagandists recorded and aired testimonies of captured soldiers.[122] French soldiers were disturbed by French prisoners of war talking on German radio:

– This is corporal DELAUSANNE Julien, 3rd Spahis. I was born on 3 October 1913 in Djidjolli, Algeria. I was taken with a few comrades three days ago but was not wounded and I am well. Here, we are well. If my wife listens, I ask her to send things to stay clean such as soap, a razor, toothpaste and underwear. If my wife does not hear this message but others do, I would be grateful if they could tell her. I thank them in advance. I live in Rouanne, near the road of Brinon.
– Is that all, M. Delausanne?
– I kiss my wife and my parents.
– Have you got anything else to ask? Clothes or... more personal things? No?
– No. I am allowed to write. I will send a letter.
– Already, this is good.
– Thank you.[123]

These interviews always followed the same format. Soldiers said who they were, in which regiments they served, greeted their families and reassured them. Talking on an enemy radio was forbidden by military authorities on 4 December 1939.[124] Soldiers could be accused of 'complicity with enemy propaganda and could face a military court in absentia'.[125] The Commissariat Général à l'Information also took a stand against German propaganda, and outlined the 'humanity' with which German soldiers were treated in France:

> We also have prisoners, German prisoners, whom we treat humanely. They are free to write to their families when they wish: the idea of forcing them to speak on the radio has never crossed our mind [...] We do not have the heart to mock the misery of a people, especially when this misery is the result of a political folly that has replaced providing food for stomachs with providing ammunition for canons. [126]

German radio shows that made French prisoners talk were nevertheless listened to by many soldiers, some of whom listened every evening at 20.30.[127] These shows were listened to by many soldiers, who were predominantly curious:[128]

> I just listened to Radio Stuttgart. What a lot of nonsense; we listen to it because we are curious. It makes us laugh and revolts us at the same time.[129]

> German broadcasts dominate everything, of course. We do not listen to the news or military reports. They are disgusting. We listen to the French broadcast, but it is often scrambled. They name French prisoners and try to look noble because, according to them, they have no quarrel with France.[130]

French soldiers on the Maginot Line were more intrigued than demoralised by the voices of fellow Frenchmen in German hands. Most realised that this was a German attempt to hurt them:

I am not surprised that Clavorie talked to his family. This is another form of propaganda used to make us know that we are not badly treated by them. A way to visit them. They are ready to do anything. [...] They try to demoralise us but will fail.[131]

Soldiers want above all to have news of their captured friends. Some soldiers even tell families of those taken by the Germans to listen to Radio Stuttgart because it is possible that a soldier might speak.[132]

On various occasions, the Germans, lacking real prisoners, read the names of soldiers who had not been captured. French soldiers were far from naive:

There are few distractions here. If we did not have Radio Stuttgart, which is really quite funny, we would die of sadness. The day we learned that one of our non-commissioned officers had been captured, we laughed a lot. Stuttgart knew his surname and first name, the rank, the unit, the squadron, etc. Very easy to find this on a discarded envelope. They had all they needed to transform him into a prisoner.[133]

This was not a unique case.[134] The Germans often recycled discarded soldiers' letters to fabricate prisoners' lists.[135] From a German perspective, airing French testimonies 'caught the attention of the French listening to German radio'.[136] To make interviews more credible, prisoners were asked to give several personal details.[137] The German army was unsure about this operation's legality. In February 1940, the OKG sought legal advice before forbidding them to 'use prisoners of war on radio'.[138] This method was against international law, including the 1929 agreement on prisoners of war.[139] Two days later, army propaganda units responded, stating that it was forbidden to 'force' a prisoner to talk but not to 'bring them to talk'. The *Auswärtiges Amt* also pressurised the army to use these interviews, the 'most influential propaganda tool'.[140] Another efficient way to attract French soldiers was simply to play popular songs. This seems to have worked and many Frenchmen approved of Radio Stuttgart's musical tastes.[141]

Radio Stuttgart even welcomed divisions arriving at the front. This deeply impressed the French. For example, soldiers of the 8th Army were sent to the Rhine at the beginning of January 1940. Many letters explained the following fact:

Stuttgart welcomed the 54th Division (which we belong to) and said bye to the 9th (that we replaced). We had just arrived and Germany was telling this to everybody... Now, you know that I belong to the 54th Division, you can listen to the German radio to know where we are.[142]

We are reaching the Rhine. If you are arriving there, they know perfectly well that you are relieving another division. They ask us to be as quiet as the previous unit. This proves that they are perfectly well informed.[143]

This situation was not exceptional and happened many times during the Phoney War. French soldiers were convinced that the Germans knew everything about them. Many believed that there were many spies, even within the EM.[144] In fact, many facts were either collected by the Germans after having fraternised with the enemy or by capturing prisoners of war. Letters collected in the no man's land were also used to understand French positions.[145]

Despite listening to the radio, the French hated the 'traitor of Stuttgart' and criticised the broadcasts:

> I heard the speaker of Stuttgart yesterday evening. What a bastard! But do not worry about his bullshit, we will get them![146]

> I just read in a newspaper an article about Ferdonnet, the bastard of Stuttgart. I do not know what effect his speeches have on the rear, but what he does to the men is totally the reverse of what the Huns hope for. He is insulted, often called a 'c' [for *con*, a very popular insult in French].[147]

Aside from Radio Stuttgart, two other 'black radios' were used, *La Voix de la Paix* and *Radio Humanité*. Both were sometimes listened to by the men and were under the control of Büro Concordia, created by Joseph Goebbels on 12 December 1939.[148] Büro Concordia was directed by Dr. Adolf Raskin, the director of the Saarbrucken transmitter during the interwar period, a man who knew a lot about broadcasting in foreign countries. He developed the *Voix de la Paix*, also known as the *Réveil de la France*, on 16 December 1939.[149] Each French broadcast followed a specific political orientation and passed as illegal.

Operating between 16 December 1939 and 25 June 1940,[150] *Radio Humanité* was supposedly communist. Its name was an obvious reference to the newspaper banned in France on 27 August 1939. *Radio Humanité* aired five shows per day, using repetition to influence its audience. Each broadcast began with 'Ici parle Radio Humanité' and was mostly made of news.[151] The Marseillaise, the Internationale and sometimes the *Carmagnole* (a revolutionary song of 1792) were also played.[152] Written and recorded in Berlin, the show was played via various transmitters (Schopfheim, Bade, Cologne, Stuttgart, Leipzig, Warsaw and, in May 1940, Luxemburg).[153] This only made more credible the story that *Radio Humanité* was broadcast by French communist on a clandestine transmitter. Texts were written by Ernst Torgler, Maria Reese and Wilhelm Kasper, all former members of the KPD (German Communist Party). Only one person spoke on the radio, a man named Thony, named by Otto Abetz in a letter written on 30 January 1940.[154] The editorial line was not dissimilar to Radio Stuttgart: the Franco-British alliance and the French government were once again the main target. However, the communist tone was reproduced:

> This war is not ours. Quite the contrary, this is a war against us, against our ideas, our material interest, our families, against everything that is dear to the poor, against everything that the lower classes are proud of.

This war is a cynical business led by international capitalism, the City of London, bankers, and reactionaries who do not want to see the world evolve.[155]

The radio also denounced the '200 richest families of France', blamed for the current level of poverty. Hitler and Germany were also criticised to reinforce further the credibility of *Radio Humanité*.[156]

The *Voix de la Paix/Réveil* also targeted French people. Broadcasted in the evening (18.30, 19.00, 20.30, 21.30, 22.30), popular songs were played between short segments on French interior politics and Franco-British relations.[157] Carmen's overture and the slogan '*Vive la France, vive la Paix*'[158] were always played first while the French national anthem concluded each broadcast.[159] Both radio stations were popular in the French army, although many soldiers identified the German influence:

> I found this *Poste de la Paix* [in fact *Voix de la Paix*], which is obviously German: 'The Huns are in Norway. Those poor guys are going to be treated like the Poles. Reynaud the Failure, who succeeded Daladier the warmonger, is to blame.' Everything they say is similar, but it is gripping. Very much ignominious. Pacifist, but Hitler's kind of pacifism, in line with Doriot-Flandin-Laval. We listen to it a lot. Radio Humanité, whose main tune is the Internationale, is also listened to by soldiers. It is said all the time that Thorez spoke. But this is a German radio station. It plays on longwave, which excludes the possibility that it is a clandestine broadcast. It reveals itself by being anti-Semitic. But many listeners are still persuaded that it is a communist or pacifist radio station. Strange and troubling aspects of this Wave War.[160]

Even if soldiers were curious enough to listen to these broadcasts, it seems that it did not greatly affect their morale. Indeed, numerous soldiers denounced the arguments of German propaganda:

> We have the radio and listen to Radio Humanité in the evening. How mean can they be to good old Edouard [Daladier]. They encourage a revolution, as if the war was not enough.[161]

Knowing that the radio stations belonged to the enemy encouraged most Frenchmen to denounce them as perfidious fabrications.[162]

Fighting German propaganda

Censorship reports and unit commanders agreed that German propaganda had only a small impact. However, its large audience was a source of concern for the French army's commanders. At the beginning of the war, listening to 'public information propaganda susceptible of causing a harmful influence on the morale of the army and the population' was declared an offence punishable by a one- to ten-year sentence as well as a 1,000-10,000-franc fine.[163] Trials, however, were rare. The archives record only a few cases of bar or restaurant owners listening to the German radio. Those found guilty were usually forced to close their business.[164] The EM relied mainly on subaltern officers to enforce the ban on German broadcasts. On 16 September 1939, a note stated that 'the authorities owning a radio set were responsible for not listening to the German radio'.[165] The matter became more complex when 8,000 radio sets were delivered to the army in December 1939:

> The multiplication of radio sets in units will make this form of entertainment easier to access. [...] However, it is not always wise to officially ban broadcasts as men could become curious and listen to them illegally. Using radio sets, in *Foyers* or meeting rooms, should be left to a man who has been designated beforehand.[166]

Listening to the radio in safe spaces and in the presence of reliable men was supposed to distract French soldiers from illegal broadcasts.[167] General Georges was particularly concerned about Radio Stuttgart.[168] Soldiers designated to turn on the radio were supposed to 'have a good spirit' and 'will be told how to use the radio set to tune into French, allied or neutral broadcasts, and to explain how uninteresting German shows were in order to detract requests'.[169] Surprisingly, listening to enemy radio was not forbidden on the Home Front, a stark contrast with Germany.[170] On the other hand, German broadcasts were jammed from September onward, with little success at first but more efficiently from April 1940.[171]

After the German offensive of May 1940, the fight against German radio broadcasts intensified. The army explained several times that *Radio Humanité* was an enemy campaign of psychological warfare:

> It hides behind the communist flag, and it is to confuse us that it talks about the 'brutal German invasion'. This trick is crude: everybody knows that *Radio Humanité* is German and based in Germany.[172]

Still in May, the 2nd Bureau of the 5th Army gave stricter punishments for 'soldiers and civilians suspected of engaging with this propaganda'.[173] Those caught were arrested on the spot and faced martial laws.

The military authorities not only adopted restrictive measures but also launched a campaign of counter-propaganda in the army. This was conceived in cooperation with the *Commissariat Général à l'Information* (CGI). This operation included speeches, army broadcasts (the *quart d'heure du soldat*), as well as contests mixing leisure and anti-espionage activities. All the methods mentioned in the previous chapter were also designed to fight against German propaganda. Leaflets, such as one named 'For whom and why are you fighting', were also distributed.[174] In these publications, Hitler was portrayed as a warmonger hiding behind pacifist propaganda. The questions raised in the title were answered as such: 'For whom? For us. Why? To retain our freedom.'[175]

The French fought German propaganda at home but also led a campaign of psychological warfare in Germany. Foreseeing the conflict, the CGI and its

Service d'information à l'étranger (SIE) were created on 29 July 1939. The department 'foreign propaganda', led by Colonel Paul Hazard, was divided in thirteen sections, including a German section.[176] It was supervised by Ernest Tonnelat, a university professor already in charge of French propaganda during the First World War, who was assisted by Edmond Vermeil and eight collaborators.[177] The section's goals were defined as such:

> The German Section has unique tasks. It designs radio broadcasts in German and works with the GQG. Its leaflets are to be distributed above enemy lines and inside Germany by plane, balloon or by other means. Its objective is to hurt German forces.[178]

Unlike the Germans, the French did not have PK companies but regular aerial companies using balloons.[179] Already used during the previous conflict, they sent balloons toward enemy lines to 'distribute leaflets'.[180] The Air Force was also ordered to drop propaganda above enemy territories.

A Franco-British alliance was also at work. Both countries designed and distributed leaflets and aired radio broadcasts in Germany.[181] As soon as May-June 1939, the idea to merge forces was secretly explored. The Committee of Imperial Defence and the *Secrétariat general du Conseil Supérieur de la Défense Nationale* met several times before creating the Franco-British War Committee for Propaganda in Enemy Countries on 7 June 1939.[182] It was presided over by Counter-Admiral J. Fernet. Initial goals were audacious and touched various fields such as leaflet distribution, printing, transportation, the creation of 'special balloonist training' for Britain,[183] and various techniques to spread propaganda (planes and balloons).[184]

These plans were not realistic. The design of collaborative leaflets, for example, was slow and sometimes even failed. The leaflet called *Darum Krieg* was made by a Franco-British team over a period of three months. The first project was completed on 17 November 1939 but was accepted only on 16 January 1940.[185] Distribution was also difficult, despite various meetings and the exchange of information.[186] At the beginning of the conflict, France did not have enough rubber balloons and had to use a paper version, capable of 'carrying 1,500 leaflets up to 40 kilometres away'.[187] The production of rubber balloons was launched on 7 October 1939, but aviation remained the most important means of distribution above enemy lines.

Despite these problems, the French and the British worked together during the whole Phoney War. In fact, the leader of the British propaganda mission, Noël Coward, worked from Paris.[188] To follow the same strategy, weekly meetings were organized between the French (Edmond Vermeil and Ernest Tonnelat) and the British (Noël Coward and Colonel Sinclair). Both countries shared information to feed propaganda and hurt the enemy. This coordination was spotted by the German headquarters in November 1939:

> French and British radio broadcasts are so similar that shows from Strasburg and Daventry have the same shape, content and construction[189]

As demonstrated by several leaflets and broadcasts, the British and the French favoured two themes.[190] They responded to German attempts to break down the union between the British and France, insisting on the importance of working together to win the war. They also tried to break the German people from Hitler and other notable leaders. Indeed, several leaflets denounced the Molotov-Ribbentrop pact and Hitler's versatility. The leaflet *Wer lacht da?* (*Who is laughing?*) showed Stalin and Ribbentrop together while insisting on Hitler's desire to fight communism.[191]

This strategy triggered a dialogue between French and German propaganda. In March 1940, the French sent a leaflet titled 'the bloodbath' to denounce Hitler's alliance with Stalin. This piece of propaganda announced that Hitler was going to be betrayed by Stalin, who was about to seize Poland while the Germans were stuck on the western front. A few months before, the Germans had sent a leaflet with the same title, but showing British and French soldiers about to jump in a bloodbath. The French soldier jumped but the British left while laughing.[192]

The French also used banners and loudspeakers, but well after the Germans. Indeed, the first report mentioning the loudspeakers was written on 25 January 1940. This form of communication had not been studied before the conflict and the authorities did not have enough material to launch an operation immediately. The army and the CGI were forced to recruit engineers to correct this problem. They designed various prototypes but faced several technical issues.[194] The first loudspeakers were installed by the 8th Army near the 'north-east of Huningue' at the end of April 1940.[195] According to various reports, the soldiers who installed the loudspeakers were not happy with what was played. They stated that the broadcasts lacked 'precise information,

Figure 4.6 French banner propaganda in Alsace[193]

numbers, quotations' and 'were too vague, wordy and not clear enough'.[196] More worrying, the German language used was average at best, a serious issue when trying to be credible.[197] Texts were inserted between songs such as 'The Blue Danube', *Das deutsche Lied*, various German drinking songs, but also the *Horst Wessel Lied* and National-Socialist tunes.[198]

The French, just like the Germans, launched various types of black (*der deutsche Freiheitssender, der Freier Deutschlandsender*) and white (Radio Strasbourg) propaganda radio broadcasts. Radio Strasbourg, the first bilingual radio in Europe, was created on 11 November 1930. It had already been used by the French in 1935 to influence the Sarre plebiscite, playing programs in German aimed at Alsatians.[199] After the beginning of the conflict, the CGI and the French authorities made German-speaking broadcasts a priority. Pascal Copeau, who supervised middle-wave broadcasts, directed the *Service des émissions en langue allemande*. This man was not a beginner as he had supervised German-speaking shows on Radio Strasbourg in 1938.[200] In April 1940, he was assisted by Germanist Pierre Bertaux.[201] These two men, both propaganda experts, worked with translators and speakers, mostly German political refugees such as director Max Ophüls, actress Anne-Marie Seekel, actor Karl Heil, but also French actress Françoise Rosay.[202] Nicknamed *Lügensender* (lie emitter) by Goebbels, Radio Strasbourg aired during the Phoney War before being shut down by the French army during the retreat of 1940.

French propagandists saw Radio Strasbourg as a riposte against German propaganda assaults and a tool to 'shake German morale'.[203] They insisted on adopting an aggressive attitude to get out of the defensive zone.[204] The station addressed topics such as the communist alliance, Hitler's bellicose attitude, the lack of food and fuel, and the strength of the Franco-British alliance. These broadcasts were played five to seven times a day.[205]

The Germans recorded 15 French broadcasts in their language in September 1939. The same month, a report explored French communication strategies:

> The French radio broadcasts eight shows in German and is openly trying to flood the German audience with an uninterrupted flow of speeches and a multitude of information to prevent it from keeping a clear head. The first evening shows of 19.00 to 21.30 give in a casual way various communiqués, press reports and pure polemics. First, remarks about the general political situation are made, then the 'news of the German internal front', and third, reports about the military and economy, always making Germany look worse than the allies. [...]
>
> Later broadcasts are pure propaganda demonstrations. Daily, the 23.45 show is presented by speaker Pascal Copeau, who talks about daily events with charisma. He brings with irony facts to divide [the German people and the government]. On 29.9, for the second time in a week, Jean Giraudoux talked about the political situation. A propaganda trick is to use the famous French actress Françoise Rosay, who talks to German women from the French radio.[206]

French propaganda was taken very seriously. The German military authorities punished both civilians and soldiers listening to French or British broadcasts or those spreading news which could 'damage soldiers' morale'.[207]

Black propaganda was used on the very first day of the war with shows like *Der deutsche Freiheitssender* and *Freier Deutschlandsender*.[208] *Der deutsche Freiheitssender* was played twice a day at 20.30 and 22.00 on different wavelengths. *Freier Deutschlandsender* was played three times each evening. There were no notable differences in terms of topics between black and white propaganda. However, French propagandists tried to give a distinct identity to each radio channel. For example, *Der deutsche Freiheitssender* was supposed to lean on the far-left, targeting oppressed people.

Conclusion

Historians have too often portrayed the French army during the Phoney War as the passive victim of German propaganda. It is correct that the enemy did its best to spread psychological warfare material on the frontline. Communists also tried to communicate with soldiers, with far less success. There is, however, enough evidence to prove without a doubt that the EM and the government did not neglect the matter. They took a defensive stance as soon as the war began to stop efforts aimed at discouraging the army and civilians. Using modern means of communication as well as experts with previous war experience, the French managed to neutralise enemy communication. It seems that soldiers were rarely affected by German arguments and mostly viewed their efforts with either amusement or disdain. The French also launched an aggressive campaign against German soldiers. Was it effective? It seems that German reports highlighted several problems. As this chapter has explained, the French and the British cooperated during the Phoney War. The last chapter will look at the relation between allies and how French soldiers saw the British army.

Notes

1   On the topic: Aristotle Kallis, *Nazi Propaganda and the Second World War* (Basingstoke, 2006); Didier Georgakakis, *La République contre la propagande: aux origines perdues de la communication d'État en France, 1917–1940* (Paris, 2004).
2   Yves Santamaria, *1939, le pacte germano-soviétique* (Paris, 1998).
3   Maurice Thorez, après avoir rejoint son poste, s'évade et part à Moscou. Henri Michel, *La drôle de guerre* (Paris, 1971), p. 199.
4   *Le Temps*, 27 August 1939 http://gallica.bnf.fr/ark:/12148/bpt6k2640422/f3. image.langFR [accessed 26 March 2018].
5   Georges Vidal, 'Le Parti communiste français et la défense nationale (septembre 1937–septembre 1939), *Revue historique*, 630 (2004), pp. 333–369.
6   *Journal Officiel de la République Française (JORF)*, 26 August 1939, p. 10743.
7   Vladislav Smirnov and Marie Tournié, 'Le Komintern et le Parti communiste français pendant la « drôle de guerre », 1939–1940. (D'après les archives du Komintern)', *Revue des Études Slaves*, 65 (1993), pp. 671–690, p. 674.
8   Ibid.

9   Ibid.
10 *JORF*, 27 September 1939, p. 1170 http://gallica.bnf.fr/ark:/12148/ bpt6k6568572r/f2.item [accessed 6 March 2018].
11 *L'Humanité*, n°1 à n° 317 (1939–1944), available on Gallica: http://gallica.bnf. fr/ark:/12148/bpt6k879113k.r=L%27Humanité?rk=343349;2 [accessed 6 March 2018].
12 *L'Humanité*, 26.10.1939. http://gallica.bnf.fr/ark:/12148/bpt6k8791126.r=L% 27Humanité?rk=21459 [accessed 6 March 2018].
13 Jean Louis Crémieux-Brilhac, *Les Français de l'an 40*, Vol. 2, *Ouvriers et soldats* (Paris, 1990), p. 478.
14 Ibid.
15 Ibid.
16 Raphael-Leygues, and Barré Jean-Luc, *Les mutins de la mer noire* (Paris, 1981); Patrick Facon, 'Les mutineries dans le Corps Expéditionnaire Français en Russie Septentrionale (Décembre 1918–Avril 1919)', *Revue d'histoire Moderne et Contemporaine*, 24 (1977), pp. 455–474. André Marty was one of the leaders of the mutiny on the Black Sea. He wrote a book about it: André Marty, *La révolte de la mer noire* (Paris, 1927).
17 Crémieux-Brilhac, *Les Français de l'an 40*, Vol. 2, p. 478.
18 *L'Humanité*, November 1939.
19 Ibid.
20 Bernard Wilkin, *Aerial Propaganda and the Wartime Occupation of France, 1914–18* (London ; New York, 2016).
21 *L'Humanité du Soldat*, 1 May 1940.
22 A French communist and later a member of the French Resistance. She was responsible for the French Communist Youth and founded the *Union des jeunes filles de France*. The French police arrested her on 15 February 1942. Danièle Casanova was deported to Auschwitz, where she died in 1943.
23 Benoît Frachon (1893–1975) was a French metalworker and trade union leader. He was a member of the political bureau of the PCF from 1928. After the defeat, he was one of the key leaders of the clandestine PCF.
24 Crémieux-Brilhac, *Les Français de l'an 40*, Vol.2, p. 478.
25 SHD AT: 27N69. General Huntzinger, commander of the 2nd Army to the General-in-chief, 31 March 1939.
26 Jean-Louis Crémieux-Brilhac, 'Les communistes et l'armée pendant la drôle de guerre', in: Jean-Pierre Rioux, Antoine Prost, Jean-Pierre Azéma (eds), *Les communistes français de Munich à Chateaubriand*, (Paris, 1987), pp. 98–118, p. 113.
27 Fernand Grenier, *Journal de La Drôle de Guerre : Septembre 1939 – Juillet 1940* (Paris, 1969), p. 74. Other examples can be found in: Crémieux-Brilhac, 'Les communistes et l'armée pendant la drôle de guerre', p. 114.
28 SHD AT: 29N318. 5th Army, direction générale de la Sureté nationale, 27 February 1940.
29 Ibid.
30 SHD AT: 27N69. CP, soldier of the GSD II, 4th Army, report, 23 February 1940.
31 SHD AT: 27N69. CP, a balloon observer to his fiancée, report, 9 December 1939.
32 SHD AT: 27N69. CP, Maréchal des logis from the 107th RAL Auto, report, 16 December 1939.
33 SHD AT: 27N69. CP, report, 9 February 1940.
34 SHD AT: 27N69. CP, Maréchal des logis of the 194th RALT, 8th Army, report, 23 February 1940.
35 Fernand Grenier, *Journal de La Drôle de Guerre : Septembre 1939 – Juillet 1940* (Paris, 1969), p. 74, and other examples: Crémieux-Brilhac, 'Les communistes et l'armée pendant la drôle de guerre', p. 117.

36 SHD AT: 29N318. EM 2nd Bureau to the General commanding the 20th region, 9 March 1940.
37 Georges Vidal, 'L'armée française face au communisme du début des années 1930 jusqu'à la « débâcle »', *Historical reflexions*, 30 (2004) 2, pp. 283–309.
38 AN: 2W68. General Gamelin about the communist threat, 20 May 1942, pp. 2, 6, quoted in: Vidal, 'L'armée française face au communisme', p. 302.
39 SHD AT: 29N318. 5th Army, EM, 2nd Bureau, instructions regarding the surveillance of individuals and revolutionary propaganda, 9 December 1939. This note refers to others sent to the GQG and the War Minister on 14 July 1939.
40 SHD AT: 28N318. 5th Army, EM, 2nd Bureau, report about revolutionary propaganda, 9 December 1939.
41 Crémieux-Brilhac, *Les Français de l'an 40*, Vol. 2, p. 483.
42 SHD AT: 29N318. 5th Army, EM, 2nd Bureau, report about revolutionary propaganda, 9 December 1939.
43 Crémieux-Brilhac, *Les Français de l'an 40*, Vol. 2, p. 484.
44 Ibid.
45 SHD AT: 29N318. 5th Army, EM, 2nd Bureau, report, 9 December 1939.
46 Ibid.
47 Crémieux-Brilhac, *Les Français de l'an 40*, Vol. 2, p. 484.
48 SHD AT: 29N318. 5th Army, EM, 2nd Bureau, report, 9 December 1939.
49 Crémieux-Brilhac, *Les Français de l'an 40*, Vol. 2, p. 485.
50 Ibid., pp. 488–490.
51 Ibid.
52 SHD AT: 28N318. GQG, report, 12 December 1939.
53 SHD AT: 29N318. Ministre de la Défense Nationale et de la Guerre, report, 9 March 1940.
54 SHD AT: 29N318. Ministre de la Défense Nationale et de la Guerre, Cabinet du Ministre, 3ème Bureau PR, Le président du Conseil, Ministre de la Défense nationale et de la guerre, à M. le commandant la 20° Région, 9 March 1940.
55 Crémieux-Brilhac, *Les Français de l'an 40*, Vol. 2, p. 487.
56 Ibid., p. 486.
57 SHD AT: 29N318. 4th Army, étapes, 2nd Bureau, strategies to surveil revolutionary parties, 27 October 1939.
58 Ibid.
59 SHD AT: 29N318. EM, 3rd Bureau, report, 27 February 1940.
60 SHD AT: 29N318. 20th military region, EM, BCR, General Fournier, 28 February 1940.
61 SHD AT: 29N318. 20th military region, État-Major, BCR, Le Général de Division Fournier, Commandant la 20ème région militaire, 28 February 1940.
62 SHD AT: 29N318. Direction des Étapes, EM, 2ème bureau, Le commandant d'étapes de Rambervillers à Monsieur le Général, Directeur des Étapes, 1 March 1940.
63 SHD AT: 29N318. Direction des Étapes, EM, 2ème bureau, Note de service, Surveillance des communistes, 4 March 1940.
64 SHD AT: 29N318. Direction des Étapes, EM, 2ème bureau, Note de service, Surveillance des communistes, 4 March 1940.
65 SHD AT: 29N318. Direction des Étapes, EM, 2ème bureau, Note de service, Perquisition, 1 March 1940.
66 SHD AT: 29N318. Direction des Étapes, EM, 2ème bureau, Note de service, Surveillance des communistes, 4 March 1940.
67 SHD AT: 29N318. Direction des Étapes, EM, 2ème bureau, Note de service 28 February 1940; SHD AT: 29N318, 5th Army, direction des Étapes, Sûreté de l'Armée, 2 May 1940

68 Férard, Nicolas, *Propaganda Kompanien: PK War Reporters of the Third Reich* (Paris, 2014), pp. 44–51.

69 Hasso von Wedel and Hermann Teske, *Die Propagandatruppen der deutschen Wehrmacht* (Vowinckel, 1962), pp. 18–22.

70 "Abkommen über die Durchführung der Propaganda im Kriege", in: Uzulis, André, 'Deutsche Kriegspropaganda gegen Frankreich', in: Jürgen Wilke (ed.), *Pressepolitik Und Propaganda. Historische Studien Vom Vormärz Bis Zum Kalten Krieg*, Vol. 7 (Köln, 1997), pp. 127–173.

71 L'OKW/WPr was led by Major Hasso von Wedel and controlled by General Alfred Jodl.

72 Bundesarchiv-Militärarchiv Freiburg im Breisgau (BArch-MA), RW4/185, Auszug aus dem Bericht der Prop. Komp. 670 vom 10.10.1939; betr.: Propagandaaktion vom 7.10.39.

73 SHD AT: 27N69. CP, 5th Army, a soldier, report, 4 November 1939.

74 BArch-MA, RW4/242, Nachricht an Verbindungsoffizier, 22 October 1939.

75 PAAA, R 60716, Anbiederungsversuche, 1940.

76 Le discours de paix d'Hitler sera repris également sous forme de tracts et d'émission radiophoniques.

77 BArch-MA, RH19 III/377, OKW/WPR, Geh. Kratzer, 7 October 1939.

78 SHD AT: 27N68. On 6 October, Hitler spoke to the Reichstag about peace and France. This speech was dismissed by Daladier and Chamberlain.

79 BArch-MA, RW4/242,Nachricht an Verbindungsoffizier, 22 October 1939.

80 Ibid.

81 PAAA, R 60716, Anbiederungsversuche, 1940.

82 BArch-MA, RW4/185, Auszug aus dem Bericht der Prop. Komp. 670 c. 10.10.39, betref. Propagandaktion v. 7.10.39, 10 October 1939.

83 Ibid.

84 BAarch-MA, RW4/261, Propagandaaktion im Westen, 10.10.1939; BArch-MA, RW4/185, Auszug aus dem Bericht der Prop. Komp. 670 c. 10.10.39, betref. Propagandaktion v. 7.10.39, 10 October 1939.

85 SHD AT: 27N69. Postal Control. Soldier 26 RI, II° DI, 4th Army. Note for the High Command, 9 November 1939.

86 SHD AT: 27N69. CP, soldier 36°GRDI, 41°DI, 4th Army, report, 28 November 1939.

87 SHD AT: 27N69. CP, maréchal des logis, 4° Hussards, 3°DC, 2nd Army, report, 28 November 1939.

88 SHD AT: 27N69. CP, soldier du 32° RI, report, 21 December 1939.

89 BArch-MA, RH/26-246, Abschrift. Betr. Besondere Feindmeldungen (Anbiederungsversuche) der 7. Kp. I.R. 283, 29 December 1939.

90 SHD AT: 27N69. CP, soldier 32° RI, report, 21 December 1939.

91 Bernard Wilkin, *Aerial Propaganda and the Wartime Occupation of France, 1914–18* (London; New York, 2016).

92 Rough estimate taken from the work of Klaus Kirchner, *Flugblatt-Propaganda im 2. Weltkrieg Europa, Flugblätter aus Deutschland*, Vol. 2 (Erlangen, 1982).

93 BArch-MA, RW4/244, March 1940. Le Rot-Weiss Geschoss was a small projectile in the form of a shell, filled with tracts that fell out on contact with the ground. It could be fired precisely at a range of 6-10km. Kirchner, *Flugblattpropaganda*, Vol. 2, p. XLI.

94 Kirchner, *Flugblattpropaganda*, Vol. 2, pp. XXXIII–WLIV.

95 Bundesarchiv Koblenz (BArch Koblenz), ee186, Bild 146-1971-080-26, Flugblattpropaganda.

96 PAAA, R 60716, Anbiederungsversuche, 1940.

97 PAAA, R 60716, Anbiederungsversuche, 1940.

98   BArch-MA, RW4/242, Reichsministerium für Volksaufklärung und Propaganda an das Oberkommando der Wehrmacht Abt. WPr, Flugblattabwurf, 18 November 1939.
99   SHD AT: 27N68.
100 SHD AT: 27N68.
101 'En avant, Pour le triomphe'. Kirchner, *Flugblattpropaganda*, Vol. 2, p. 118.
102 'Où le Tommy est-il resté ?', 10x15cm, early Aapril until the beginning of June 1940. Kirchner, *Flugblattpropaganda*, Vol. 2, p. 118.
103 SHD AT: 27N69. CP, 4th Army, report, 13 November 1939
104 SHD AT: 27N69. CP, Vth, report, 13 November 1939.
105 SHD AT: 27N69. CP, sergeant, 71st RI, 19th DI, 4th Army, report, 28 November 1939.
106 SHD AT: 27N69. CP, report, 28 November 1939.
107 SHD AT: 27N69. CP, soldier, 160th RI, 41st DI, 4th Army, report, 28 November 1939.
108 On the relationship between the British and the French, see chapter 5.
109 SHD AT: 27N69. CP, soldier, 44th Brigade de Chasseurs 70th DI, 5th Army, report, 3 December 1939.
110 SHD AT: 27N69. CP, soldier, 160th RI, 41st DI, 4th Army, report, 28 November 1939.
111 Kichner, Flugblattpropaganda, Vol. 2, pp. 253–302.
112 SHD AT: 27N69. GQG, EMG, 2nd Bureau, N° 1833 / 2 FT, report on morale, 15 April 1940.
113 'Soldats de couleur! Déposez les armes', 21x30cm, June 1940, around 80,000 copies. Kirchner, *Flugblattpropaganda*, Vol. 2, p. 213.
114 For a detailed analysis of the radio war carried out by France and Germany, see Maude Fagot [Williams], 'La guerre des ondes entre la France et l'Allemagne pendant la "drôle de Guerre"', *Revue Historique*, 3 (2014), pp. 630–654.
115 Crémieux-Brilhac, *Les Français de l'an 40*, Vol. 1, p. 373.
116 Sendelaufplan SDR, 11.01.1990, 4, quoted in: Uzuli, 'Deutsche Kriegspropaganda gegen Frankreich', p. 136.
117 AN F43/95.
118 12.45 to 12.55, 14.15 to 14.25, 17.15 to 17.25, 20.15 to 20.25, 21.15 to 21.30, 22.45 to 23.00, 0.15 to 0.25, quoted in: Crémieux-Brilhac, *Les Français de l'an 40*, Vol. 1, p. 380.
119 AN 72AJ/582, Institut d'Études Européennes de Strasbourg, Vues sur la propagande et sur les problèmes alsaciens, 25 October 1939.
120 SHD AT: 27N69. Brigadier SF Haguenau, 5th Army, report, 3 December 1939.
121 SHD AT: 27N69. Artillery soldier to his wife, 5th DINA, 3rd Army, report, 3 December 1939.
122 From February 1940, French soldiers refused to participate in this type of program, which forced German propagandists to find ways of making them talk immediately after their capture, 'When they are still under the influence of being captured.' BArch-MA, RW4/243, WPr, Geheim, 10 February 1940.
123 SHD AT: 29 N 198. Extrait du bulletin d'écoute radiophonique n°219 de l'office régional d'information du 7 avril. Émission de la radio allemande du 6 avril, 21h15.
124 SHD AT: 29 N 198. Note n°I.645/FTCE, 4 December 1939.
125 SHD AT: 29 N 198. IVth armée, 1er Bureau, communications faites à la radio allemande par des militaires français prisonniers, 27 April 1939.
126 BDIC: 4 res 0057. Bulletin n°9, 16 December 1939.
127 SHD AT: 27N69. CP, pioneer of the 3rd bataillon, 8th Army, report, 28 November 1939.
128 SHD AT: 27N69. CP, pioneer of the 3rd bataillon, 8th Army, report, 28 November 1939.

129 SHD AT: 27N69. CP, soldier to his wife, 103rd RI, 2nd Army, report, 15 January 1940.
130 SHD AT: 27N69. CP, soldier to his wife, 13rd RAD, 41st DI, 4th Army, report, 28 November 1939.
131 SHD AT: 27N69. CP, soldier 67th RI, 8th DIM, 4th Army, report, 18 January 1940.
132 SHD AT: 27N69. CP, soldier of the 413rd Pionnier to his wife, E.O. 2nd Army, report, 21 February 1940.
133 SHD AT: 27N69. CP, soldier 30th GRDI, 18th DI, 9th Army, report, 6 January 1940.
134 SHD AT: 27N69. CP, soldier 131st RI, 25th DIM, 7th Army, report, 2 February 1940.
135 BArch-MA, RW4/243, Abschrift. Betr. Abhören des Senders Stuttgart in Frankreich, January 1940.
136 BArch-MA, RW4/243, WPr, Geheim, 10 February 1940.
137 Ibid.
138 BArch-MA, RW4/243, WPr, Gefangenen Rundfunkreportagen, 20 February 1940.
139 Art. 5 Capture, in: Abkommen vom 27.07.1929 über die Behandlung der Kriegsge-fangenen (RGBl. 1934 II 227), Convention relative to the Treatment of Prisoners of War Geneva, 27 July 1929, quoted in: Nobert Wagner (ed.), *Archiv des Humani-tären Völkerrechts in bewaffneten Konflikten* (Brühl; Weseling, 2012), pp. 203–220.
140 BArch-MA, RW4/243, WPr, Gefangegen Rundfunkreportagen, 20 February 1940.
141 SHD AT: 27N69. CP, soldier 120°RAL, CA, 4th Army, report, 3 December 1939.
142 SHD AT: 27N69. CP, a soldier to his wife, 317th RI, 54th DI, 8th Army, report, 6 January 1940.
143 Ibid.
144 SHD AT: 27N69. CP, a soldier, 5th DI, 4th Army, report, 28 December 1939.
145 BArch-MA, RH26/246, Abschrift. Besondere Feindmeldungen, January 1940.
146 SHD AT: 27N69. CP, a soldier, 3rd DC, 3rd Army, report, 28 December 1939.
147 SHD AT: 27N69. CP, a soldier to his wife, 21st RAC, 5th DIC, 4th Army, report, 18 January 1940.
148 Willi A. Boelcke, *Wollt ihr den totalen Krieg?: Die Geheimen Goebbels-Konferenzen 1939-1943* (Stuttgart, 1967), p. 22.
149 *La Voix de la Paix* and *Le Réveil de la France* turned out to be one single radio station that was named differently to create the image of un difficile établissement des radios françaises to reinforce its credibility in the eyes of the French.
150 Ortwin Buchbender and Reinhard Hauschild, *Geheimsender gegen Frankreich: Die Täuschungsoperation Radio Humanité 1940* (Herford, 1984), p. 8.
151 Politisches Archiv des Auswärtigen Amts, Berlin (PAAA), R 67492–67494.
152 Buchbender and Hauschild, *Geheimsender gegen Frankreich*, p. 8.
153 Ibid., 44.
154 Ibid., 48.
155 PAAA, R67492, Radio-Humanité, 11 January 1940.
156 PAAA, R67492, Radio Humanité, 2 February 1940.
157 Crémieux-Brilhac, *Les Français de l'an 40*, Vol. 2, p. 380.
158 Sadoul, *Journal de guerre*, p. 183.
159 BArch-MA, RW4/312a, 25 January 1940.
160 Sadoul, *Journal de guerre*, p. 178.
161 SHD AT: 27N69. CP, a soldier of the 326th RI, 62nd DI, 5th Army, report, 11 March 1940.
162 SHD AT: 27N69. CP, a soldier of the 413rd Pionnier to his wife, E.O. 2nd Army, report, 21 February 1940.
163 SHD AT: 30N39. CP, 5th Army, EM, 2nd Bureau, report, 18 December 1939.

164 SHD AT: 30N39. CP, 5th Army, EM, 2nd Bureau, Général Duron, commander of the 30rd DI, 3 December 1939.
165 SHD AT: 30N59. GQG, EMG, 2nd Bureau, note for the armies, 29 December 1939.
166 Ibid.
167 SHD AT: 29N269. 5th Army, EM, 2nd Bureau, report, 29 December 1939; SHD AT: 30N59. GQG, EMG, 2nd bureau, note for the armies, 29 December 1939.
168 SHD AT: 30N59. GQG, EMG, 2nd Bureau, report, 29 December 1939.
169 Ibid.
170 *Verordnung über außerordentliche Rundfunkmaßnahmen*, 1.09.1939, RGBl. 1939 I, S. 1683. On the subject of forbidding listening to foreign radio in Germany, see: Michael P. Hensle, *Rundfunkverbrechen: das Hören von 'Feindsendern' im National-sozialismus* (Berlin, 2003).
171 ADBR: 98AL649. Institut d'Études Européennes de Strasbourg, propagande et contre-propagande radiophonique de guerre, 30 September 1939; ADBR: 98 AL 658. Institut d'Études Européennes, L'écoute de la Radio en Alsace, 14 April 1940.
172 SHD, 29N318. 5th Army, EM, 2nd Bureau, counter-propaganda, 18 May 1940.
173 Ibid.
174 SHD, 27N67. 4th Army, 2nd Bureau, 'Why do you fight?', 29 April 1940.
175 Ibid.
176 AN F41/14–15, Attribution du service d'information à l'étranger, 6 December 1939.
177 AN F/41/979, civilian and military members of the department, 16 November 1939.
178 AN F41/14–15, Attribution du service d'information à l'étranger, 6 December 1939.
179 AN F/41/980.
180 Ibid.
181 For a detailed analysis of common preparations and outcomes regarding propaganda material, see: Williams, Maude, 'La coopération franco-britannique en matière de propagande, 1939–940', *Relations Internationales*, 162 (2015), pp. 45–62.
182 AN F/41/ 980, The French-German propaganda committee, 7 September 1939.
183 AN F/41/980, balloon staff, 8 June 1939.
184 AN F/41/ 980, Report on the meeting of 8 June 1939.
185 AN/F/41/980, Meeting of 17 November 1939 and 16 January 1940.
186 AN F/41/991, 'M' Balloon Manual, report on rubber balloons, 17 November 1939.
187 Kirchner, *Flugblattpropaganda*, Vol. 2, p. 34.
188 AN F/41/991, 17 November 1939.
189 BArch-MA, RW4/241, 7 November 1939.
190 On leaflets, see: Klaus Kirchner, *Flugblattpropaganda im Zweiten Weltkrieg*, Vol. 2, *Flugblätter aus England* (Erlangen 1982); Klaus Kirchner, *Flugblattpropaganda im Zweiten Weltkrieg*, Vol. 3, *Flugblätter aus Frankreich* (Erlangen, 1982). On radio propaganda, see: Michael Balfour, *Propaganda in War, 1939–45: Organisations, Policies and Publics in Britain and Germany* (London; Boston, 1979); Fagot, 'La guerre des ondes'.
191 Kirchner, *Flugblätter aus Deutschland*, p. 42.
192 SHD AT: 27N68. The bloodbath.
193 PAAA, R 60716, Anbiederungsversuche, 1940.
194 AN F/41/979. Propaganda report, 15 November 1939.
195 SHD AT: 28N52. 8th Army, 3rd Bureau, loudspeakers, 22 April 1940.
196 SHD AT: 28N52. Report on German loudspeaker propaganda, 1 May 1940.
197 SHD AT: 28N52. Report on German loudspeaker propaganda, 1 May 1940.

198 SHD AT: 28N52. 8th Army, loudspeaker propaganda, 3 May 1940, 9 May 1940 and 5 May 1940.
199 BBC Europe only started in 1938. Tim Brooks, *British Propaganda to France, 1940–1944: Machinery, Method and Message* (Edinburgh, 2007), 11.
200 Laurent Douzou, 'Pascal Copeau', in: Marcot (ed.), *Dictionnaire historique de la Résistance* (Paris, 2006); Pierre Leenhardt, *Pascal Copeau (1908–1982). L'histoire préfère les vainqueurs* (Paris, 1994).
201 Pierre Bertaux, *Mémoires interrompus* (Asnières, 2000), 133.
202 German collaborators were also named in a CGI report: M. Dyck, M. Levi, M. Wronkow, M. Handler, M. schlesinger and M. Lewy, AN F/41/21–22.
203 Radio-Paris, Paris Mondial, Lyon, Paris PTT, Rennes, Lille. BArch-MA, RW4/241, Technischer Einsatz, 24 September 1939.
204 ADBR: 98AL 649, Institut d'Études Européennes de Strasbourg, propagande et contre-propagande radiophonique de guerre, 30 September 1939.
205 AN F 41/21-22; BArch-MA, RW4/241, Technischer Einsatz, 24 September 1939.
206 BArch-MA, RW4/241, Technischer Einsatz, 24 September 1939.
207 BArch-MA, RW4/284, Abhören ausländischer Rundfunksender, 26 January 1940. On the fight against radio propaganda see: Hensle, *Rundfunkverbrechen.*
208 There was also a show in German targeting Austrians (*Der österreichische Freiheitssender*).

5 Interacting with British soldiers

In the interwar period, Britain and France witnessed the rise of Nazism. Hoping to secure peace after the annexation of portions of Czechoslovakia, Chamberlain and Daladier signed the Munich agreement on 30 September 1938. On 15 March 1939, both countries witnessed the collapse of the agreement after the German invasion of what remained of Czechoslovakia and Hitler's proclamation of a Protectorate of Bohemia and Moravia. Following this event, France and Britain renewed their pledge to protect Poland, Greece, Romania and Turkey.[1] On 3 September 1939, the Allies declared war on Germany in response to the invasion of Poland. Infantry and air force units were sent to France to fight. The British presence was a source of tensions and jealousy. This chapter will look at interactions between French and British soldiers. It will first detail the British presence in France before looking at the French perception and relations between allied soldiers.

Military collaboration

The Franco-British alliance, already effective in 1914–1918, was kept alive in the interwar period.[2] On 22 February 1939, the British Expeditionary Force (BEF) was formed: the Cabinet ordered 'five regular infantry divisions, one mobile division and four Territorial divisions be equipped for European warfare'.[3] The first soldiers of the BEF arrived in France on 4 September. On 27 September, the BEF had 152,031 men.[4] According to British reports, this figure included 9,392 airmen along with 21,494 army vehicles, 2,470 RAF vehicles, 36,000 tons of ammunitions, 25,000 tons of fuel and 60,000 tons of frozen meat.[5] Leaving from Bristol, Plymouth and Southampton, most soldiers landed between 10 September and 10 October 1939 at Le Havre, Cherbourg, Brest and Nantes-Saint-Nazaire.[6]

General Lord Gort, 'a highly decorated Guardsman who had commanded at battalion and brigade level in the Great War'[7], commanded the BEF. He was nominated after lengthy debates and landed at Cotentin on 14 September.[8] Lieutenant-General Henry Pownall, Director of Military Operations and Intelligence, was appointed Chief of the General Staff and Lieutenant-General Sir Wellesley Brownrigg, Director General of the Territorial Army, became the BEF's

Adjutant-General.[9] General Gort and the BEF, in agreement with General Ironside, Chief of the Imperial General Staff, were placed directly under the command of General Alphonse Georges, C-in-C of the French North-East theatre of operations. As a result, the BEF followed French orders at the beginning of the war, although it was agreed that the expeditionary corps would become independent toward the end of 1940, once reaching the size of an army.[10]

Gort and Georges got along well, the British commander even stating that he was 'happy to be his subordinate', but relations were more difficult with General Gamelin.[11] Georges was also supported by the British, who had 'absolute faith' in him.[12] Military liaisons were established: French General Voruz stayed at the British GHQ at Arras (Pas-de-Calais), British Brigadier John Swayne was based at the HQ of General Georges at La Ferté sous Jarre and Major-General Sir Richard Howard-Vyse worked with Gamelin from Vincennes.[13] During the first months of the Phoney War, the British were eager to cooperate, understanding that their numbers were a mere fraction of the French army and that they had to learn by their side.[14]

The British army was included in various scenarios to win the war. Georges believed that the Franco-British forces 'needed to occupy parts of the Belgian territory to block the enemy's access to the ports' while Gamelin wanted larger movements to reach the Netherlands.[15] On 17 November, Gamelin's strategy was chosen by the *Conseil Suprême*.[16] In the event of a German invasion of Belgium, Franco-British forces were to occupy the Dyle river (from Leuven to Wavre) and the area of Gembloux (Wavre to Namur on the Meuse river) as quickly as possible.[17] This plan was modified by the Bréda variable on 12 March 1940.[18] The allies intended on positioning British troops on the Dyle river while French units of the 7th Army of General Giraud raced for the southern point of the Netherlands to join with the Dutch Army.[19] This strategy was used in May 1940 but soon became obsolete, due to the speed of German territorial gains.[20]

By October 1939, only a fraction of the BEF was on French soil but more troops arrived during the next months. On 10 May 1940, 10 divisions, or 237,000 men, were in France:

Army Corps:

- I Corps of Lieutenant-General Barker, made of the 1st, 2nd et 48th Infantry Divisions,
- II Corps of Lieutenant-General Brooke, made of the 3rd, 4th Infantry Divisions and the 50th Motor Infantry Division (arrived February 1940),
- III Corps of Lieutenant-General Adam, arrived in March 1940 and made of the 42nd and the 44th Infantry Divisions (and 51st Highland Division)

Reserve units (under French command in 1940):

- 1st Armoured Division with Mark VI tanks (arrived in May)
- 51st Highland Infantry Division, arrived at the beginning of February 1940, commanded by Major-General Victor M. V. Fortune and attached

to the 3rd French Army in the fortified region of Metz from 30 April to 7 May 1940.[21]

Others:

- a regiment of mechanised cavalry,
- a regiment of armoured cars,
- a regiment of tanks (the 4th Royal Tank Regiment),
- the Air Component, 29 RAF squadrons, under the command of Vice-Marshal C. H. B. Blount.[22]

General Gort set his temporary General Headquarters in the castle of Blancharsière, near Mans, before settling for the castle of Habarcq (Arras).[23] Three weeks after landing, the BEF was stationed in the sector of the first GA on the Belgian border, between Maulde and Halluin.[24] The local commander, General Billotte, served as an intermediary between Georges and Gort, a measure criticised in May-June 1940.[25] A few units were also integrated in the French command, such as the 3rd Infantry Brigade of Brigadier Curtis, which was on the Lorraine front in December 1939. In January 1940, the 51st Highland Infantry Division was positioned close to the Sarre.

The RAF was also on French territory. Twenty-two squadrons, or 363 planes, were sent to France in September 1939 to form the Advance Air Striking Force (AASF) and the Air Component of the BEF.[26] The Air Component, led by Air Vice-Marshal Charles Blount, went to France to support the BEF.[27] Its HQ was based at Marœuil-sur-Scarpe, near Arras, from 9 September onward. French General Jeaunnaud was its overall commander before being replaced by General Armengeaud.[28] Mission n.1, commanded by Air Marshal Arthur Barratt, was in liaison with French aerial forces and General Vuillemin.[29] Reconnaissance plans were prepared in coordination with General Mouchard, commander of the air forces on the North-East front.[30] By September 1939, the Air Component had 5 squadrons of Westland Lysanders, two squadrons of Bristol Blenheim I, two squadrons of Hurricanes and a squadron of Gladiators.[31]

The Advanced Air Striking Force (AASF), led by Air Vice-Marshal Patrick Playfair, was composed of detachments from Bomber Command and operated from French airfields. The HQ was at Polignac castle (Reims).[32] The AASF was independent from the BEF and Lord Gort. To link with the French Air Force, mission n.2 was created.[33] However, it was decided that in case of German offensive Air Marshal Barratt would lead the AASF if needed.[34] On 1 September 1939, 10 squadrons of Fairey Battles were sent to France. On 8 September, two squadrons of Hurricanes also reached France. By September, the AASF had 32 Hurricane and 160 Fairey Battle. In May 1940, the AASF and the Air Component had 29 squadrons with 464 planes.[35]

On 9 October 1939, the British created the Allied Central Air Bureau of Chauny to link together the Air Ministry, Bomber Command, the BEF and the AASF.[36]

Table 5.1 The RAF in France from 3.09.1939 to 10.05.1940.[37]

Planes	3 September 1939		10 May 1940	
	Squadrons	Planes	Squadrons	Planes
AASF				
Hawker Hurricane	2	32	3	48
Fairey Battle	10	160	8	128
Bristol Blenheim	0	0	2	32
TOTAL AASF	12	192	13	208
RAF Air Component				
Hawker Hurricane	2	32	6	96
Gloster Gladiator	1	17	0	0
Bristol Blenheim	2	32	4	64
Westland Lysander	5	90	5	90
Supermarine Spitfire PR	0	0	1	6
TOTAL Air Component	10	171	16	256

At the beginning of 1940, The British reorganised aerial forces in France.[38] On 15 January 1940, the British Air Forces in France (BAFF), led by Air Marshal Arthur Barratt, was constituted to unify all RAF bases in France.[39] Air-Marshal Barratt controlled and coordinated all actions of the Air Component and the AASF.[40] Before the German offensive, BAFF's HQ was close to the HQ of General Vuillemin at Coulommiers. Liaison officers were sent to Generals Georges, Vuillemin and Gort.

Several airfields and landing strips were made available to the BEF. The French and the British had agreed before the war that their construction and renovation would be taken care of by the BEF.[41] However, a great deal of work was needed to make them functional.[42] During the Phoney War, 10,000 men built and improved them. 47 air stations were constructed or renovated, including at 19 new locations; by 15 May, 8 out of these 19 new sites were usable.[43]

The French authorities saw the BEF as too small and feared the effect this would have on their country's morale. The presence of British soldiers was the best weapon to fight the idea that the French population was about to suffer catastrophic losses, just as it had during the First World War. In September 1939, Daladier insisted on placing the BEF on the Belgian border and next to the Sarre region to make the British more visible. However, the imbalance between armies weighed on Franco-British relations. At the beginning of the conflict, the French mobilised 6 million soldiers while the British sent 200,000 men.[45] In January 1940, official communiqués announced that 2 million British soldiers were headed for France. In reality, the British government mobilised men slowly, a fact denounced by Senator Camille Ferrand during a secret

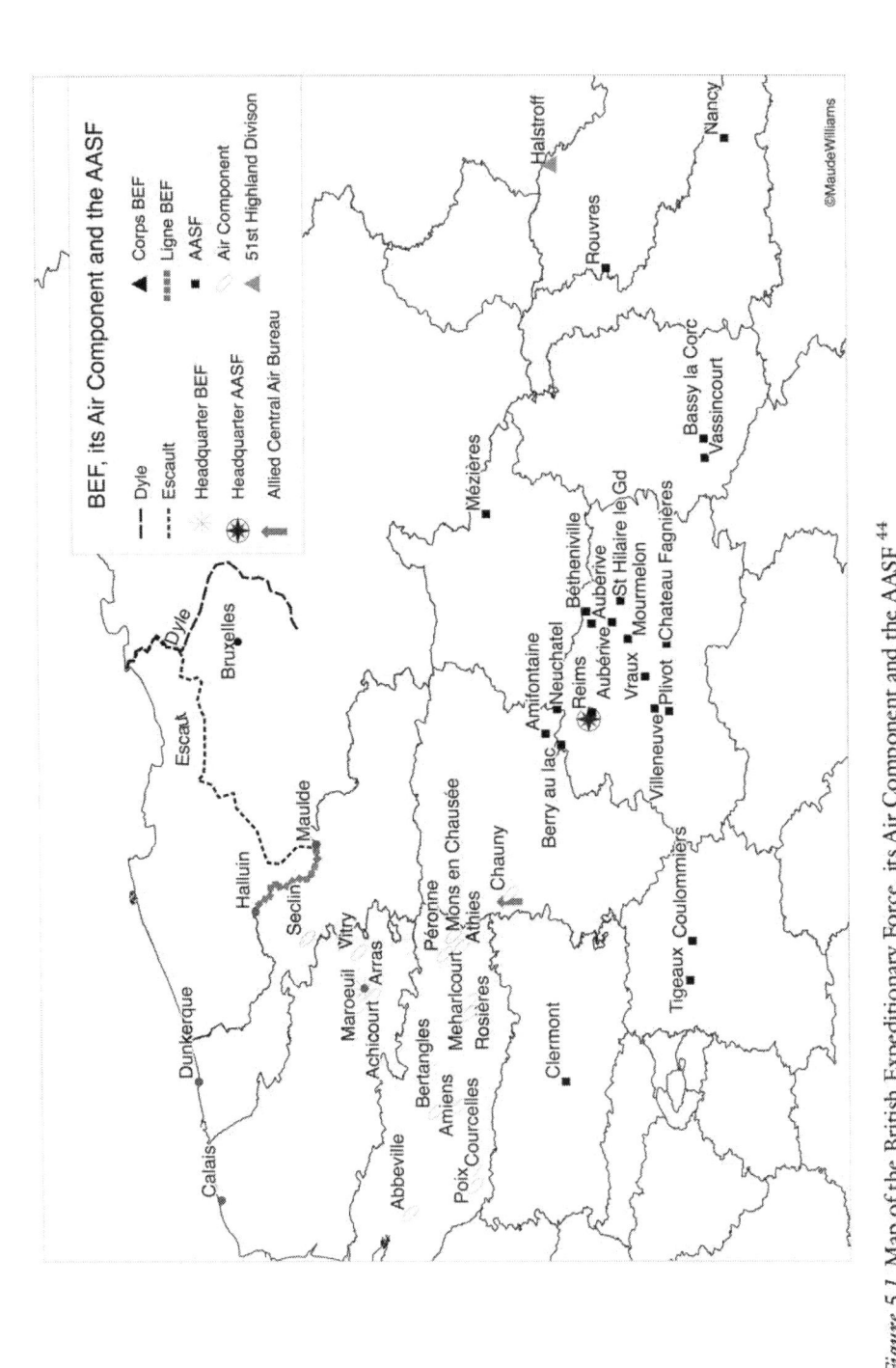

Figure 5.1 Map of the British Expeditionary Force, its Air Component and the AASF [44]

Credit: Maude Williams

Senate meeting.[46] The French were disappointed by the British, who had promised 400,000 soldiers as well as logistical support by spring 1940. Daladier had hoped for more fighting squadrons but this wish never materialised.[47] In parliamentary, military and government circles, greater British commitment was vainly expected.

The organisation and coordination of British and French troops on the North-East front must be examined. During the interwar period, First World War institutions were revived.[48] In April 1938, Gamelin asked during a meeting of the *Conseil Supérieur de la Défense National* for the creation of an interallied committee.[49] A year later, the *Conseil suprême interallié* was born. Formed of politicians and superior officers of both countries, this council met ten times from 12 September 1939 to 27 April 1940, and five times between 26 May and 13 June 1940.[50] During the meetings common military strategies were discussed.[51] It is important to highlight that communication existed at the highest level to coordinate efforts not only in France, but also in other theatres of operations.

Cooperation was not fine-tuned at the beginning of the war. Important considerations such as how to host the BEF had not been settled, a fact triggering inevitable conflicts. In Saint-Nazaire and Le Havre, the British requisitioned private properties (factories, depots, etc.) and occupied spaces where frozen meat for the French army was stored.[52] Tension was high where the British were stationed. The far-right, traditionally against Britain, talked about 'English pillage'.[53] In the north, men of the AASF illegally occupied private properties and took resources without paying or asking beforehand. These problems triggered tensions between British and French soldiers, as well as civilian populations and authorities. On 2 October 1939, these conflicts were summarised in a 'note relative aux *répercussions particulières de la mainmise anglaise sur notre mobilisation industrielle et le ravitaillement général*.[54] This report, forwarded to General Gamelin, was debated by British generals and French civilian authorities on 26 October 1939:

> All English relations with French civilian ministries will go through the military regions and all questions will be centralised by the 4th Bureau of the EM. [...] There will be a British liaison officer for each military EM and an French liaison officer or an interpreter will help British officers during all important steps. Finally, a reminder aimed at the British will be published jointly.[55]

Fifteen days later, another Franco-British meeting was called to agree on how to buy or mobilise equipment for the British army. The creation of '3 joint military commissions to coordinate matters of transportation, men and accommodations, deliveries and disputes' was decided.[56] Liaison officers were also tasked with identifying and reporting local problems.[57] Even if most structural and hierarchical disputes were resolved by November 1939, British soldiers continued to face conflicts with French troops and civilians.

The French soldier and his perception of the British

It is important to make a distinction between French soldiers who were in contact with British units and those, mostly men serving on the Maginot Line, who rarely saw them. French troops close to the British belonged to the GA1 and GA2. At first, French soldiers were impressed by the British and their equipment: 'They are well-equipped, look shiny, have formidable material'.[58] 'The English are numerous and their equipment is formidable'.[59] By December, French soldiers were mostly jealous:

> The arrival of the British is the cause for general satisfaction. Troops' morale is improving and the first contacts have been courteous. A little bit of jealousy because they are better paid, better equipped and enjoy accommodations made by us.[60]

The CP mentioned jealousy for the first time in October 1939 and blamed living conditions.[61] The fact that British soldiers were better paid than the French was an important source of tension:[62]

> British soldiers are among us and we do not get along very well. They earn nearly 35 frs [francs] per day and us 0.50. They are condescending but their phlegm is not obvious on the frontline.[63]

> It is sad here but those English bastards can dance on a daily basis with their 35 frs. It is the good life. Us, with our 15 *sous*, pay 2frs for a beer. We cannot party often.[64]

This situation reinforced the idea, common among French soldiers, that Britain was very rich but invested little in the war.[65] Several incidents occurred between French and British troops:

> On 7 October 1939, at 21.30, the manager of the brothels in the rue de la Charrière called us to resolve a fight about beverage prices between English and French soldiers as well as women working there. After the police's intervention, calm was restored.[66]

Violent confrontations were reported, especially in the North and in the Champagne region where most British troops were stationed. This triggered several problems, such as noise and brawls, in Lille during the weekends.[67] To solve this issue, British commanders only authorised their men to go to Lille during the other days of the week. This measure, coupled with strict sanctions for those caught behaving badly, calmed the atmosphere.[68] From mid-January to mid-April 1940, regional commanders noted with satisfaction that the situation had 'very greatly improved'.[69] British military authorities of the GHQ of the BEF, including Lieutenant-General Sir Brownrigg, took incidents seriously and asked for a thorough investigation when ill-disciplined soldiers were reported.[70]

They firmly believed in the importance of getting along well with the local population and the mayors.

Fights between French and British soldiers were often fuelled by alcohol. As we have seen before, the French army was heavily dependent on wine and other drinks during the Phoney War.[71] The British were equally tempted to drink, especially considering the fact that alcohol was cheaper than at home:[72]

> In March 1940, the British Government considered any overseas military facility that sold draught beer at six-pence per pint as good value and competitively priced with a 6d Bass on Third Class Rail. However, it was distinctly uncompetitive with Phoney War France where British soldiers could 'get very drunk on two francs [3d]' (sic) a night. A beneficial exchange rate of one franc = 1.36d (176.5 francs = £1), and fortnightly pay issues in 20 franc notes, further encouraged excessive drinking habits.[73]

British soldiers, better paid than their ally, were able to drink expensive bottles of champagne and strong alcohol. These drinking sessions sometimes led to violent episodes but also brought together allied military men, especially when the British paid the tab:

> Here, we see many English, they seem to earn a lot, and in the evening they cannot walk straight. Despite everything, they are good looking guys and they often pay for drinks when we meet. They are really friendly.[74]

> In this region, the English are here and yesterday afternoon, we celebrated the entente cordiale. We were quite drunk because they offered strong drinks and cigarettes. These guys have deep pockets.[75]

In Champagne, the presence of thousands of RAF airmen was another source of problems. More than 500 airplanes operated from Champagne airfields while 651 British lived in the village of Béthenville (717 inhabitants).[76] British soldiers spent their free time in the closest cities such as Châlons-en-Champagne and Reims. There, their inappropriate behaviour was badly perceived both by French civilians and soldiers.[77] French and British authorities tried to adopt common rules to improve the matter. On 26 September, French Lieutenant-Colonel Tapie, who worked with the AASF, sent a letter to the general commanding the 6th region to better understand local regulations in the area.[78] Asking questions about troops in the city of Reims, he also enquired about sexual matters. This problem was also explored by the GHQ of the BEF. Brownrigg wrote that 'the question of licensed brothels is one which requires the most delicate handling', before admitting that 'I'm afraid my hands are not delicate enough'.[79] Steps were taken to know more about brothels' opening hours and measures taken to fight underground prostitution as well as pornographic movies, which had 'nefarious effects' on 'young English officers who have a different education and are younger at the same age'.[80] Answering this query, General Cabotte explained that soldiers were allowed to visit brothels from 18.00 to 20.00 and that illegal prostitutes were frequently arrested. Moreover, pornographic movies had already been 'banned for a few days already'.[81] British and French officers strongly disagreed on the opening hours of drinking establishments. On 12 October, an officer of the 2nd Bureau of the EM of the 6th Region met two officers of the RAF Provost Company (Reims). The British 'did not see any reason for which NCO and soldiers should come home by 20.30'.[82] In Britain, they were allowed to come back at 23.00 and there was no evening call. In Reims, drinking places were closed at 20.00 and the evening call was organised at 20.30. During the meeting, it was agreed to keep drinking places open until 21.00 and delay the evening call until 22.00. However, the French EM refused these modifications.[83] On 16 December 1939, the EMG ruled that cafes and restaurants in the British sector could open until 21.30.[84] When French and British were together, they were forced to follow French rules. This decision, however, was not respected by the British in the 6th region.[85] The matter was complex. For example, airmen of the AASF did not belong to the BEF and were part of 'an independent force obeying only Air-Marshal Barratt (HQ-BAFF), who was not subordinate to the French command'. Coordination problems remained a fact of life during the whole Phoney War, despite various attempts to ease the situation. Several problems, such as illegal requisitions, military salutes, or relations with women, were never solved.[86]

In French bistros, local women were seen with British soldiers. The French saw them 'kissing in the street' with 'children aged 15 at most'.[87] They wrote about what they had seen:

> A friend travelled near Reims. He said that the English are behind the front and party with French women. It is revolting. There will be a fight when the poilus of this sector come back. The French are holding the lines but the English sleep in our beds.[88]

Rumours of French women cheating with British soldiers were amplified in various letters:[89]

> It is like in 14–18. While the French are at the front, the English are behind fucking our women. No shame. They even tattoo their breast when they sleep. It is said that such a drama occurred in Rennes.[90]

The topic of corrupted French women was used heavily by German propaganda, as we saw in the previous chapter.[91] French soldiers played a huge part in spreading such rumours. Nearly all problems occurred in the rear area of the front. This lack of visibility meant that the French were convinced they were doing more:

> I hope that we will see soon English soldiers elsewhere than on the great boulevards. They really should relieve us because we have been here too long.[92]

This situation had negative consequences on morale. The BEF realised that the lack of British troops near the French sector was detrimental. On 3 October 1939, the British Foreign Office's political intelligence department warned against this:

> The period of getting British troops into line with the French troops is a trying one for French public opinion. There is belief in France in the strength of the British blockade ... but it is the presence of the British troops in the line that is being eagerly awaited. And it is during this intermediate period while the British army is being lined up and got into position that it is felt that German propaganda could best work on French defeatist elements.[93]

The situation was different when British soldiers were on the frontline with the French. In the third army, British units were stationed next to French soldiers. In their letters, the French were positively impressed:

> The guys who are with me watch the sector, 400 metres from the Huns, with the English, because there is only one French regiment. We have no complaint, they give us as much tobacco and cigarettes as we want.[94]

> We have so much fun with the English lost in our sector. They are charming.[95]

> We are all on the frontline. We put in all our energy. The English reach the line. Many of them. We begin to admire them.[96]

> We have with us detachments of English aviation, artillery, etc. They are mostly very young, 24 or 25 years, but they have a lot of enthusiasm, which is good.[97]

The British were deemed as polite, courteous, real 'gentlemen'.[98] Seeing them was 'comforting'.[99] Having British soldiers on the frontline was also the best argument against Anglophobic propaganda and rumours:

> Here, we have English soldiers, who fight with a lot of courage. It is good to say it on the home front.[100]

> I have met the English. They are close to us. They are lovely. Hurrah to the entente cordiale![101]

> From time to time, we see convoys of English. No matter what the Hun radio says, English soldiers hold the 1st line.[102]

> The Tommies are going on the line. They are not only found in Paris or in the big cities of the rear.[103]

French soldiers' letters had a big impact on their families. Waiting for an offensive, both nations got to know each other. They spent Christmas together, went to the theatre, joked, organised football matches, a sport loved by both armies.[104] During the Phoney War, several tournaments took place. In April 1940, the CP stated that 'Franco-British football matches are always a success and contribute to the spirit of camaraderie between allied troops.'[105] After having played together, teams kept in touch. French aviators, having met a team made of British airmen, went to their barracks.[106] Longer-lasting friendship even developed:

> Give us news, what was your first impression of the line? If you come back to Saulny, tell me a few days in advance so we can organise a football match with your team, and a cordial handshake with French soldiers.[107]

French soldiers on the Franco-German line were in a different situation. British troops served on the Belgian frontier since October and others arrived in Moselle and Lorraine in December 1939.[108] However no British served in Alsace during the Phoney War, despite the recognition of how beneficial this would have been.[109] The absence of British soldiers was felt by soldiers of the 4th and 5th Armies on the German border. Unlike others, they did not meet them even when resting in bigger towns or cities. Many unfavourable stories were spread:

> When talking about army matters, such as the English, our pals are furious, having never met one since we reached the frontline. We have not seen them elsewhere. There must be only a handful of them at the rear. And they are well fed and earn 19 francs. They even have better clothes than us, as the lieutenant told us.[110]

The idea, shared by a few members of the EM and the government, that French soldiers were not really helped by the British was common:

> I can see that you are trying to make me feel better by saying that the English are coming with their material. I believe you, but I can tell you that there is not even one around here and I really would like to see them. Perhaps they would understand a bit better what it is like. They should not send 150.000 men but a million, such a power is not acceptable. They have plenty of pounds, which makes French restaurants happy, but not us.[111]

These negative remarks must be put in perspective. They were not common among soldiers and did not represent a wave of Anglophobia or deep anti-British feelings.[112] We must remember, when reading letters like the one reproduced above, that the soldier was answering his mother. She had probably told him about the massive arrival of allied troops and material. This information was found in the French media as journalists were doing their best to provide a positive picture of the Franco-British alliance. A strong British army and a perfect harmony between armies often featured in the French newspapers during the Phoney War. Not a single day passed without the media celebrating their ally and the positive atmosphere between armies. The biggest selling newspapers, the

Petit Parisien (about 1 million copies sold) and *Paris-Soir* (2,5 million in April 1940) were entirely devoted to the Entente Cordiale.[113] They followed guidelines given by the CGI on how to portray the alliance favourably.[114] Articles tried to counteract anti-British propaganda from Germany, the Communist Party or left- and right-wing defeatists.[115]

The most frequent topics were the arrival of the BEF, the work done by the British in the military zone, aerial or naval warfare, and the visit of British leaders or personalities to the frontline. In September 1939, newsreels showed the arrival of British troops, 'led to the frontline and given to the authority of the French High Command'.[116] They were seen landing on French beaches with 'absolute order', carrying 'a lot of supplies'.[117] On the screen, long columns of British soldiers, cars and trucks, were shown. British soldiers were portrayed as disciplined, friendly young men.[118] This campaign of propaganda gave the feeling that the British expeditionary corps was enormous. As we have seen, this was to have negative consequences for how the French imagined the British presence.

At the end of October 1939, a meeting with General Gamelin and General Lord Gort was filmed. The commentator talked about 'great cordiality and a perfect understanding' between leaders.[119] George VI's visit to the Maginot Line, with his brother the Duke of Gloucester, on 5–7 December 1939 was also used by the political world and the media.[120] He was also filmed when meeting Gamelin, Daladier and the French President of the Republic Lebrun. This visit was instrumentalised by the French media to show the support of the British Empire, the 'biggest empire in the world'.[121] Other visits of British dignitaries, such as Chamberlain, the Duke of Windsor, the brother of the King, etc., were reported with enthusiasm.[122] In newsreels, many references to the First World War were made to show the continuity and the links uniting both countries.[123] On 11–12 November 1939, a big 'day of Franco-British solidarity' was organised to commemorate the end of the First World War.[124]

The CGI also launched a poster campaign in the streets of Paris.[125] The respective floral symbols of remembrance, British poppies and French *Bleuets* (cornflowers) were sold together. During the Phoney War, many Franco-British links were created and advertised by the press: calls for help, trade unions, etc.[126] The BBC equally broadcast French shows.[127] This propaganda campaign worked with civilians but had adverse effects in sectors of the front where the British were absent:

> I have not seen a single English. At the beginning, we saw a few of their planes, but now: NO-THING, done. However, all the newspapers are full of their exploits. The English at the front here, the glorious British allies fighting there. But where? On the côte d'Azur, the Jura or the North? Where there are blows to be given, not a single one of them. They could relieve us.[128]

> We have not seen an Englishman. They must be in Marseille or London. The pictures of 'Match' and company are just bluff.[129]

— Aoh !... Well !!...
quand je sors... moi, demander à
John, pourquoi « ATTENTION ».!!!

Figure 5.2 Caricature of a British soldier[135]

The portrayal of the British in the press was so far away from reality that soldiers compared it to First World War *bourrage de crâne*. In frontline newspapers, French soldiers made fun of their ally. In those designed by units serving on the front of Lorraine, unflattering 'English stories' were written. A joke explained:

An Englishman travels in a railway compartment. His suitcases occupy most nets. One of his bags is not closed properly, probably, because a few drops of

a golden liquid fall from it and land on another [French] traveller. This traveller, believing that a bottle has broken, tastes a drop.
– 'Whisky?' he says, while looking at the Englishman.
– 'No', said the Englishman, 'Fox-Terrier'.[130]

In this story, most French clichés are reproduced: a well-equipped soldier drinking Whisky, a beverage often mocked.[131] As can be seen in the above-mentioned joke, the French were equally keen to mock their own country.[132] Articles, caricatures and jokes give several clues about the relationship between allies. In the newspaper *L'Isard de Metz*, a two-part article published in January 1940 told the story of a Franco-British relief. The author began by stating that he had been 'surprised' to be relieved by the British.[133] He also explained, not without humour, that it was difficult to communicate. British troops were described as well-dressed and 'a bunch of guys with good equipment, comfy and rainproof, all very jolly, although a bit impressed to be so close to the "Germans"' [in English in the original text].[134] The same article remembered amusing situations, including stories about the British becoming familiarised with the French line. A corner was filled with empty cans and other tools near the shooting position and called the *piège à cons*. Despite being asked to keep quiet, a British soldier fell in the pile of cans during the night, causing great uproar and a 'furious need to laugh' among the French. In this story, the author of the article made a caricature in which the British soldier did not look at his best.

Stories published in frontline newspapers about the British were closer to the reality of war than what the French media produced. Most talked about daily difficulties or interesting anecdotes and offered a more balanced picture of the alliance. However, it should be remembered that frontline newspapers were censored, meaning that writers were not entirely free to express their doubts. As such, humour was the best way to express frustrations and describe problems.

Conclusion

French interactions with the British army cannot be reduced to a single attitude. During the Phoney War, relations between allies were influenced by factors such as unit locations, social levels or political opinions. Fighting next to the British on the frontline was the best guarantee of positive views. By contrast, meeting behind the lines in bars or restaurants made salary differences obvious and brought jealous reactions. French soldiers serving on the German border were rarely exposed to the British army, a fact triggering rancour. German propaganda, recognising this, used different arguments to tarnish the British. On the home front, the French media launched a campaign of communication to shed a positive light on the British. French soldiers, far from convinced by the press, used their own newspapers to denounce daily problems.

The British arrival in September caused several coordination and cohabitation issues. This problem, resolved at the end of 1939, was replaced by the British army's lack of visibility. However, there was never a wave of Anglophobia at the front. The lack of British soldiers or material was denounced mostly by the far-right. The situation changed in June 1940, when men like Pétain or Weygand came to power. Faced with the British retreat in Belgium, the Battle of Sedan, and the Dunkirk evacuation, anti-British feelings became prominent. The French public felt betrayed by their ally after Dunkirk. On 20 June 1940, a brutal campaign of Anglophobia began in the French press, peaking after the Mers-El-Kébir incident.

Notes

1 Jean-Baptiste Duroselle, *Histoire diplomatique de 1919 à nos jours* (Paris, 1997), pp. 239–241.
2 Colloque franco-britannique (ed.), Les relations franco-britanniques de 1935 à 1939: communications présentées aux colloques franco-britanniques tenus à Londres (Imperial War Museum) du 18 au 21 octobre 1971, Paris (Comité d'histoire de la Deuxième Guerre mondiale) du 25 au 29 septembre 1972 (Paris, 1975).
3 Edward Smalley, *British Expeditionary Force, 1939–40* (New York, 2015), p. 17.
4 Ibid., p. 19.
5 Major L. F. Ellis, *War In France And Flanders 1939–1940: History Of The Second World War*, ed. by J. R. M. Butler (London, 2009).
6 Jean-Louis Crémieux-Brilhac, 'L'opinion publique française, l'Angleterre et la Guerre (Septembre 1939-Juin 1940)', in: Comité international d'histoire de la Deuxième Guerre mondiale (ed.), *Français et Britanniques dans la drôle de guerre: actes du colloque franco-britannique tenu à Paris du 8 au 12 décembre 1975* (Paris, 1979), pp. 1–49, p. 28.
7 Smalley, *British Expeditionary Force, 1939–40)*, p. 17; Max Schiavon, 'Les relations entre hauts commandements français et britannique en 1939–1940', *Revue historique des armées*, 264 (2011), pp. 59–74, p. 61.
8 Smalley, *British Expeditionary Force, 1939–40*, p. 17; Cochet, *Les soldats français*, p. 57.
9 Smalley, *British Expeditionary Force, 1939–40*, p. 18.
10 Ibid.
11 SHD AT: 30 N 180. Journal de marche du général Fagalde, 2 Novembre 1939, p. 9, quoted in: Schiavon, 'Les relations entre hauts commandements français et britannique en 1939–1940', p. 62.
12 Ibid., p. 63.
13 Watt Donald Cameron, 'Le moral de l'armée française tel que se le représentaient les Britanniques en 1939 et 1940: Une faillite des services de renseignement ?', in: Comité international d'histoire de la Deuxième Guerre mondiale (ed.), *Français et Britanniques dans la drôle de guerre* (Paris, 1979), pp. 197–211, p. 206.
14 Schiavon, 'Les relations entre hauts commandements français et britannique', p. 62.
15 Ibid.
16 François Bédarida, *La Stratégie Secrète de La Drôle de Guerre: Le Conseil Suprême Interallié; Sept. 1939 à Avril 1940* (Paris, 1979), p. 149.
17 Martin Alexander, '"Fighting to the Last Frenchman"? Reflections on the BEF Deployment to France and the Strains in the Franco-British Alliance, 1939–40', *Historical Reflections/Réflexions Historiques*, 22 (1996) 1, p. 250.
18 Ibid., p. 262.
19 Ibid.

20 Simmonet Stéphane, Prime Christophe and Claire Levasseur, *Atlas de la Seconde Guerre mondiale: La France au combat: de la drôle de guerre à la Libération* (Paris, 2015), p. 14.
21 Second Dispatch, Commander-in-chief Gort, 1941, in: John Grehan and Martin Mace, *The BEF in France 1939–1940: Manning the Front Through to the Dunkirk Evacuation* (Pen and Sword, 2014), p. 23
22 ECPAD. Le corps expéditionnaire britannique (BEF, British Expeditionary Force) en France, septembre 1939 –mai 1940, http://archives.ecpad.fr/wp-content/uploads/2013/03/Dossier-La-BEF.pdf [accessed 13 April 2018]. For a list, see: Ellis, *War In France And Flanders 1939–1940* (London, 2009).
23 Cochet, *Les soldats français de la drôle de guerre*, p. 57.
24 First Dispatch, Covering the period from 3rd September to 31st January, 1940, Comander-in-Chief Lord Gort, 25.04.1940, in: John Grehan and Martin Mace, *The BEF in France 1939–1940: Manning the Front Through to the Dunkirk Evacuation* (Barnsley, 2014), p. 5.
25 Schiavon, 'Les relations entre hauts commandements français et britannique en 1939–1940', p. 62.
26 Peter Masefield, 'La Royal Air Force et la production d'avions de guerre en Grande-Bretagne, 1934–1940', in: Comité international d'histoire de la Deuxième Guerre mondiale, *Français et Britanniques dans la drôle de guerre* (Paris, 1979), pp. 411–456, p. 426.
27 First Dispatch, Covering the period from 3rd September to 31st January, 1940, Commander-in-Chief Lord Gort, 25.04.1940, in: John Grehan and Martin Mace, *The BEF in France 1939–1940: Manning the Front Through to the Dunkirk Evacuation* (Barnsley, 2014), p. 10.
28 Ibid.
29 Haslam E.B., 'La préparation à la guerre: Étude de quelques éléments de l'efficacité opérationnelle des forces aériennes sur le front du Nord-Est', in: Comité international d'histoire de la Deuxième Guerre mondiale (ed.), *Français et Britanniques dans la drôle de guerre. actes du colloque franco-britannique tenu à Paris du 8 au 12 décembre 1975* (Paris, 1979), pp. 517–528, p. 523.
30 First Dispatch, in: Grehan and Mace, *The BEF in France 1939–1940*, p.10.
31 Masefield, 'La Royal Air Force et la production d'avions de guerre en Grande-Bretagne', p. 428.
32 Ibid., p. 428.
33 Haslam, 'La préparation à la guerre', p. 523.
34 Ibid.
35 Masefield, 'La Royal Air Force et la production d'avions de guerre en Grande-Bretagne', p. 428.
36 Haslam, 'La préparation à la guerre', p. 524.
37 Ibid., p. 429.
38 Haslam, 'La préparation à la guerre', p. 523.
39 Second Dispatch, Covering the period from 1st February, 1940, to 30st May, 1940, with an Appendix covering operations of the 1st Corps from 6 p.m. 31st May, to midnight 2nd/3rd June), 25.07.1940, in: John Grehan and Martin Mace, *The BEF in France 1939–1940: Manning the Front Through to the Dunkirk Evacuation* (Barnsley, 2014), p. 26.
40 Haslam, 'La préparation à la guerre', p. 523.
41 First Dispatch, in: Grehan and Mace, *The BEF in France 1939–1940*, p. 10.
42 Haslam, 'La préparation à la guerre', p. 521; p. 525.
43 Second Dispatch, in: Grehan and Mace, *The BEF in France 1939–1940*, p.27.
44 Based on: British positions on 9th May 1940, in: Major L. F. Ellis, *War In France And Flanders 1939-1940: History Of The Second World War*, ed. by J. R. M. Butler

(London, 2009), https://www.ibiblio.org/hyperwar/UN/UK/UK-NWE-Flanders/maps/UK-NWE-Flanders-1.jpg [accessed 30 April 2018].

45 Crémieux-Brilhac, 'L'opinion publique française', p. 23.
46 Henri Michel, *La drôle de guerre* (Paris, 1971), p. 188.
47 Crémieux-Brilhac, 'L'opinion publique française', p. 23.
48 Anne-Laure Anizan, '1914–1918, le gouvernement de guerre', *Histoire@Politique*, 22 (2014) 1, pp. 215–232; J. William Philpott, 'The Benefit of Exeprience? The Supreme War Council and the Higher Management of Coalition War, 1939–1940', in: Martin Alexander and William Philpott (eds), *Anglo-French Defence Relations Between the Wars* (London, 2002), pp. 209–226.
49 Christian Cavan, 'Le Commandement Interarmés franco-britanniques en 1939–1940', *Guerres Mondiales et Conflits Contemporains*, 1992, pp. 59–69, p. 61.
50 François Bédarida, 'La rupture franco-britannique de 1940. Le conseil suprême interallié, de l'invasion à la défaite de la France', *Vingtième Siècle. Revue d'histoire*, 25 (1990) 1, pp. 37–48, p. 37 and François Bédarida, *La stratégie secrète de la drôle de guerre: Le conseil suprême interallié; Sept. 1939 à avril 1940* (Paris, 1979).
51 Ibid.; CEl W.B.R. Neave-Hill, 'L'évolution de la stratégie franco-anglaise (1939–1940)', in: Comité international d'histoire de la Deuxième Guerre mondiale (ed.), *Français et Britanniques dans la drôle de guerre* (Paris, 1979), pp. 333–359.
52 Crémieux-Brilhac, 'L'opinion publique française', p. 29.
53 Ibid.
54 Ibid.
55 Ibid., pp. 18–19.
56 Ibid.
57 Haslam, 'La préparation à la guerre', p. 523; SHD: AT: 31 N 77; Watt, 'Le moral de l'armée française', p. 206.
58 SHD AT: 27N69. 405th Pionniers, 5th Army, 16 November 1939.
59 SHD AT: 27N69. 3rd Army, 9 December 1939.
60 SHD AT: 27N69. 16 December 1939.
61 SHD AT: 27N69. 3rd Army, 17 October 1939.
62 In November 1939, 10 francs were given to frontline soldiers. Crémieux-Brilhac, 'L'opinion publique française', p. 30.
63 SHD AT: 27N69. Soldier 42°DI, 3rd Army, 16.12.1939.
64 SHD AT: 27N69. 1st DIM, 1st Army, 6 January 1940.
65 SHD AT: 27N69. 19 October 1939.
66 SHD AT: 31N77. Daily report, 10 October 1939.
67 Crémieux-Brilhac, 'L'opinion publique francaise', p. 31.
68 Ibid., p. 32.
69 National Archives London (NA): CAB 63–144. Perth, to Ministry of information, 3 January 1940.
70 NA: CAB 63–144. WDS Brownrigg, AG BEF, A, Relations between British and French, 3 December 1939.
71 See chapter 2.
72 Edward Smalley, In the Courts or Off the Record: Discipline in the British Expeditionary Force, September 1939–June 1940, *University of Sussex Journal of Contemporary History*, 16 (2015), pp. 75–91, p. 83.
73 Ibid.
74 SHD AT: 27N69. 163rd Rgt Infanterie de forteresse, 3rd Army, 9 December 1939.
75 SHD AT: 27N69. Soldier, IDIC, 3rd Army, 2 January 1940.
76 Cochet, *Les soldats français de la drôle de guerre*, p. 59.
77 SHD AT: 31N77. Lt.-Colonel Tapie, 6 October 1930; Cochet, *Les soldats français de la drôle de guerre*, p. 59.
78 SHD AT: 31N77. Lt.-Colonel Tapie, 26 September 1939.

79 NA: CAB 63-144. WDS Brownrigg, A branch GHQ 1st Echelon, BEF, 15 December 1939.
80 SHD AT: 31N77. Lt.-Colonel Tapie, 26 September 1939.
81 SHD AT: 31N77. General Cabotte to Lt.-Colonel Tapie, 30 September 1939.
82 SHD AT: 31N77. 2nd Bureau, 13 October 1939.
83 SHD AT: 31N77. Chief of 2nd Bureau, 13 October 1939.
84 SHD AT: 31N77. GQG, EM, report about British troops, 16 December 1939.
85 SHD AT: 31N77. General Foise to Lt.-Colonel Tapie, 10 February 1940.
86 SHD AT: 31N77. Crémieux-Brilhac, 'L'opinion publique française', p. 34.
87 SHD AT: 27N69. A soldier of the 306th RI, 56th DI, 3rd Army, 9 February 1940.
88 SHD AT: 27N69. 136th RI zone Chiers Meuse, 2nd Army, 24 November 1939.
89 SHD AT: 27N69. 171st Bat. de Génie Réserve Générale, 9th Army, 16 December 1939.
90 SHD AT: 27N69. 207ª RALD, 20° DI, 2nd Army, 21.12.1939.
91 See chapter 3, leaflet 'Où le Tommy est-il ?'.
92 SHD AT: 27N69. 19 October 1939.
93 Foreign Office Weekly Political Intelligence Summaries, Vol. I, no. 1 (3 Oct. 1939), p. 4, quoted in: Martin S. Alexander, '"Fighting to the Last Frenchman"? Reflections on the BEF Deployment to France and the Strains in the Franco-British Alliance, 1939–40', in: *Historical Reflections/Réflexions Historiques*, 22 (1996) 1, pp. 235–262, p. 257.
94 SHD AT: 27N69. 306th RAP, RF Metz, 3rd Army, 21 February 1940.
95 SHD AT: 27N69. 4th hussards, 3rd DC, 2nd Army, 28 November 1939.
96 SHD AT: 27N69. 408th DCA-E0, 3rd Army, 16 December 1939.
97 SHD AT: 27N69. Soldier of the 32nd DI, 3rd Army, 24 November 1939.
98 SHD AT: 27N69. 221st Radio, SF Metz, 3rd Army, 21 February 1940.
99 SHD AT: 27N69. 3rd Army, 2 March 1940.
100 SHD AT: 27N69. 132nd RP, RF Metz, 3rd Army, 21 February 1940.
101 SHD AT: 27N69. 164th RIF, 3rd Army, 15 January 1940.
102 SHD AT: 27N69. 30th B., 3rd Army, 10 January 1940.
103 SHD AT: 27N69. SF of Boulay, 3rd Army, 16 December 1939.
104 SHD AT: 27N69. Officer BCG, QG, 3rd Army, 11 March 1940; 1st DIM, 7th Army, 15 April 1940 and 221st Génie -RIF Metz, 3rd Army, 6 January 1940.
105 SHD AT: 27N69. 12 April 1940.
106 SHD AT: 27N69. Soldier Air 2/22, FA, 3rd Army, 11 March 1940.
107 SHD AT: 27N69. A soldier about a British soldier 402nd DEA, 3rd Army, 29 January 1940.
108 ADBR: 98AL653. IEE, British soldiers in Alsace, 21 December 1939.
109 Ibid.
110 SHD AT: 27N69. 187th Rt. Heavy artillery, 5th Army, 20 November 1939.
111 SHD AT: 27N69. 19 October 1939.
112 Crémieux-Brilhac, 'L'opinion publique française', p. 44.
113 Ibid., p. 10.
114 BDIC, 4 delta res 0057.
115 Crémieux-Brilhac, 'L'opinion publique française', pp. 15–16.
116 Archives Pathé-Gaumont (APG): PJ 1939 516 13. Journal-Actualité, 27 September 1939.
117 APG: 3942GJ 00013. Journal-Actualité, 19 October 1939.
118 APG: PJ 1939 529 9. Journal-Actualité, 27 December 1939.
119 APG: 3943GJ 00015. Journal Gaumont, 26 October 1939.
120 *Le Populaire*, 5 December 1939; *Le Petit Parisien*, 5 December 1939; *Le Matin*, 5 December 1939; APG: PJ 1939 527 8. Journal-Actualité, 13 December 1939.
121 APG: 3950EJ 31406. Gaumont (Journal Éclair), 14 December 1939.

122 APG: PJ 1939 529 7. Pathé, Journal-Actualité, 27 December 1939; APG: 4004EJ
　　31572. Gaumont, Journal Éclair, 25 January 1940.
123 APG: PJ 1940 539 9. Journal-Actualité, 7 March 1940.
124 APG: PJ 1939 521 10. Journal-Actualité, 1 November 1939.
125 Poster « journée franco-britannique », 11–12 November 1939. http://gallica.bnf.fr/
　　ark:/12148/btv1b9013939g.item [accessed 17 April 2018].
126 Crémieux-Brilhac, 'L'opinion publique française', p. 20.
127 Ibid., p. 26.
128 SHD AT: 27N69. 309th Rt. artillery, 5th Army, 20 November 1939.
129 SHD AT: 27N69. 152nd RI, 14th DI, 4th Army, 2 February 1940.
130 *Cambronne*, January 1940.
131 *Cambronne*, April 1940. *Le pied lourd*, 21 January 1940.
132 *Coup de Bambi* (3ᵉ Bat 156 RIF), January 1940.
133 *L'isard de Metz*, 15 January 1940.
134 Ibid.
135 Ibid.

Epilogue

The Phoney War ended on 10 May 1940 when Hitler launched *Fall Gelb* (Case Yellow).[1] The German strategy was to surround the Allies and advance to the Channel coast. To execute this plan, Hitler's men needed to go through the Ardennes, considered as impenetrable, before reaching the Meuse and the Channel, trapping in the process Allied troops engaged in the area. A diversion in the Netherlands and Belgium was designed to attract Allied armies towards the North. The next step of the offensive was called *Fall Rot* (Case Red) and was conceived to turn the Allied armies stationed on the Maginot Line down to Switzerland. This successful plan led to the defeat of France and the armistice of 22 June 1940.

On 10 May, the Netherlands, Belgium and Luxemburg were invaded simultaneously by the Wehrmacht.[2] Gamelin launched the Dyle-Bréda plan. The 1st Army Group of General Billotte and the BEF moved toward Belgium but the Belgian Army was unable to last long enough to let the Franco-British troops reach their planned positions. Three days later, General Guderian and his panzers of the 19th Army Corps crossed the River Meuse near Sedan. They exploited this breach to race towards the Channel and successfully split Allied forces. On 16 May, the day the Dutch army surrendered, Gamelin ordered a retreat. Counter-assaults against German tanks were unable to slow the enemy. On 19 May, Rommel took Cambrai with the 7th Tank Division while Guderian reached Abbeville and set off in the direction of Boulogne-sur-Mer on 20 May. General Weygand, who had replaced Gamelin on 19 May, tried to stabilise the front on the Somme and on the canals of Crozat and Ailette. Despite ferocious allied counter-assaults, the troops broke, leaving 500,000 allied soldiers trapped in the city of Dunkirk.[3] The French wanted to launch an offensive to free them but the British launched Operation Dynamo to evacuate their troops.[4] In total, 235,000 British, 115,000 French and 16,000 Belgians escaped under artillery and aviation fire from Dunkirk.[5]

Before the end of the evacuation on 4 June, German troops went south to complete Operation *Fall Rot*. Weygand reorganised the defence of the French army to avoid a linear line.[6] Violent fighting was not enough to make up for the inequality between German and Allied forces (104 German Divisions against 66 Allied Divisions, including 2 from Britain).[7] In nine days, Paris was declared an open city and occupied. Once they crossed the River Seine, Guderian's men went towards the Swiss border.[8] The 2nd, 4th and 6th Armies tried to retreat toward Besançon but were crushed while the 3rd, 5th and 8th Armies were surrounded in the region of Épinal and Saint-Dié.[9]

The Germans also took Cherbourg and Brest and captured the cities along the Loire, the Saône and the Rhône. Langres and Dijon were taken on 15 and 16 June. On 10 June, Italy joined the war against France. 300,000 Italians fought against 85,000 French but were kept at bay by General Olry. The only notable Italian success was in the region of Menton but elsewhere, Mussolini's army was pushed back.

Facing the German assault, the French Government left the capital on 10 June for the south, first reaching Tours, before settling for Bordeaux on 14 June. Two days later, Reynaud, the *Président du Conseil*, resigned. Marshal Pétain, who enjoyed great popularity, formed a new cabinet. On 17 June, Spanish diplomats forwarded German and Italian armistice conditions. On 22 June, the armistice was signed at Rethondes, in the very same wagon used 22 years before to end the First World War. Two days later, another treaty was signed with Italy. On 25 June, the armistice took effect.

In less than two months, three-fifths of the French territory was occupied by German forces. About 55,000 to 65,000 French soldiers were killed, 123,000 wounded and 1,850,000 captured. The German army lost 63,7000 men, 110,000 were wounded and 18,000 went missing in action. 60,000 Allied soldiers (from Britain, the Netherlands, Belgium and Poland) were either killed or wounded.[10]

Notes

1 Karl-Heinz Frieser, *The Blitzkrieg Legend: The 1940 Campaign in the West* (Annapolis, 2013).
2 Stéphane Simmonet, Christophe Prime, Claire Levasseur, *Atlas de la Seconde Guerre mondiale: La France au combat: de la drôle de guerre à la Libération* (Paris, 2015), p. 14.
3 Ibid.
4 Frieser, *The Blitzkrieg Legend*, p. 347.
5 Simmonet, Prime, Levasseur, *Atlas de la Seconde Guerre mondiale*, p. 14. Other figures were given in : Jean Quellien, Françoise Passera, Jean-Luc Leleu, and Michel Daeffler (eds), *La France pendant la Seconde Guerre mondiale: Atlas historique* (Paris, 2010), p. 41.
6 Quellien, Passera, Leleu, Daeffler (eds), *La France pendant la Seconde Guerre mondiale*, p. 42.
7 Ibid., p. 42.
8 Ibid.
9 Simmonet, Prime, Levasseur, *Atlas de la Seconde Guerre mondiale*, p. 18.
10 Ibid., p. 21.

Conclusion

This book has aimed to suggest that nuance is required when trying to understand French morale during the Phoney War. The experience of fighting for France in 1939–1940 cannot be summarised easily as life on the frontline varied greatly. Men in forward bases were exposed to the weather, those manning the Maginot Line suffered from the lack of sunlight. Soldiers stationed further away from the frontline were better off but still found it hard to live far away from home and relatives. Bored and ill-equipped, all soldiers felt at odds with this strange conflict. The growing urbanisation of France after the First World War did not help. Parisian intellectuals were far more likely to dislike digging a trench than experienced rural men.

This study divided soldiers' morale into three different phases. The first, during which the French Army showed confidence, matched the mobilisation period and the early stage of the war. During the winter phase, the French military was burdened by climatic conditions and the lack of action. The last phase saw morale improving greatly, helped by warmer weather and the hope of launching a major offensive to defeat the German Army.

Military authorities and the French Government were far from passive during the Phoney War. Indeed, morale was closely monitored to make sure that the Army was ready for combat. Two broad strategies were designed to safeguard the fighting spirit: work and entertainment. Ordering soldiers to do farm work or build new fortifications proved detrimental as they complained bitterly. Sport, movies, newspapers, and various other forms of entertainment, were far more effective. Several primary sources showed that soldiers' morale improved greatly after having enjoyed various activities organised by the authorities.

France also led a war of propaganda against German and communist psychological warfare. The Communist Party, banned after the Molotov-Ribbentrop pact and the invasion of Poland, was perceived by the military as a major threat. In fact, communist propaganda failed to convince most men. The German war of words was a much bigger danger. Enemy psychological warfare was very active on the frontline. A specialised propaganda company used radio broadcasts, posters, loudspeakers, and various other means, to demoralise French soldiers. Their Anglophobic campaign asking for immediate peace was countered by French propaganda. It is clear that French soldiers were intrigued by the German war of words but they rarely fell for it.

Anglophobia was present in various parts of the front but did not represent the mainstream feeling. Moreover, this book argued that anti-British arguments were predominantly located in places where the BEF was not present. As soon as September 1939, the BEF and the RAF came to France. French soldiers living on the frontline with the British saw them as good friends with whom they could play football or share drink. Those who saw the British further away from the frontline, in cities for example, were more inclined to feel jealous about their higher salary or their popularity with women. French soldiers were far more likely to dislike the British if they did not serve alongside the BEF. As such, Maginot Line men and forward post soldiers posted on the Franco-German border were more inclined to believe German propaganda.

There is still a lot of work to do to understand the French Army in 1939–1940 but this book hopes to demonstrate that morale was far from catastrophic. Future historians, when trying to understand the reasons for the 1940 defeat, will have to look for other explanations than German propaganda, communism or a lack of spirit on the frontline. There is no doubt that French soldiers were determined to fight the Germans to secure peace for future generations.

Bibliography

Primary sources

Archives

National Archives London (NA)

CAB 63-144

Bibliothèque Documentaire Internationale Contemporaine (BDIC)

4 res 0057, Bulletin n°9, 16.12.1939.

Bundesarchiv-Militärarchiv Freiburg im Breisgau (BArch-MA)

RW4/185
RW4/241
RW4/242
RW4/243
RW4/244
RW4/261
RW4/284
RW4/312a
RH19/III/377
RH/26-246

Bundesarchiv Koblenz (BArch Koblenz)

ee186, Bild 146-1971-080-26, Flugblattpropaganda

Politisches Archiv des Auswärtigen Amts, Berlin (PAAA)

R 67492–67494

Archives nationales Paris (AN)

72AJ582
72AJ580
F41/14–15

F41/19–20
F41/21–22
F41/980
F41/979
F41/991
F43/95
2W68
566Mi/1

Archives départementales du Bas-Rhin (ADBR)

98AL283
98AL490
98AL635
98AL649
98AL450
98AL651
98AL653

Archives Gaumont-Pathé (AGP)

Journal-Actualité Pathé
PJ 1940 538, 29 February 1940
PJ 1939 517, 29 September 1939
PJ 1939 518, 12 October 1939
PJ 1939 516 13, 27 September 1939
PJ 1939 529 9, 27 December 1939
PJ 1939 527 8, 13 December 1939
PJ 1939 529 7, 27 December 1939
PJ 1940 539 9, 7 March 1940
PJ 1939 521 10, 1 November 1939

Gaumont-Journal

3942GJ00013, 19 October 1939
3943GJ00015, 26 October 1939
3950EJ31406, 14 December 1939
3952GJ00017, 28 December 1939
4004EJ31572, 25 January 1940
4008EJ31725, 22 February 1940

Service Historique de la Défense – Armée de Terre (SHD AT)

2N224
7N2486
27N65
27N67
27N68
27N69
27N178
28N13
28N52

29N130
29N290
29N198
29N259
29N269
29N318
30N39
30N59
31N77
31N102

Établissement de Communication et de Production Audiovisuelle de la Défense (ECPAD)

Journal de guerre, n. 5, week of 20 October 1939, http://www.ecpad.fr/journal-de-guerre-5-semaine-du-20-octobre-1939/ [accessed 18 April 2017]
Journal de Guerre, n. 7, week of 11 November 1939, http://www.ecpad.fr/journal-de-guerre-7-semaine-du-11-novembre-1939/ [accessed 5 January 2018]
Journal de guerre, n. 10, 29 November 1939.
http://www.ecpad.fr/journal-de-guerre-10-semaine-du-29-novembre-1939/ [accessed 12 November 2017]
Journal de Guerre, n. 14, week of 6 January 1940, http://www.ecpad.fr/journal-de-guerre-14-semaine-du-6-janvier-1940/ [accessed 17 April 2017]

Archives épiscopales de Strasbourg (AES)

Guerre 1939–40. 22nd RIF, 1st CEO, Hochwald, 18 September 1939.

Newspapers

Le Petit Parisien
Le Matin
L'Époque
Le Petit Journal
Le Temps
Le Populaire
Gringoire
Le Figaro
Paris-Soir
L'œuvre
Le Miroir
L'Illustration
Journal officiel de la République Française (JORF)
Strasbourg en Périgord

Frontline newspapers

Terre à cheval
Et avec ça ?
L'Hirondelle
La cage à douille
La nation
Le poilu du 6-9

Le poilu lorrain
Le réveil de Beauséjour
Lorraine Gironde
Secteur postal
Cambronne
Coup de Bambi
CQ
Hausse 400
Je passe partout
L'Isard de Metz
La rose Maginot
La voix de la voir de 60
Le cheval Vapeur
Le chic à Nied
Le cri du béton
Le pied lourd
Rouge vert
L'Humanité
L'Humanité du Soldat

Posters

« journée franco-britannique », 11–12 November 1939. http://gallica.bnf.fr/ark:/12148/btv1b9013939g.item [accessed 17 April 2018].

Secondary sources

Alary, Eric, L'exode (Paris, 2010).
Alexander, Martin S., '"Fighting to the Last Frenchman"? Reflections on the BEF Deployment to France and the Strains in the Franco-British Alliance, 1939–40', Historical Reflections/Réflexions Historiques, 22.1 (1996), pp. 235–262.
Amouroux, Henri, Le peuple du désastre, 1939–1940 (Paris, 1976).
Anizan, Anne-Laure, '1914–1918, le gouvernement de guerre', Histoire@Politique, 22 (2014) 1, pp. 215–232.
Anselmini, François, 'Alfred Cortot et la mobilisation des musiciens français pendant la Première Guerre mondiale', Vingtième Siècle. Revue d'histoire, 118 (2013), pp. 147–157.
Audoin-Rouzeau, Stéphane, 'Les soldats français et la Nation de 1914 à 1918 d'après les journaux de tranchées', Revue d'Histoire Moderne & Contemporaine, 34 (1987) 1, pp. 66–86.
Balfour, Michael, Propaganda in War, 1939-45: Organisations, Policies and Publics in Britain and Germany (London; Boston, 1979).
Baudelaire, Charles, Les Fleurs du mal (Paris, 1857).
Beauvoir, Simone de, La force de l'âge (Paris, 2000).
Becker, Jean-Jacques, 1914: Comment les Français sont entrés dans la guerre, contribution à l'étude de l'opinion publique, printemps-été 1914 (Paris, 1977).
Bédarida, François, La stratégie secrète de la Drôle de Guerre: Le Conseil Suprême Interallié; Sept. 1939 à avril 1940 (Paris, 1979).
Bédarida, François, 'La rupture franco-britannique de 1940. Le conseil suprême interallié, de l'invasion à la défaite de la France', Vingtième Siècle. Revue d'histoire, 25 (1990) 1, pp. 37–48.
Berstein, Serge and Pierre Milza, Histoire de la France au XXe siècle, Vol. 2, 1930–1958 (Paris, 2009).
Bertaux, Pierre, Mémoires interrompus (Asnières, 2000).

Blazy, Olivier, 'La presse militaire française à destination des troupes indigènes issues des différents territoires de l'Empire puis de l'Union française', Revue historique des armées, 271, (2013), pp. 51–59.

Boelcke, Willi A., Wollt ihr den totalen Krieg?: Die Geheimen Goebbels-Konferenzen 1939–1943 (Stuttgart, 1967).

Boniface, Xavier, 'Au service de la nation et de l'armée: Les aumôniers militaires français de 1914 à 1962', Guerres Mondiales et Conflits Contemporains, 187 (1997), pp. 103–113.

Boniface, Xavier, 'Les aumôniers militaires', in: Robert Vandenbussche (ed.), De Georges Clemenceau à Jacques Chirac: L'état et la pratique de la loi de Séparation (Lille, 2012), pp. 131–147.

Boswell, Laird, 'Fissures Dans La Nation Française: Les réfugiés alsaciens et lorrains En 1939–1940', in: Max Lagarrigue (ed.), 1940. La France du repli, l'Europe de la défaite (Toulouse, 2001), pp. 197–208.

Boterf, Hervé, Le Théâtre en uniforme: le spectacle aux armées, de la drôle de guerre aux accords d'Évian (Paris, 1973).

Brooks, Tim, British Propaganda to France, 1940–1944: Machinery, Method and Message, (Edinburgh, 2007).

Bruge, Roger, Faites sauter la ligne Maginot! (Paris, 1975).

Buchbender, Ortwin and Reinhard Hauschild, Geheimsender gegen Frankreich: Die Täuschungsoperation Radio Humanité 1940 (Herford, 1984)

Cabanes, Bruno and Édouard Husson, Les sociétés en guerre: 1911–1946 (Paris, 2003).

Cavan Christian, 'Le commandement interarmés franco-britannique en 1939–1940', Guerres Mondiales et Conflits Contemporains, 168 (1992), pp. 59–69.

Challéat, Violaine, 'Le cinéma au Service de la défense, 1915–2008', Revue Historique des Armées, 252 (2008), pp. 3–15.

Charpentier, Pierre-Frédéric, La drôle de guerre des intellectuels français (Lavauzelle, 2008).

Cochet, François, Première Guerre mondiale: dates, thèmes, noms (Quétigny, 2001).

Cochet, François, Les soldats de la drôle de guerre (Paris, 2004).

Cochet François, '1914–1918: L'alcool aux armées. Représentations et essai de typologie', Guerres Mondiales et Conflits Contemporains, 222 (2006) 2, pp. 19–32

Colloque franco-britannique (ed.), Les relations franco-britanniques de 1935 à 1939: communications présentées aux colloques franco-britanniques tenus à Londres (Imperial War Museum) du 18 au 21 octobre 1971, Paris (Comité d'Histoire de la 2ème Guerre Mondiale) du 25 au 29 septembre 1972 (Paris, 1975).

Conférence Universitaire de Démographie et d'Étude des Populations, La population de la France, (2005), URL: http://cudep.u-bordeaux4.fr/sites/cudep/IMG/pdf/La_popula tion_de_la_France-2.pdf

Crémieux-Brilhac, Jean-Louis, Les Français de l'an 40, Vol. 1, La guerre, oui ou non ? (Paris, 1990).

Crémieux-Brilhac, Jean-Louis, Les Français de l'an 40, Vol. 2, Ouvriers et soldats (Paris, 1990).

Crémieux-Brilhac, Jean-Louis, 'L'opinion publique française, l'Angleterre et la Guerre (Septembre 1939–Juin 1940)', in: Comité international d'histoire de la Deuxième Guerre mondiale (ed.), Français et Britanniques dans la drôle de guerre: actes du colloque franco-britannique tenu à Paris du 8 au 12 décembre 1975 (Paris, 1979), pp. 1–49.

Crémieux-Brilhac, Jean-Louis, 'Les communistes et l'armée pendant la drôle de guerre', in: Jean-Pierre Rioux, Antoine Prost and Jean-Pierre Azéma (eds), Les communistes français de Munich à Chateaubriand (Paris, 1987), pp. 98–118.

Delaporte, Sophie, 'Névroses de guerre', in: Stéphane Audoin-Rouzeau and Jean-Jacques Becker (eds), Encyclopédie de la Grande Guerre (Paris, 2014), pp. 357–365.

Delporte, Christian, La Troisième République, 1919–1940. De Poincaré À Paul Reynaud (Paris, 1998).

Département de la Moselle (ed.), Un exil intérieur: l'évacuation des Mosellans de septembre 1939 à octobre 1940 (Lyon, 2009).

Deroo, Eric and Pierre de Taillac, Carnets de déroute 1939–1940: Lettres et récits inédits (Paris, 2010).

Derry, Thomas K., The Campaign in Norway (London, 1995).

Dorgelès, Roland, La Drôle de Guerre: 1939–1940 (Paris, 1957).

Doughty, Robert, Pyrrhic victory: French strategy and operations in the Great War (Harvard, 2005).

Douzou, Laurent, 'Pascal Copeau', in: Marcot François (ed.), Dictionnaire historique de la Résistance, (Paris, 2006).

Dowling, Timothy, Personal Perspectives: World War I (California, 2006)

Duhard, Jean-Pierre, Écrits de guerre et de captivité (Paris, 2015).

Duroselle, Jean-Baptiste, Histoire diplomatique de 1919 à nos jours (Paris, 1997)

Eck, Hélène, La guerre des ondes: histoire des radios de langue française pendant la Deuxième Guerre mondiale (Paris, 1985).

ECPAD, 'Le corps expéditionnaire britannique (BEF, British Expeditionary Force) en France, septembre 1939-mai 1940', URL: http://archives.ecpad.fr/wp-content/uploads/2013/03/Dossier-La-BEF.pdf

Ellis, Major L. F., War In France And Flanders 1939–1940: History Of The Second World War, ed. by J. R. M. Butler (London, 2009).

Facon, Patrick, 'Les mutineries dans le Corps Expéditionnaire Français en Russie Septentrionale (décembre 1918-avril 1919)', Revue D'histoire Moderne et Contemporaine, 24 (1977), pp. 455–474.

Fagot [Williams], Maude, La drôle de guerre: Une guerre d'influence. La propagande antibritannique allemande et la guerre psychologique française pendant la drôle de guerre du 3 septembre 1939 au 10 mai 1940, (Masterthesis, Albert-Ludwig Universität/Université Lumière Lyon II, 2013).

Fagot [Williams], Maude, 'La guerre des ondes entre la France et l'Allemagne pendant la ,drôle de guerre', Revue Historique, 671 (2014), pp. 630–654.

Férard, Nicholas, 'La campagne de Norvège. 9 avril – 13 juin 1940, dossier n°1: la campagne vue du côté français', ECPAD, URL: http://archives.ecpad.fr/wp-content/uploads/2010/06/norvege.pdf

Férard, Nicholas, Propaganda Kompanien: PK War Reporters of the Third Reich (Paris, 2014).

Flack, Werner, Wir bauen am Westwall: ein Fronterlebnis deutscher Jugend im Frieden (Berlin, 1939).

Folcher, Gustave, Les carnets de guerre de Gustave Folcher, paysan languedocien, 1939-1945, ed. by Rémy Cazals (Paris, 2000).

Fonvieille-Alquier, François, Les Français dans la Drôle de guerre (Paris, 1971).

Frieser, Karl-Heinz, The Blitzkrieg Legend: The 1940 Campaign in the West, (Annapolis, 2013).

Gaber, Stéphane, Quatre siècles de fortifications en Lorraine: Des premiers bastions à la ligne Maginot (Metz, 2012).

Gallo, Max, Et ce fut la défaite de 1940: la cinquième colonne (Paris, 1980)

Garraud, Philippe, 'L'action de l'armée de l'air en 1939–1940: Facteurs structurels et conjoncturels d'une défaites', Guerres mondiales et conflits contemporains, 203 (2001), pp. 7–31.

Garraud, Philippe, 'La politique de fortification des frontières de 1925 à 1940: logiques, contraintes et usages de la ligne Maginot', Guerres mondiales et conflits contemporains, 226 (2007), pp. 3–22.

Georgakakis, Didier, La République contre la propagande: aux origines perdues de la communication d'État en France, 1917–1940 (Paris, 2004).

Gide, André and Jean Malaquais, Correspondance: 1935–1950 (Paris, 2000).

Grehan, John and Martin Mace, The BEF in France 1939–1940: Manning the Front Through to the Dunkirk Evacuation (Barnsley, 2014).

Grenard, Fabrice, La drôle de guerre –L'entrée en guerre des Français (Paris, 2015).

Haslam, E.B., 'La préparation à la guerre: Étude de quelques éléments de l'efficacité opérationnelle des forces aériennes sur le front du Nord-Est', in: Comité international d'histoire de la Deuxième Guerre mondiale (ed.), Français et Britanniques dans la drôle de guerre: actes du colloque franco-britannique tenu à Paris du 8 au 12 décembre 1975 (Paris, 1979), pp. 517–528.

Hensle, Michael P., Rundfunkverbrechen: Das Hören von 'Feindsendern' im Nationalsozialismus (Berlin, 2003).

Hiegel, Henri, Ils disent drôle de guerre ceux qui n'y étaient pas … 3 septembre 1939–10 mai 1940, (Sarreguemines, 1983), pp. 219–254.

Hiegel, Henri, La Drôle de Guerre en Moselle, 1939–1940 (Sarreguemines, 1983).

Imlay, Talbot, 'Mind the gap: The perception and Reality of Communist Sabotage of French War Production during the Phoney War 1939–1940', Past and Present, 189 (2005), pp. 179–224.

Jacobsen, Hans-Adolf, Fall Gelb: Der Kampf um den Deutschen Operationsplan zur Westoffensive 1940 (Wiesbaden, 1957).

Jahr, Christoph, Gewöhnliche Soldaten (Göttingen, 1998).

Jeanneney, Jean-Noël, 'Les Archives des Commissions de Contrôle postal aux Armées (1916-1918). Une source précieuse pour l'histoire contemporaine de l'opinion et des mentalités', Revue d'Histoire Moderne & Contemporaine, 15 (1968) 1, pp. 209–233.

Jeanneney, Noël, 'L'opinion Publique En France Pendant La Première Guerre Mondiale', Publications de l'École Française de Rome, 54 (1984), pp. 209–227.

Johansson, Alf, 'La Neutralité Suédoise et Les Puissances Occidentales Entre 1939 et 1945', Revue d'histoire de La Deuxième Guerre mondiale, 28 (1978), pp. 9–31.

Jovelin, Hervé, 'Poilu's Park (1914–1919) Un parc d'attractions pour soldats sur le front', Guerres mondiales et conflits contemporains, 183 (1996), p. 111–123.

Kallis, Aristotle, Nazi Propaganda and the Second World War (Basingstoke, 2006)

Kersaudy, François, Norway 1940 (Lincoln, 1998).

Kirchner, Klaus, Flugblattpropaganda im Zweiten Weltkrieg, Vol. 1, Flugblätter aus England, (Erlangen 1982).

Kirchner, Klaus, Flugblatt-Propaganda im 2. Weltkrieg Europa, Vol. 2, Flugblätter aus Deutschland, (Erlangen, 1982).

Kirchner, Klaus, Flugblattpropaganda im Zweiten Weltkrieg, Vol. 3, Flugblätter aus Frankreich (Erlangen, 1982).

Kiszely, John, Anatomy of a Campaign: The British Fiasco in Norway, 1940 (Cambridge; New York, 2017).

Landau, Philippe-Efraïm, 'La communauté juive de France et la Grande Guerre', Annales de démographie historique, 103 (2002), pp. 91–106.

Lasserre, André, 'En Suisse, aux frontières de la politique et du militaire: "armée et foyer" 1939–1945', Revue d'histoire de la Deuxième Guerre mondiale et des conflits contemporains, 33 (1983) 130, pp. 77–89.

Leenhardt, Pierre, Pascal Copeau (1908–1982). L'histoire préfère les vainqueurs (Paris, 1994).

Lefèvre, Bernard, 'La légende du bromure durant la drôle de guerre', Arkheia, Revue d'histoire. Histoire, Mémoire du Vingtième siècle en Sud-Ouest, http://www.arkheia-revue.org/La-legende-du-bromure-durant-la,296.html [Consulted 18 April 2017].

Leygues, Raphael and Jean-Luc Barré, Les mutins de la mer noire (Paris, 1981)

Liss, Ulrich, Westfront 1939–1940 (Neckargemünd, 1959).

Malaquais, Jean, Journal de guerre, journal du Métèque (1939–1942) (Paris, 1997).

Marseille, Jacques and Daniel Lefeuvre, 1940 au jour le jour (Paris, 1989).

Marty, André, La révolte de la mer noire (Paris, 1927).

Mary, Jean-Yves and Alain Hohnadel, Hommes et Ouvrages de La Ligne Maginot, Vol. 1 (Paris, 2000).

Mary, Jean-Yves and Alain Hohnadel, Hommes et Ouvrages de La Ligne Maginot, Vol. 3, (Paris, 2000).

Masefield, Peter, 'La Royal Air Force et la production d'avions de guerre en Grande-Bretagne, 1934–1940', in: Comité international d'histoire de la Deuxième Guerre mondiale (ed.), Français et Britanniques dans la drôle de guerre: actes du colloque franco-britannique tenu à Paris du 8 au 12 décembre 1975 (Paris, 1979), pp. 411–456.

Méadel, Cécile, 'Programme en masse, programmes de masse? La diffusion de la radio en France pendant les années trente', in: Régine Robin (ed.), Masses et culture de masse dans les années trente (Paris, 1991), pp. 51–68.

Melchior-Bonnet, Christian, Lettres du temps de guerre: 1939–1942 (Paris, 1999).

Michel, Henri, Le Procès de Riom (Paris, 1979).

Molinier, Jean, 'L'évolution de la population agricole du XVIIIe siècle à nos jours', Economie et statistique, 91 (1977) 1, pp. 79–84.

Naour, Jean-Yves Le, Misères et tourments de la chair durant la Grande Guerre. Les mœurs sexuelles des Français, 1914–1918 (Paris, 2002).

Naour, Jean-Yves Le, 'Épouses, marraines et prostituées. Le repos du guerrier, entre service social et condamnation morale', in: Evelyne Morin-Rotureau (ed.), Combats de femmes, 1914–1918. Les Françaises, pilier de l'effort de guerre (Paris, 2014), pp. 63–79.

Neave-Hill, CEI W.B.R., 'L'évolution de la stratégie franco-anglaise (1939–1940)', in: Comité international d'histoire de la Deuxième Guerre mondiale (ed.), Français et Britanniques dans la drôle de guerre: actes du colloque franco-britannique tenu à Paris du 8 au 12 décembre 1975 (Paris, 1979), pp. 333–359.

Nizan, Paul, Intellectuel communiste, Vol. 2 (Paris, 1970).

Nizan, Paul and Jean-Jacques Brochier, Paul Nizan, Intellectuel Communiste, 1926–1940. Articles et Correspondance Inédite (Paris, 1967).

Passera, François, 'Premiers témoignages publiés de la guerre 1939–1940. Des histoires vraies cousues de fil blanc?', in: Bertrand Fonk and Amable Sablon du Corail (eds), 1940, l'empreinte de la défaite: Témoignages et archives (Rennes, 2014), pp. 179–199.

Pernot, Georges, Journal de guerre, 1940–1941 (Besançon, 1971).

Philpott, J. William, 'The Benefit of Experience? The Supreme War Council and the Higher Management of Coalition War, 1939–1940', in: Martin Alexander and J. William Philpott (eds), Anglo-French Defence Relations Between the Wars (London, 2002), pp. 209–226.

Poulain, Martine, Livres pillés, lectures surveillées (Paris, 2013).

Prost, Antoine and Jay Winter, Penser la Grande Guerre: Un essai d'historiographie (Paris, 2004).

Quellien, Jean, Françoise Passera, Jean-Luc Leleu, and Michel Daeffler (eds), La France pendant la Seconde Guerre mondiale: Atlas historique (Paris, 2010).

Sadoul, Georges, Journal de guerre: 2 septembre 1939–20 juillet 1940 (Paris, 1977).

Santamaria, Yves, 1939, le pacte germano-soviétique (Paris, 1998).

Sartre, Jean-Paul, Carnets de la Drôle de Guerre: Septembre 1939–Mars 1940, ed. by Arlette Elkaïm-Sartre (Paris, 1995).

Schiavon, Max, 'Les relations entre hauts commandements français et britannique en 1939–1940', Revue historique des armées, 264 (2011), pp. 59–74.

Simmonet, Stéphane, Christophe Prime, and Claire Levasseur, Atlas de la Seconde Guerre mondiale: La France au combat: de la drôle de guerre à la Libération (Paris, 2015).

Smalley, Edward, British Expeditionary Force, 1939–40 (New York, 2015).

Smalley, Edward, 'In the Courts or Off the Records: Discipline in the British Expeditionary Force, September 1939–June 1940', University of Sussex Journal of Contemporary History, 16 (2015), pp. 75–91.

Smirnov, Vladislav and Marie Tournié, 'Le Komintern et le Parti communiste français pendant la « drôle de guerre », 1939–1940. (D'après les archives du Komintern)', Revue des Études Slaves, 65 (1993), pp. 671–690.

Soudagne, Jean-Pascal and Michel Mansuy, Comprendre la ligne Maginot: Nord, Ardennes, Lorraine, Alsace, Savoie, Dauphiné, Alpes-Maritimes (Rennes, 2009).

Stein, Luise, Grenzlandschicksale – Unternehmen evakuieren in Deutschland und Frankreich, 1939/1940 (PhD, Ruhr-Universität Bochum, 2017).

Thibault, Richard, Des forêts d'Alsace aux chemins de Normandie (Condé-sur-Noireaut, 1985).

Thies, Klaus-Jürgen, Der Westfeldzug, 10. Mai Bis 25. Juni 1940: Ein Lageatlas der Operationsabteilung des Generalstabs des Heeres: Neu gezeichnet nach den Unterlagen im Bundesarchiv/Militärarchiv (Osnabrück, 1994).

Tuffrau, Paul, De la 'drôle de guerre' à la libération de Paris (1939–1944): Lettres et Carnets (Paris, 2002).

Uzulis, André, 'Deutsche Kriegspropaganda gegen Frankreich', in: Jürgen Wilke (ed.), Pressepolitik Und Propaganda. Historische Studien Vom Vormärz Bis Zum Kalten Krieg, Vol. 7 (Köln, 1997), pp. 127–173.

Vaïsse, Maurice (ed.), Défaite française, victoire allemande sous l'œil des historiens étrangers (Paris, 2000).

Vaïsse, Maurice, 'Der Pazifismus und die Sicherheit Frankreichs 1930-1939', Vierteljahrshefte Für Zeitgeschichte, 33 (1985), pp. 590–616.

Vidal, Georges, 'Le Parti communiste français et la défense nationale (septembre 1937– septembre 1939)', Revue historique, 630 (2004) 2, pp. 333–369.

Vidal, Georges, 'L'armée française face au communisme du début des années 1930 jusqu'à la 'débâcle'', Historical reflexions, 30 (2004) 2, pp. 283–309.

Wagner, Nobert (ed.), Archiv des Humanitären Völkerrechts in bewaffneten Konflikten (Brühl/Weseling, 2012).

Wahl, Jean-Bernard, Jours Tranquilles et Bruits de Guerre Au Mont Des Welches: Août 1939 - Juillet 1940; (Petite)Histoire, La 'Drôle de Guerre' Sur La Ligne Maginot (Huningue, 2007).

Wahl, Jean-Bernard, La Ligne Maginot En Alsace: 200 Km de Béton et d'acier (Ellange, 2013).

Watt, Donald Cameron, 'Le moral de l'armée française tel que se le représentaient les Britanniques en 1939 et 1940: Une faillite des services de renseignement ?', in: Comité international d'histoire de la Deuxième Guerre mondiale (ed.), Français et Britanniques dans la drôle de guerre (Paris, 1979), pp. 197–211.

Wedel, Hasso von, and Hermann Teske, Die Propagandatruppen der deutschen Wehrmacht (Vowinckel, 1962).

Wilkin, Bernard, Aerial Propaganda and the Wartime Occupation of France, 1914–18 (London; New York, 2017).

Wilkin, Bernard and René Wilkin, Fighting for Napoleon: French Soldiers' Letters 1799–1815, (Barnsley, 2015).

Williams, Maude, Kommunikation in Kriegsgesellschaften am Beispiel der Evakuierung der deutsch-französischen Grenzregion, 1939/40 (PhD Thesis: Tübingen/Sorbonne Université, 2016).

Williams, Maude, 'La coopération franco-britannique en matière de propagande, 1939–1940', Relations Internationales, 162 (2015), pp. 45–62.

Williams, Maude, 'La communauté catholique d'Alsace-Lorraine face aux évacuations (septembre 1939-juin 1940)', Annales de l'Est, 2 (2014), pp. 203–224.

Williams, Nicholas, An 'Evil Year in Exile'. The Evacuation of the Franco-German Border Areas in 1939 under Democratic and Totalitarian Conditions (Berlin, 2018).

Williams, Nicholas, 'Les évacuations de 1939 en Moselle et en Sarre: cadres et plans stratégiques pour la prise en charge des populations civiles', Vingtième Siècle. Revue d'histoire, 128 (2015), pp. 91–104.

Zay, Jean, Lettres de la Drôle de Guerre (Paris, 2015).

List of abbreviations

BEF	British Expeditionary Force
CA	*Corps d'Armée*
CAC	*Corps d'Armée Colonial*
CAF	*Corps d'Armée de Forteresse*
CEC	*Commandant en chef*
CGI	*Commissariat Général à l'Information*
CP	*Contrôle Postal*
DIC	*Division d'Infanterie Coloniale*
DIF	*Division d'Infanterie de Forteresse*
DIM	*Division d'Infanterie Motorisée*
DINA	*Division d'Infanterie Nord-Africaine*
EM	*État-Major*
EMG	*État-Major Général*
EOCA	*Eléments Organiques de Corps d'Armées*
FCP	*Parti Communiste Français*
GQG	*Grand Quartier Général*
IFOP	*Institut Français d'Opinion Publique*
OKW	*Oberkommando der Wehrmacht*
PCF	*Parti communiste français*
PK	*Propagandakompanien*
PR	*Propagande Révolutionnaire*
RALD	*Régiment d'Artillerie Lourde Divisionnaire*
RF	*Régions Fortifiées*
RIF	*Régiment d'infanterie de Forteresse*
RMVP	*Reichsministerium für Volksaufklärung und Propaganda*
SD	*Secteurs Défensifs*
SF	*Secteurs Fortifiés*

Chronology

1939

March

15   German invasion of Bohemia and Moravia
28   End of the Spanish Civil War

August

23   Signature of the Molotov-Ribbentrop pact
25   Signature of the Anglo-Polish military alliance
       Newspapers *L'Humanité* and *Ce Soir* are banned
26   The communist press is banned
27   Censorship is established

September

1   German invasion of Poland
     General mobilisation in France is declared
2   The French vote war credits (69 billion francs)
3   Britain and France declare war on Germany
     Lord Gort becomes Commander in Chief of the newly formed British Expeditionary Force
4   Advance parties of the BEF begin arriving in France
6   The French army enters the Sarre region
10   Landing of the BEF (Cherbourg)
11   Landing of the BEF (Saint-Nazaire and Nantes)
12   First French-British Supreme council meeting
17   The Soviet troops enter Poland
18   The CGT breaks with the PCF
21   The French army leaves the Sarre region
26   The PCF is dissolved
28   Warsaw is taken by Germany

October

6   Hitler peace speech at the Reichstag
       The names of the 'Stuttgart traitors' are revealed: Ferdonnet et Obrecht
7   The newspapers announce that Thorez deserted on 4 October
8   35 communist MPs are arrested
9   Haut-Rhin MPs, Rossé et Sturmel, are arrested
10   Hitler's peace offer is rejected

November

2   Winston Churchill travels to France
30   Finland is attacked by the USSR
       The French Parliament gives all powers to Daladier

December

12   The French and the British help Finland

1940

February

16   The *Altmark* tanker is captured by the Royal Navy in Norwegian waters
21   Thorez loses his French citizenship

March

6   Ferdonnet and Obrecht are sentenced to death
7   The American sub-secretary Summer Welles is in Paris for a European
       mission of information
12   Signature of the peace treaty between Finland and the USSR
16   The Finnish Parliament ratifies the peace treaty
20   Daladier resigns
       Paul Reynaud becomes the new *Président du Conseil*
21   Reynaud picks Cabinet members
22   The new Cabinet is confirmed by the French Parliament
28   The French and the British agree not to seek separate peace

April

9   German operation *Weserübung*, invasion of Denmark and Norway
12   French and Polish units embark for Norway
10–13 Battle of Narvik
14   British Forces begin landing in Norway
19   Allied landing in Namsos

| 20 | Bombing and destruction of Namsos by the German army |
| 27 | Operations in the Narvik sector |

May

2	British forces begin evacuating Norway
10	Invasion of Belgium and the Netherlands
	Churchill becomes Prime Minister
13	German offensive in the Ardennes
15	Capitulation of the Netherlands
18	Pétain becomes *Vice-Président du Conseil*
19	Weygand replaces Gamelin
24	Beginning of the Narvik evacuation
25	Gort abandons his counter-attack
27	Capitulation of Belgium
26	Dunkirk evacuation (Operation Dynamo)
29–4.6	Allied offensive toward the Swedish border

June

8	Evacuation of remaining British troops and French troops in Norway
14	The Germans take Paris
	The government retreats toward Bordeaux
15	The last French troops of the CEFS reach Breast
16	resigns; Marshal Pétain is called
18	BEF operations in France officially end
22	The armistice is signed with Germany
24	The armistice is signed with Italy
25	National mourning day
29	The government leaves Bordeaux for Vichy

Index

Printed in Great Britain
by Amazon

16596863R00097